SOARING WITH FIDEL

SOARING WITH FIDEL

AN OSPREY ODYSSEY
FROM CAPE COD TO CUBA AND BEYOND

David Gessner

BEACON PRESS, BOSTON

Beacon Press
25 Beacon Street
Boston, Massachusetts 02108-2892
www.beacon.org

Beacon Press books
are published under the auspices of
the Unitarian Universalist Association of Congregations.

10 09 08 07   8 7 6 5 4 3 2 1
This book is printed on acid-free paper that meets the uncoated paper
ANSI/NISO specifications for permanence as revised in 1992.

Composition by Wilsted & Taylor Publishing Services

Library of Congress Cataloging-in-Publication Data

Gessner, David
  Soaring with Fidel : an osprey odyssey from Cape Cod to Cuba and beyond /
by David Gessner.
    p. cm.
  ISBN-13: 978-0-8070-8578-3 (hardcover : alk. paper)
  ISBN-10: 0-8070-8578-2 (hardcover : alk. paper)
  1. Osprey—Migration. 2. Osprey—Anecdotes. 3. Gessner, David—Travel.
I. Title.

QL696.F36G485 2007
598.9'3—dc22   2006031402

To the two who migrate with me,
Nina de Gramont and Hadley Gessner

And to Jason Starfire,
who united avocation and vocation

WHEN WE TRY TO PICK OUT ANYTHING
BY ITSELF, WE FIND IT HITCHED TO
EVERYTHING ELSE IN THE UNIVERSE.

John Muir

I DON'T LOOK AT THE SKY.

A mechanic in Venezuela

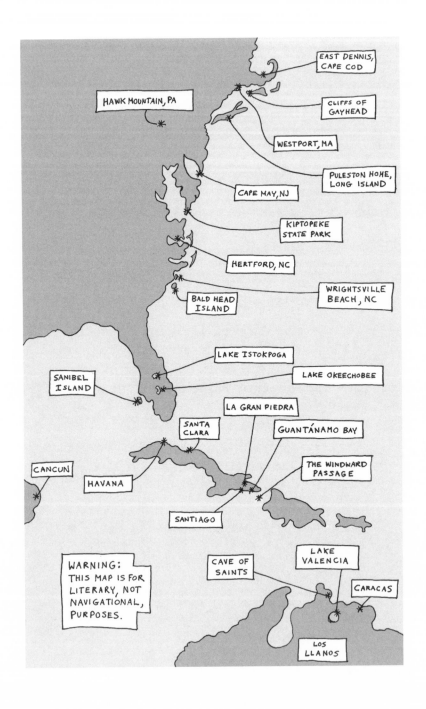

EAST DENNIS, CAPE COD

HAWK MOUNTAIN, PA

CLIFFS OF GAYHEAD

WESTPORT, MA

PULESTON HOME, LONG ISLAND

CAPE MAY, NJ

KIPTOPEKE STATE PARK

HERTFORD, NC

WRIGHTSVILLE BEACH, NC

BALD HEAD ISLAND

LAKE ISTOKPOGA

LAKE OKEECHOBEE

SANIBEL ISLAND

LA GRAN PIEDRA

GUANTÁNAMO BAY

SANTA CLARA

CANCUN

THE WINDWARD PASSAGE

HAVANA

SANTIAGO

WARNING:
THIS MAP IS FOR LITERARY, NOT NAVIGATIONAL, PURPOSES.

CAVE OF SAINTS

LAKE VALENCIA

CARACAS

LOS LLANOS

CONTENTS

TO THE READER

This is not a bird book.

Okay, yes, sure there are birds in it. Lots of them, in fact. But it is *not* a bird book. It is a book, among other things, about the nature of human happiness. About what happens when human beings, instead of focusing on themselves, turn their attention to things with feathers that fly. As you'll see, many of the characters in this book have done just that and seem the better for it. The high points in their lives have corresponded, not coincidentally, with the flight of the birds they follow. And they have, to a certain extent, become what they watched—that is, have become imbued with the avian attributes of flight and freedom. Of course, I don't want this all to sound *too* healthy; there was an element of obsession in almost every bird person I met. But in an increasingly restrictive and xenophobic world, birds have pulled these people across borders. More than that: you might say their empathy with these birds is a kind of flight in itself.

We all sometimes feel the tug of migration, of moving from one home to another, of leaving our old lives behind. Each fall and spring, the times of the great migrations, the world shifts into movement, with almost every winged thing heading somewhere else. It's an immense drama of movement playing out right before our eyes, and one year I decided not just to notice but to partake in that drama. My own life had recently been unsettled by a move away from the place I had long called home.

And so I joined the great unsettling, the biannual feathered disruptions when urgency fills the air. My trip was, among other things, a different way to see the year. Not merely as days on a calendar or things to check off a list but as a dangerous journey along seasonal edges. And as a larger experiment in living in between.

Now, after a year of following birds and following people who follow birds, I have reached this not-so-scientific or original conclusion: humans are never happier than when they are chasing something.

So this is a book about people and flight and obsession and freedom and empathy. And okay, yes, it's also a bird book.

FIRST CONTACT

The journey will end, or rather culminate, atop La Gran Piedra, a massive rock in the Sierra Maestra mountains of Cuba, as I stare down the spine of those majestic peaks, while ospreys—known locally as *águilas pescadoras,* or "eagle fishermen"—appear out of the clouds above the city of Santiago and glide toward the rock I'm standing on. But it begins, more prosaically, with hose socks.

Let me explain:

On September 9, 2004, I flew from my new home in North Carolina to my former home on Cape Cod. It was a business trip of sorts, though my business was a strange one. I was leaving behind my new job as a professor, my wife, Nina, and my one-year-old daughter, Hadley, so that I could follow some birds. I had never considered myself an ornithologist, or even much of a birder, but back when I lived on Cape Cod I became interested in the local ospreys, and that interest gradually transformed into obsession. Ospreys are large, nearly eagle-sized birds with almost six-foot wingspans, known for their swashbuckling dives for fish and distinguished by their dark brown masks and vivid brown-and-white wing patterns. I had gotten to know the birds well when I lived on the Cape but had observed them only during their five-month summer nesting season. This year, however, a migrant myself, I'd decided to see where they went when they left in the fall. The plan was to fly north so that I could then turn around and drive back south again, following the birds on their migration.

But the trip began poorly. My new home was on a small barrier island in North Carolina, and the night before I left I barely slept. My family always piled together in one bed, and when the storm hit, my daughter, a little bald monkey, clung to my chest. Lightning flashed, rain pelted, and high winds off the water buffeted the windows. We'd already lost part of our roof during a hurricane early that summer, and it felt like we might lose the rest of it. The same winds rattled my plane—"choppy air," the pilot euphemistically called it—as I flew north. I clapped along with the other passengers when we finally landed in Providence, Rhode Island. There I rented a white Pontiac Grand Am and drove to Cape Cod, where I spent the afternoon racing around, going from nest to nest, managing not to see a single osprey.

My plan had seemed like a brilliant one back in North Carolina, but it seemed decidedly less so now. After a couple of hours my pants were covered with muck and ticks, and my spirits were sagging. All the local nests were empty. Since this was mid-September, these results were not all that surprising. Ospreys are fairly obvious birds—bandit-masked, loud, big, and unselfconscious—and if they are in your neighborhood, you know it. During the spring and summer months, the time of breeding and chick-rearing for raptors, the nests act as great magnets, holding the birds fast. But by late summer the magnets lose their attraction, and the ospreys that haven't already migrated tend to hang out in the woods, lying low, being much less conspicuous than during the summer. I had somehow counted on getting lucky, but all afternoon I searched futilely.

I had vast experience in not seeing birds. Because I'd become obsessed with ospreys while on Cape Cod, some people considered me an "expert," but an expert I was not. I'd become particularly adept at not seeing the birds dive. The dive is the osprey's tour de force: the bird first hovers in the air like a giant hummingbird, then hurtles down at reckless speed, headfirst, until, at the last possible second, right before hitting the water, it pops a wheelie and enters the water talons first, often snaring a live fish. Though other people seem to see these dives all the time, while sunbathing or boating or fishing, I have witnessed precious few given the hours I've devoted to watching. Once, after presenting a slide show and talk on the birds at a lodge in Colorado, I walked outside and saw an osprey flying above a mountain lake. It was a beautiful sight, the bird flashing its dark-to-light semaphore wings: a perfect moment. I walked closer to the lake, until I was standing about fifteen feet behind an old couple, retirees who'd just attended my lecture and were now sitting on a bench watching the bird. I planned on saying hello to the old folks, basking in my role as birder celebrity, maybe imparting some osprey knowledge, but first I had a practical matter to attend to. My laces had become loose, so I dropped down to tie my sneakers.

It was as I was looping the second bow that I heard the woman squeal: "Oh, my goodness, did you see that?"

"I did," said the man. "Amazing. Right into the water!"

I looked up to see the osprey flying off, the glint of a fish shining in its talons. The bird had apparently waited until the exact moment I bent my head to make its strike.

Now I was meeting with similar luck during my search of the Cape Cod nests. Deciding to give up on the birds and turn toward human informants, I drove over to the house of Don MacKenzie. Don is a craftsman and violin-and-bow-maker who lives beside Route 6A in the town of Brewster, and a nest I'd once regularly observed stands in the marsh behind his home. A few years back I'd spent many hours on that marsh, watching a pair of ospreys build up their bulky nest while watching Don build his home out of mostly recycled materials. As impressive as that home is, the jewel in the property's crown is the enormous wood-floored, window-filled violin studio overlooking the marsh, and on this day that is where I found Don.

We chatted for a while before the talk turned, inevitably with us, to ospreys. He smiled as he looked out at the empty osprey nest, a shaggy head of hair on top of a human-made pole and platform. Ragged clouds blew east across the bay. Don was in his sixties, and he spoke in a quiet voice, but I sensed a kind of wild exuberance below that quiet, and he had many projects going on out there in the studio. Though he didn't consider himself a birder, really, he had lived so long with the birds as neighbors that he had gotten to know their habits and markings. To his way of thinking, it was simply polite to get to know your neighbors. Unlike most people, he could tell male and female ospreys apart fairly easily, or at least could tell the difference between *his* male and female. He took the calendar off the wall and flipped back to March, where he'd penciled in the day the birds had returned from the south: the twenty-first. Then he flipped ahead and found the other date he was looking for.

"I'm afraid you're kind of late," he said. "They left early this year. The last time we saw those guys was on the seventeenth of August."

He looked at me. I looked back in silence.

"You've got some catching up to do," he said with a quiet laugh.

I agreed that I did. But I knew that just because he hadn't seen the birds, that didn't mean they had begun their true migration. Before they launched off on their big trip south there would be a period of dispersal behavior, dry runs during which the birds, particularly the young birds, made practice excursions out into the world.

We chatted for a while more and Don told me about a friend who regularly watched ospreys on a nearby lake. The friend had gotten to know the local birds as individuals, including a male that had been coming back for years, whom he called "Ol' Never Miss." While the other birds he watched caught fish about half the time they dove, Don's friend had never seen the old male come up with empty talons. Don also told me the story of an osprey adult trying to drown a young bird, something I had never heard of. Then I thanked him and was on my way. I planned on spending the night at my mother's house, which is just down the street from Don's. But before retiring, I had one last nest in mind, and I headed out to it as the sun set into the bay.

I saw a beautiful sunset, red-tailed hawks, blue herons, harriers. But no ospreys. Frustrated, I let my thoughts turn toward beer and the lamb chops my mother had promised to cook. That would be nice, a consolation, but wouldn't make up for the lack of birds. At the moment the trip didn't seem like such a great idea: my bank account was almost empty and I was running around after birds, while back home my classes went untaught and my wife and daughter waited. I drove to my mother's house wondering just what the hell I was doing.

Just what the hell *was* I doing?

It had begun earlier that summer, when I had briefly returned to Cape Cod from North Carolina. Over the previous seven years I had come to believe I would spend the rest of my life on the Cape, but that had not come to pass and now I returned as a visitor, a tourist. That June morning I hiked out to one of the nests where I used to waste so much time, a sprawling, unkempt nest that my daughter could have fit in quite comfortably. But she wasn't up in the nest; instead it was filled with other children, three dark-brown-and-white juvenile birds whose insistent cries sounded like yearning distilled. At that point, in late June, they had been alive for only a month or so, but they were already larger than crows and were comparatively far more advanced in their development than my daughter. They were being so loud because they wanted food, and since they were ospreys, food meant fish. They were not yet able to fish for themselves, however, so their food was provided by their parents. I watched as one of those parents, the male, flew to a nearby juniper with a freshly caught flounder. After he had chewed on the fish awhile, the female flew over to the tree, wrested away the bottom half from him, and carried it back to the young. She landed on the edge of the nest, where she tore off chunks of white, nearly translucent flesh and doled them out, inequitably, to the three nestlings.

It was summer solstice, and a silver-edged green spilled over the world. These young birds would imprint this place, the place they were born, and then, in less than three months, they would head out on a daunting journey of thousands of miles to South America. Almost two years later they would return as adults to this same neighborhood to build their own nests. Ospreys are fanatically committed to their large, sloppy nests. In fact, though they are said to mate for life, most ornithologists believe that it is the commitment to the nest, not the mate, that binds pairs together. It was this commitment to their homes that first attracted me to the birds as I got to know them during their summer nesting seasons. I believed that I too had imprinted this neighborhood and would never leave. In fact, I had written a book —about the place, about the ospreys—that ended in precisely that way, with my promising to "commit forever to Cape Cod."

What happened next was kind of funny, and consistent, in my experience, with what always happens when you make that kind of grand pronouncement. Some professors at a university in the South read the book and liked it, especially the fancy lines about how I would never leave, and so they asked me to come teach at their school. All my high-flown yapping about loving and committing forever had been nice, but we were expecting a child, and they were offering a salary and health insurance. In the end, the decision was easy. I moved South for the same reason birds migrate: to feed myself and my family.

A year after that move, standing there on solstice, I regarded the birds differently, more casually than I had before. After the nestlings had eaten their fish dinner, the largest and most likely the oldest of the chicks made what looked like his first weak attempt at flight, lifting up like an off-balance helicopter and landing almost instantly. Then, as the bird again lifted and fell, I felt my mind lifting too, reordering, redefining. It occurred to me that the birds, for all their ferocity in defending their nests, were, like me, only visitors to Cape Cod. After all, wasn't it somewhat presumptuous of me to call Cape Cod home to the birds, seeing that they spent less than half the year there? Who knew what the ospreys considered home? Home might be the South American rainforest where they passed their winter months, or the migration itself, since they lived on the wing for so much of the year. Home might be a place in between, and this thought was reassuring to my newly unsettled self.

My old question had been *how to nest*. My new question was *how to be at home in movement*. And it was then and there that I made my decision to follow the birds when they left Cape Cod at summer's end. While before I'd seen these birds as relatively sedentary, as nesters, I now wanted to get to know their other, more flamboyant selves. I wanted to see the year as a journey, a long, precarious trip, a cycle of exodus and return. I felt an old excitement stirring. With solstice the sun starts a journey of its own, making its annual about-face and not returning to the same spot in the sky for 365 days. What better day to begin? And what better bird to follow? Ospreys are one of the world's most cosmopolitan birds, one of only six species to appear on every continent except Antarctica. Each year the adult Cape Cod birds undertake a round trip of about 8000 miles. Each osprey becomes an annual Ulysses, making these epic journeys with regularity, leaving in mid-September and returning in late March. And this year I would follow them.

But back to hose socks.

If September 9 began inauspiciously, it ended disastrously. The plan was to have dinner and spend my first night at my mother's home in East Dennis. On the way over, tired of bird watching, I switched on the radio. Soon I was tapping my fingers to the distinctive chords of Alice Cooper's "No More Mr. Nice Guy," though as I sang along, I had little sense of what the song foreshadowed. As it ended, my wheels crunched over the pebble driveway at my mother's house, a modest yellow-trimmed Cape that sits on a small hill. My mother was living with her boyfriend, Jim, her first real relationship since my dad's death ten years earlier. My father had been a volcanic, charismatic character, with all the excitement and anxiety that go along with that temperament. Jim, in contrast, was quieter, apparently as steady and reliable as a backboard. He had even used my telescope to watch the ospreys behind the house for me while I was in North Carolina, reporting on their progress over the phone. To date, my only mild point of conflict with Jim was the fact that he had taken to trimming and pruning my mother's property with an enthusiasm bordering on fanaticism. It was a sweet and steady fanaticism, however, so even as he reduced the lawn to a putting green, I made a point never to mention that I preferred it shaggy and wild.

The visit went swimmingly at first, all hors d'oeuvres and red wine and catching up with the two of them. But then politics came up. Jim and I had had a couple of playful debates in the past, but nothing angry. But these were divisive times, and we resided at the opposite ends of the national spectrum: he was red, conservative and ex-military, and I was the bluest of blue, the stuff of Republican nightmares, the clichéd overeducated liberal from Massachusetts. We watched a little TV before dinner, and I, exhausted from the trip and frustrated by my failure to see any birds, became despondent about the latest polls for the November election. I said as much as we sat in the living room, and soon we were jousting. The jousting lasted for a little while, and then, unexpectedly, it became something more. The dance we were dancing was no different from the dance so many others were dancing all over the country, but to us it felt personal. We were going pretty strong, almost yelling, when my mother called us to dinner.

We turned to other subjects, and to the delicious food. And that might have been it had the phone not rung. It's been my experience that people of my mother's generation often react to the ringing of a phone like startled cavemen, furrowing their brows and looking about as if to say, "Where is that strange noise coming from?" Though my mother had an answering machine, she had no concept of using it to screen calls. "She wouldn't screen a call from the devil," my sister said. If a phone rang, you picked it up. It was a rule of life.

The ringing threw her into the usual tizzy, and she leapt up and ran around the table. She grabbed the phone just after the machine picked up, which meant her whole conversation was recorded along with screeching feedback like that of a bad garage band. "Hello," she yelled. "Hello? Hello? How do you stop this thing?"

With my mother battling the phone, Jim and I returned to our debate. It didn't take long to build up our former steam. Soon the lamb chops were ignored (though the wine was not) and our voices rose. I don't remember the exact moment when we officially went over the edge, but the next thing I knew, I was acting out an ugly Oedipal drama with my mother's lover. I think I started the true escalation by comparing George W. Bush to Joe McCarthy, and then Jim, in turn, compared him to Winston Churchill. Churchill has always been one of my heroes, so his statement was like the lighting of a fuse. A short fuse. I jumped up from the table and slammed down my glass. Since Jim was a military man, I tried to explain that I wasn't your run-of-the-mill effete blue-stater. I attempted to put September 11 and the Iraqi war in personal terms.

"If someone hurt my daughter," I said, "I would track them down and find them. But I wouldn't go out and attack a random person."

He paused dramatically and then said, "If someone hurt your daughter, you would punch the first person you saw."

At that moment there was little question whom I wanted to punch. Instead I stormed out of the dining room. I headed, appropriately, up to my old childhood room, where I grabbed my suitcase before charging back downstairs to pull my wet clothes from the washer. I then marched out of the house, slamming the door after me for effect, leaving my poor mother speechless and the lamb chops half eaten on the table.

It was an interesting way to begin an adventure in nature. As I drove around the town of Dennis, heart beating fast, I considered taking my sleeping bag out to one of the osprey nests and sleeping there. But it was cold, and after a half-hour of driving—and sputtering and fuming—I finally called a friend who owned a small farm. He laughed when he heard my story, then offered me a bed in the cabin he had on his property.

And so, as it turned out, there was an upside to my tantrum: thanks to my fit, I spent the first night of my osprey quest in a one-room cabin almost exactly the size of Thoreau's cabin. Walden. Not that my mood was pastoral. While the leaves rustled and the wind blew, I tried to sleep. But mostly I just lay there in that state of guilt and embarrassment that always comes after rage. Over the next eight hours I spent a lot of time staring out the plate-glass window as black clouds streamed across the moon. At one point I stumbled outside and watered my friend's flower garden, then back inside into a half-sleep.

The next morning I rose at dawn. I knew that Jim, like me, was an early riser. So I drove over to my mother's house, and sure enough, there he was in the dining room, reading the paper. He too had barely slept. I apologized, he apologized, we shook hands, we embraced, we laughed. "Welcome to the family," I said.

My mother came out and joined us in her bathrobe and we all had a nice peaceful discussion about the Red Sox. Before I took off, my mother wrapped the leftover lamb chops in tinfoil for me.

But while the day's first crisis was taken care of fairly quickly, another, more pressing one was not. I had come all this way to see ospreys, and so far the count was zero. I spent the morning once again hustling from one nest site to the next and finding all the local nests still empty. After a while I just gave up and tried to be Zen about the whole thing. After all, part of the idea behind my quest was to fall into the rhythm of the natural year. So why race around at 1000 rpms? I decided to spend my last hour on Cape Cod walking along the beach below the bluff.

The bluff was a clay bank near the house Nina and I had once rented, the same place where I had first watched ospreys forage and where I'd also seen humpback whales breach and seals lounge on rocks. This beach, which I'd walked since I could walk, was the closest thing I had to a real home. This was the

ind. While living here I'd kept a close watch
ting the water boiling with fish in early fall,
he cranberries, the seals returning from the
lying in, the peepers and swallows heralding
walked over the rocky beach, a belted king-
fisher ratcheted off ahead of me. I followed the bird, then hiked
up into the dunes, a bowl of sand and beach grass between woods
that Nina and I called "the land in between." After a minute or
two I came upon a doe and two fawns, one lightly spotted and
the other darker. They just stared at me until the mother snorted
a signal and ran off, her children following, all three bouncing
over the duned landscape, their white tails waving behind like
flags of surrender.

I cut through some trees to a small isolated sandy spot, hidden from the rest of the dunes by tree branches and brush, where
Nina and I had made a small shrine to a child we'd lost to a mis-
carriage. At the far end of the clearing, under a gnarled post oak,
we had carefully piled up a tiny cairn of sea glass and shells. I
paid my respects but noticed that the neighborhood grave rob-
bers had been at it again. Blue sea glass is the rarest kind on our
beaches, and this time, as always, all the blue we'd placed there
was gone.

I hiked back to the car, thinking that it had been a good decision to walk the beach, despite the fact that I was now pretty
sure I'd see no ospreys. But time considerations pressed in on my
peace when I looked down at my watch. My schedule had to be
tight if I was going to make it back south in a week, and I had to
leave Cape Cod by midday. The morning had been nice, but I
needed to get going.

And now I return, finally, to hose socks. Despite the fact that
I was just forty-three, I had developed severe varicose veins in
my right leg. Studying birds had taught me that preparation was
necessary before migration, and I had to make a preparation of

my own. If I was really going to follow the ospreys, it would mean driving a thousand miles and then flying a few thousand more, and to do that I would require an item of clothing commonly associated with shuffleboard-playing Floridians. And so, before leaving Cape Cod, I made one last stop, driving down White's Path to Foley's medical supply store to buy some socks. Once inside I picked out the kind I liked—medium tension, black, knee high—and handed them to the woman behind the counter. She mentioned offhandedly that I seemed kind of young to be buying hose socks, and I tried to explain to her that the veins had formed during the many years I'd spent playing Ultimate Frisbee seriously. ("Yes," I insisted when she laughed. "There *is* such a thing as playing Frisbee seriously.") She, like most people, had never heard of the sport and asked me the usual question, the question I always get: "Is that the thing you do with dogs?" I decided to change the subject and started to tell her about my trip chasing the birds, but her eyes went blank at my mention of ospreys. "Never mind," I said, smiling as I paid.

Once back inside my Pontiac, I tore open the pack and pulled one of the long elastic socks up over my right leg, my bad leg. Well aware of how dorky the lone black sock looked below my shorts, I started the car and pulled out of the parking lot. Then I headed down White's Path to Route 6, resigned to leaving Cape Cod without seeing a single bird.

It was a fact that I had conceived of my osprey quest during that one epiphanic moment watching the nestlings on summer solstice. But truth be told, I'd had a lot of grand romantic impulses in my life, most of which I'd never followed through on. Though I immediately jotted down plans for my great migration trip, this idea too could easily have faded into nothing. What kept it from fading was two strokes of good luck.

The first came when, during some routine Internet explorations and calls to birder friends, I learned of a relatively new aspect of osprey migration, or rather, an aspect familiar to ospreys but new to humans. Recently I had heard murmurings about ospreys migrating through Cuba, but now I uncovered more of the story, which centered on Freddy Rodriguez Santana, a young Cuban scientist who'd found a dead osprey with a band on its leg in 1996. Through the information on the band, Freddy got in touch with Keith Bildstein, a raptor expert at Hawk Mountain, Pennsylvania, and over the next few years the two played large parts in unraveling one of the great mysteries of osprey migration.

Ospreys had always been considered broad frontal migrants. This meant that though they sometimes migrated together in small groups, they were rarely seen migrating the way broad-winged hawks did, for example, together in a big gang made up of their own kind. It was also assumed that once they left the United States they migrated more or less individually, again unlike the millions of turkey vultures and broad-winged hawks that stream through Mexico each fall. This assumption was based on the simple fact that no one had ever seen ospreys migrating in large groups. But as it turned out, there was a good reason for this: people had been looking in the wrong place.

As Freddy Santana soon discovered, ospreys did migrate together; they just took a different route. Most birds, including most raptors, are hydrophobic, and therefore migrate to South America across Mexico. But ospreys, strong flyers and expert fishermen who live near and sometimes on the water, have less reason to fear the overseas route. As Freddy learned, each September thousands of ospreys course through the Sierra Maestra mountains in southeastern Cuba. Osprey experts had long been aware of this route, but not of the density of the migration. Satellite studies had recently begun to paint a clearer picture of this island-hopping, over-water route, and the most prominent osprey satellite tracker, Mark Martell, now believed that nine out of ten East Coast birds flew through Cuba rather than Mexico. But this was all theory until Freddy began exploring his own country, sniffing around and searching out the ancient route that he suspected was there. He knew that ospreys would naturally travel along Cuba's mountain ridges so that they could glide on the updrafts the ridges created, and so he focused much of his search in the mountains. Then, on one glorious day in August of 2003, as he stood on La Gran Piedra, Freddy Santana confirmed all he had suspected. While he watched, over six hundred ospreys streamed and soared along the beautiful mountain ridge toward the peak where he stood. The huge birds seemed to materialize out of the clouds above the city of Santiago and fly at him in flocks of up to fifty birds—*flocks!* No one had ever heard of osprey flocks before!—while he clicked away on the mechanical counter in his hand.

The more I pieced Freddy's story together, the more excited I got. It seemed to tie my place to his, to link us in some way, and I liked the idea of this man sharing my obsession in another country. Furthermore, I'd always found the sight of two or three ospreys wild and magnificent, and I could barely picture hundreds of the birds soaring over the mountains. I didn't know quite how I was going to get to Cuba, since the government had recently tightened travel restrictions, but I knew I had to try. Soon I began attempting to contact Freddy Santana through the birding grapevine, which, as it turned out, wasn't that hard. Bird people tend to be both generous and garrulous, and that generosity and garrulousness tend to cross international lines. Freddy and I were soon exchanging simple caveman-style e-mails—my bad Spanish mixed with his passable English—as we began to plan a trip for the fall.

It was in late summer, while I was still planning my itinerary, that I had my second stroke of good luck. I'd always been a technophobe, barely able to operate my cell phone, and I hadn't planned on using satellite telemetry—the most current technology, in which the birds are outfitted with and tracked through transmitters that bounced beams off satellites—to follow the birds. Instead I wanted to watch the general flow of the birds south, experiencing the ospreys' world as they traveled their ancient route. I imagined that my attempt to follow ospreys would be a primitive affair, involving equal parts guesswork, intuition, and perhaps research of the older satellite maps. But then something fell in my lap. One of my birding friends called to ask if I had heard about the documentary the BBC was planning. No, I hadn't, I said, and listened slack-jawed as he told me that a BBC team planned to follow ospreys down the East Coast using satellite telemetry and that their trip, and film, would culminate in Cuba. The news left me both nonplussed and excited. On the one hand, someone else was going to be following *my* birds, which rendered my journey less than original. But on the other hand, despite my prejudice against satellite technology, I now had a way to follow specific ospreys. What's more, it turned out that the satellite birds had been caught and radio-tagged on Martha's Vineyard, which meant that the BBC's quest, like mine, would start on Cape Cod.

Not long after I learned about the project, I contacted the BBC by e-mail. A staff person there wrote back a friendly note, asking if the BBC could show my book *Return of the Osprey* onscreen and have the presenter, an English TV celebrity named Steve Leonard, read from the book's pages. Leonard, I discovered, had made it big during his last year of veterinary school, when the BBC had decided to film a reality show called, appropriately, *Vets School.* Steve had been one of a handful of students selected to have his final year filmed and had emerged as the star.

I also learned that the documentary would focus on the work of the scientist Rob Bierregaard, who had placed the satellite transmitters on the ospreys on Martha's Vineyard. The documentary presented a rare opportunity for Bierregaard: usually scientists can't afford the technology necessary for ground-to-bird tracking, but in this case, the BBC, with its deep pockets, had spent around twenty grand to wire five birds. I soon got in touch with both Rob Bierregaard and the BBC's top scientist. Rob was a great guy, funny and easygoing, and the BBC scientist was enthusiastic on the phone as we compared notes on our coming journeys. It was all looking quite cozy. I would still take my more primitive trip, camping at night and hiking along known osprey routes, but what would it hurt to bump into the BBC occasionally? To drop in and say hi and hitch a ride in the TV crew's van, plane, boat, or helicopter and sneak a peek through the cameras at the birds wearing transmitters? Why not?

The answer to that question came in the form of a long e-mail from the documentary's producer. She was quite polite. "Fascinating to hear about your forthcoming trip," she wrote. "What a coincidence!" But gradually, still polite, the note took a turn toward its real purpose. She continued: "Our remit—to actually travel with the ospreys *as they do their migration*—has never been done before. This is naturally one of the *Unique Selling Points* of our series. To this end, I think our co-producers will want the detailed story of *our* tagged birds to remain under wraps until the programmes are aired." She graciously offered to let me look at some of the film and to compare notes *after* the crew had made their trip. But I got the point. In a very proper British way, she was telling me to fuck off. *We want to do it first.*

This, it turned out, was the wrong thing to tell me. If her goal was to get me to defer quietly, then she couldn't have picked a worse strategy, short of challenging me to a duel. Because in my mind it immediately *became* a duel. My vague plans solidified from abstract to concrete, from theory to fact. Now I was going to do it. Within days I was casting our twin journeys as a kind of John Henry battle. Though I had been momentarily intoxicated by the idea of following the satellite ospreys, I now suddenly remembered how much the thought of these radiocollared robobirds chafed against my sense of what was "natural." Yes—what I cared about, after all, was *wild nature,* and when I thought of *wild nature,* the image that sprang to mind was not one of birds wearing creepy little electronic backpacks feeding signals to satellites in space in a kind of avian video game. The BBC could have its fancy gizmos and technology and its vans and trains and planes, and I, the simple primitive, the noble savage, would have my feet and binoculars and nose and guts (and, of course, my rental car).

My capacity for self-romanticizing is fairly deep, and in my mind what had been a basically friendly e-mail became a declaration of war. The BBC crew was going to fly over on September 10 to begin following the birds down from Martha's Vineyard. But I would arrive on Cape Cod the day before to start my own trip. The British were coming, and once again a small rebel force would be waiting, ready to take them on.

Of course the rebel leader was feeling more than a little demoralized as he drove down White's Path, single hose sock up and on, ready to retreat from Cape Cod. Gnawing on the leftover lamb chops that my forgiving mother had packed, I sped down the road until I almost rear-ended a bargelike Oldsmobile. The Oldsmobile was going about three miles an hour and at first seemed to be driving itself—a ghost ship. But then, squinting, I made out two gnarled hands reaching up from below the steering wheel, and the top of a gray Brillo pad of hair. If I could barely see the woman, then it was a good bet that she could barely see the road. But this is a given on Cape Cod, where retirees drive until they are dead, and sometimes beyond. In fact there are distinct similarities between the many elderly motorists and that other group of drivers that make driving on Cape Cod so treacherous: stoned teenagers. Both groups drive in a slow but sometimes weaving fashion, semiblind but simultaneously overcautious to the point of paranoia.

But I am thankful for the old woman. The course of migrations hinges on accident, and mine hinged on the fact that I had had to visit Foley's medical supply store for hose socks and now found myself trapped behind a crawling oldster. Because of these factors I had time to daydream, and because I had time to daydream I remembered the one nest I hadn't inspected, and because I remembered that one nest I made a sudden, impulsive decision. I waited until the coast was clear and pulled a U-ey. Only a couple of miles away was the nest at Gray's Beach, a spot I didn't visit much though one I'd once observed with the great Cape Cod nature writer John Hay. As I drove toward the beach, passing roads with names like Pequod Place and Ahab Circle, I knew it was unlikely that I would find any birds there. But what I didn't know was that I was about to have a wild string of osprey luck, like a gambler in Vegas who can't stop rolling sevens and elevens.

Sure enough, no sooner had I stepped out of the car than I heard it: that high-pitched *kew, kew, kew* that means osprey. I looked to my left, and there were two young birds, siblings in all likelihood, engaged in a midair battle over a fish. A second later the larger of the birds, a young female, ripped the fish away, and then, after much elaborate circling (the bird equivalent of gloating), she landed on the huge osprey nest that sat in the middle of Gray's Marsh.

She was a powerful young bird, and I got my telescope from the car to study her while she tore apart her still-living meal. Ospreys are ruthlessly suited to their constant pursuit of fish. This bird's long white legs and huge talons pinned the dying fish, her rich chocolate-brown wings occasionally beat, her eyes shone orange. A checkered necklace of brown, like a string of large freckles, spotted her white-feathered throat. As she ate, she established a familiar osprey rhythm: dipping down to tear at the fish, shoulders hunched, ripping the fish to reveal its pink insides, then lifting her head before gulping the bite down, slurping the strands of fish like spaghetti.

Through the scope I could see the perfect roundness of her orange eyes, eyes capable of seeing at least six times farther than a human's, eyes capable of peering down into water from 100 feet above to spy a fish. I stepped away from the scope and studied the nest through my binoculars. Like most of the Cape Cod nests, it was built on a platform and pole erected by human hands. The pole looked like a telephone pole, only shorter and thinner, and the horizontal platform nailed on top had roughly the surface area of a basketball backboard. The nest itself was as haphazard as the bird was elegant: ospreys are classic packrats and will jam anything into the walls of their nests. In years and nests past I had found everything from checkbooks to belts to naked Barbie dolls. Here pieces of fishing line and white sheets of plastic and ropes and what looked like Easter basket stuffing all blew in the wind like wild hairs.

The osprey's plumage shone white and brown-black, distinct against a backdrop of gray, bulked-up clouds. The bird was all angles: the tucked wings jutting up like shoulder blades, the bill jabbing the fish, the beautiful crown sharply pointing to the sky.

Osprey feathers are a dark brown that appears black from a distance, and the ends of the feathers look like they have been dipped in a bucket of white paint. I hate to anthropomorphize, but if you happen to be a human being, it is hard not to have the word *proud* pop into your head when you look at a bird like this. My own thoughts were no less basic: *God, what a beautiful bird.*

And then I heard almost the same words said out loud. I pulled away from the telescope and turned around to see a short woman with a floppy hat and wild curly hair. She made a quick glance down at my single hose sock but was kind enough not to say anything. Instead she smiled and pointed. "What kind of bird is that?" she asked.

I told her and adjusted the telescope so she could look through it. At first she had a hard time with the scope and saw nothing. I fiddled with the lens for her and she tried again. This time she finally saw the osprey up close.

"Oh my God," she said quietly.

She asked me about the bird, and before I knew it I had told her about my trip, as well as launching into a little osprey lecture. She introduced herself as Susan Schwalb, a painter who taught at Brandeis. After staring for a few minutes, she called her husband over from where he had been standing on the beach, and he looked through the scope too. Then another couple came by, a man in a floppy hat similar to Susan's, who seemed to have some bird knowledge, and his wife, a tiny Asian woman who was thrilled to see the bird and was the first to notice it preening. I adjusted the scope for them as they took turns oohing and ahing, and I passed my binoculars around. Soon we'd created a little community, a phenomenon that I've found to be common among osprey watchers. Since there was no one else handy, I played the role of expert, dispensing tidbits.

"When do they migrate?" Susan asked. And "How will they

find their way?" Her husband said he had heard that birds had a kind of built-in GPS system, and I said that that about matched what I'd read. The truth is, no matter how scientifically you try to explain the concept of migration, it comes off as farfetched. Some ornithologists believe that birds have an internal map of the stars, I tried to explain, and some believe that they are led by magnetism. Though this all came from science books, it sounded more like science fiction, or like the far-out theories of the ancient naturalists, who believed, among other things, that when swallows migrated, they were actually wintering below the ice in ponds.

After I finished my lecture, I decided to head down the long wooden walkway over the marsh. I left Susan in charge of the telescope. Tidal creeks wound through the lime-green marsh, and the outgoing tide seethed over barnacled rocks, creek beds glistening a murky grayish brown. Soon after I returned, our little group broke up, Susan and I exchanging e-mail addresses. I liked her right away; she knew nothing about birds but had an obviously sharp and inquisitive mind. Later I found a quotation of hers that appeared in an anthology of writing by women artists: "When I'm working in my studio, at that moment it's all worth it, it's worth the struggle, it's worth the fact that I have no money, it's worth the fact that my life is ridiculous in most people's terms." Like following ospreys, I thought.

Once she and the others had left, I lost myself in the telescope's viewfinder. I claim to hate technology, but I am pure hypocrite, at least when it comes to telescopes. It's a strange thing, but these awkward and intrusive-looking optic tools can be a portal allowing you to enter a bird's world. Through the looking glass and into the nest. Now the osprey stood at nest's edge with her head up like a ship's figurehead, wind ruffling her feathered crown. Having arrived at this point in just her fourth month of life—able to procure a fish, either by diving or by wrangling it away from a sibling—was a good sign, though no guarantee of success during the trying year to come. What lay ahead was uncertain, but what was already behind was a remarkable period of growth whose rapidity was enough to make your head spin.

Born in May in all likelihood, this bird before me had emerged slimy, black, reptilian, no more capable of flight than a rock. The transformation over the next month, from a miniature dinosaur stuck full of pinfeathers to an approximation of an adult bird, occurred at a fast-forward pace that made daily growth seem like time-lapse footage. That that awkward-looking creature would, after many clumsy attempts, learn to fly seemed surprising; that it would learn to fish with any competence seemed more so. But that it would then, after barely earning its wings, turn around and begin a 4000-mile trip to South America was beyond astounding.

Yet that was what this bird would soon attempt. She was faced with an intimidating itinerary. With most first-year birds, the parents leave the nest first while the young stay behind to hone their hunting skills and fatten up on local fish. Then the young birds, prodded by instinct, head south too, and if they are very resilient and lucky, they make their way to South America. The juveniles don't return the following spring but spend the whole next year in South America. Then, as two-year-olds, they fly back north, usually right to the neighborhood they left as youngsters. It is by any standard a journey bordering on the preposterous.

But as I watched this individual bird, I felt something like confidence, or at least hope, that she would have a chance. The odds were against her—only about a third of the birds survive their first year—but she looked athletic and capable. And big—

that was important too, a possible indicator that she was the firstborn of her brood and had not been left to scrounge for scraps of fish like nestlings further down in the pecking order. Who knew? Maybe this bird would be strong and lucky enough to make it all the way to Cuba and beyond. Travel is the weak point in the year, a time when danger and death are one wrong turn away, and for each of these birds the trip south is a high-risk endeavor, a wild risk that requires a great exercise in energy and exuberance. It is always a gamble, but here was a bird, I thought, worth putting your chips on.

And I felt hopeful for another reason. Over the past twenty-four hours I had begun to question the sanity of my decision to follow the ospreys. But now, watching this juvenile, her checkered feathers gleaming, I remembered what had drawn me to the birds in the first place. Wind soughed through the spartina grass while bulky clouds sailed across a blue sky, and the bird couldn't have looked nobler. I felt part of that world, part of the marsh, and I also felt suddenly—and wildly—happy. I remembered how much I loved being close to these birds, and remembered why I was chasing them. Soon the marsh would tint toward orange, undergoing its regularly scheduled death, but I didn't feel the season's usual melancholy. Autumn was the time for travel, and this had always been the time of year when I said goodbye to the birds, resigning myself to waiting until March to see them again. But not this year. This year I was going along for the ride.

One of the things I had forgotten was just how big ospreys are. To use a basketball analogy, they may not be the centers of the bird world—like eagles or condors or pelicans—but they are certainly power forwards. As I watched, this large young female finished her meal. She sat still—digesting, I suppose—and then dropped her head so her neck formed an *S*, like a snake, poised to push off. Then she sprang into the air and, after banking in front of the sun, disappeared into the trees. I tried to keep my binoculars trained on her, but in a second she was gone, invisible.

Which is what she would have been to me if I had not had the good luck to arrive right during her lunchtime, just after I'd finished my own lunch. The sheer randomness of the sight hit me: I wouldn't have seen the bird if I hadn't needed hose socks or if I hadn't eaten those leftover chops or if I hadn't stormed out of my mother's house the night before. Accident and chance were, as usual, life's guiding factors.

I packed up my telescope and headed toward the car, still thinking about accident. In the parking lot a drunken woman was yelling at her husband or boyfriend, who stood next to a white pickup truck. The guy was wearing some sort of Vin Diesel getup, a dark blue tank top with dark blue pants, tattoos of barbed wire encircling his large biceps. He was completely bald and might have been scary-looking if not for his docile expression and hunched posture. In fact, it was his drunken girlfriend or wife who was the aggressive one, and as I drove off she was still yelling.

This time as I headed down White's Path past Foley's I no longer felt despondent. *We must have contact,* Thoreau had said. And that was what I felt upon seeing the bird: *contact.* The sight had lifted me and the day.

But I'll admit that as I pulled onto Route 6, I also experienced a less noble emotion. There was this added satisfaction in seeing the bird: Gessner 1, BBC 0.

CHAPTER TWO

SHRINE

The birds were on the move and so was I. The whole world jittered with movement. I had recently read about the Nukak tribe, the last human hunter-gatherers, who lived in the jungles of Colombia and became sick as soon as they gave up their nomadic lives. Then I thought of the way that elder deer stomp their hooves nervously before the herd moves. We so often look to nature for clichéd notions of peace, of calm and quiet. We are looking in the wrong place. During migration the natural world shakes and stomps with unease.

As I crossed the silver glinting hump of the Sagamore Bridge, leaving Cape Cod behind, the sun broke through a bank of high clouds. The weather reports had been bad, but so far those reports hadn't affected the actual weather, which was quite nice. Before I left, my friend Alan Poole, a biologist who literally wrote the book on ospreys (*Ospreys: An Unnatural History*), had blessed me with an Arab traveling prayer: "God willing and weather permitting."

As I pointed the Pontiac south, it was Alan's house I was aiming for. Westport, Massachusetts, less than an hour's drive from the bridge, can also be considered the home of osprey true believers. It was there, in the late 1960s and 1970s, that a remarkable comeback story began. People and ospreys have always gotten along well, and for centuries sailors looked at the birds' annual return as a sign of spring. But it's only been during the past thirty to forty years that the ospreys' status has been elevated. The birds probably regard themselves as they always have, their self-images unwavering, but people now see them as a kind of fish-eating phoenix. Ospreys sparked so much passion in so many people by using one of the oldest tricks in the book: they became rare. By almost going away forever they made themselves noticed, and missed.

What led to this decline was the liberal use of the chemical DDT during the post–World War II era, when the birds suffered devastation and were almost entirely wiped out in New England. For two decades or so pesticides were embraced by Americans as a symbol of hope and progress for our squeaky-clean, Jetsonian future, and were sprayed over marshes to kill mosquitoes. But it turned out that it wasn't just mosquitoes the chemical killed. Like some over-the-top movie villain, DDT destroyed ospreys in an almost perversely evil fashion, thinning their eggshells so that mothers crushed their young when they tried to incubate. For a period of close to twenty years after World War II, many of the birds in the contaminated landscapes could not reproduce, and it began to look like ospreys would no longer come back each March to signal spring for coastal New Englanders. But thanks to the banning of DDT in the early 1970s and the work of several passionate individuals, the birds did return. Westport had been the center of one of their earliest and strongest comebacks and was still home to the largest and densest osprey colony in New England, a kind of shrine for osprey lovers.

As I drove, I fingered the osprey skull and shoulder bone that sat in the passenger seat. While I hadn't found any ospreys at the nests back on that first futile day, I had discovered some bones at the base of one of the nests. They looked to be the remains of a young bird, and I'd decided to bring them along, with the idea of perhaps placing the skull at another nest along the route of my trip. Of course I felt a little silly about this idea. Once, a few years before, I'd had an encounter with a famous nature writer that made me suspicious of just this sort of New Age ritual. I was attending a writing conference and was out on the lawn throwing a Frisbee with a few people when I noticed the famous writer walking out of the woods. I tossed the Frisbee to a friend and ran up to say hello. The writer didn't shake my hand or introduce himself but instead stepped back a little and spoke in a hushed voice as if delivering a eulogy. Like many nature writers, he seemed to enjoy indulging in the role of high priest, exuding a kind of pompous humility, and there was a moment when I almost felt that he expected me to get down on my knees to receive his blessing. Instead I asked him what he'd been doing in the woods.

"I was down at the beaver dam," he said in his sacred whisper. "I was paying homage to the dam, spreading the wood chippings of my beavers from my home dam back in Oregon."

I didn't know what to say to that, though Woody Allen's line from *Annie Hall* occurred to me: "Excuse me, but I'm due back on Planet Earth."

But if I liked to mock that sort of groovy ritual, I also occasionally liked to indulge in it. During my years on Cape Cod I had collected various skulls and bones that I'd found along the beaches and marshes, and in a way I regarded these as totems and talismans, physical manifestations of the love I felt for the place. In truth I wasn't so different from High Priest Beaver Chippings. I had developed various strange rituals, like walking out every day to check the spot where I'd hidden a coyote skull under the rocks below the bluff. If at times these rituals seemed silly, mere fluff, at other times they really did seem to connect me to the natural world in a way beyond reason.

As I drove through New Bedford the clouds split even further, and soon I was heading into the opening credits of *The Simpsons:* white cartoon clouds interspersed with an unreal pastel blue. What better place to begin an obsessive quest after an animal? New Bedford, after all, was Melville territory, and it was here that Ahab headed out after his whale. I understood that Ahab was not a particularly healthy role model, but despite myself I admired his obsessiveness. There were ospreylike qualities to the crazy captain's quest. I'd read more than one story of an osprey sinking its talons into a too-large fish and being pulled underwater, dying Ahab-fashion, drowned by what it sought. Although I didn't want to die chasing ospreys, I never forgot the good points of obsession. For one thing, it does a fine job of filling the void. On the same day that I had encountered the famous nature writer, I'd heard him give a talk about the human need for "emptiness, quiet, and stillness." I didn't buy it. As I drove, chasing the ospreys, I enjoyed the opposite sensations: fullness, excitement, and engagement.

And, to be honest, nervousness. Unlike me, Ahab didn't have to compete with the BBC. I glanced at my watch, knowing that the British were probably landing soon. I'd taken some small competitive pleasure in the next day's forecast for Cape Cod, since the BBC team would be making camp on drizzly Martha's Vineyard through the weekend. Meanwhile, according to the admittedly inaccurate reports, I would be leaving the rain behind. But the truth was, I didn't really wish the TV people ill luck. I was feeling more magnanimous after my sighting of the young female bird. There were plenty of ospreys for everyone.

Of course it wasn't really a competition, or if it was, it was a competition only in my mind. Certainly the Brits weren't losing any sleep dreaming up ways to impede me. I couldn't quite picture their team of chipper producers, directors, and scientists whispering into their walkie-talkies, "We just got word that that bloke Gessner saw a juvenile female in Yarmouth . . . We've got to stop him." In fact, far from being secretive, the BBC was helping, not hindering, my own adventure. The movements of their satellite ospreys were available online for anyone to read. Rob Bierregaard, the American scientist I'd talked to, was posting the movements of the birds, along with concise and sometimes funny travelogues. Each day Rob would also chart the course of the five birds he was following on a color map. When I'd dropped by my mother's house that morning, it had taken just five minutes to check the Internet to see what the BBC birds were up to.

My original idea had been to follow the general path of migrating ospreys. But now, thanks to Rob and the BBC, I could also gauge the movements of individual birds. The five Martha's Vineyard birds that had been outfitted with small satellite transmitters included an adult female that Rob named Elsie (since her nest was on Cow Bay) and Elsie's sole offspring, Bunga (named for the same reason, as in *Cowabunga!*); Jaws, a fledgling male, and Bluebeard, an adult male, both tagged on the west end of the island, in Chilmark and Gay Head, respectively; and Tasha, a first-year female tagged in the center of the island, near Vineyard Haven.

Putting the satellite transmitters on the birds was unavoidably invasive. During the summer Rob had traveled to Martha's Vineyard, climbed up to each osprey nest, and placed something called a noose carpet over the nest while the ospreys were off fishing. A noose carpet, or noose carp, is a piece of chicken wire threaded with nooses made of fishing wire. Rob placed a fish below the noose carp, and when an osprey returned, it would get its talons tangled in the fishing line. Then he would climb the pole and, using a special seat he had invented, similar to a bosun's chair, swing up to the nest. There he would grab the bird and put a hood over its head to calm it and then carry it back down. On the ground he fitted each bird with a small elastic backpack containing a transmitter and an antenna that jutted out below the pack. My admittedly limited understanding of what the transmitter did was this: it shot a signal up to a satellite, which shot a signal down to some scientist in France, who, after some Doppler-shift calculations, e-mailed the location to Rob.

As you can imagine, some of the ospreys weren't crazy about being kidnapped. Jaws had earned his name by biting Jennifer, Rob's grad student assistant. They'd had to pry his bill apart to free her hand. "It was just like how they tear the meat off fish," she said later. While Jaws reacted with aggression, Bunga grew depressed, becoming so traumatized after Rob put the backpack on that he didn't fly for two days.

Rob admitted that the process stressed the birds. What's more, the transmitters literally ruffled their feathers, which was a problem, since consistency of feather formation aids a bird's flight. Add to this the extra weight (though slight) and you certainly weren't doing the individual birds any favors. Migration was tough enough, both the odds and the miles, without any other hindrances.

On the other hand, while this wasn't anybody's idea of wild nature, transmitters were the obvious future of osprey research. Almost all the big recent advances in osprey knowledge had come thanks to satellite technology, and in particular to Mark Martell, who was the pioneer. And like cell phones and the Internet, the technology wasn't going away. The big unanswered questions about the birds could be answered only with the new technology.

One of the questions that Rob Bierregaard was helping answer through that technology concerned the nature of early dispersal behavior before migration. Simply put, what did the birds do in the weeks after they left the nest and before they flew south? This was one of the great unknowns of osprey behavior, and already Rob had added to the scant store of knowledge. The three juvenile birds he had put transmitters on, Jaws, Bunga, and Tasha, were only the eighth, ninth, and tenth young birds ever to be tracked, almost doubling the total data.

The main thing he was learning was that young birds, in fact all the birds, do a lot of moving before the main move. In August, Bunga had taken an unexpected trip *north*, over 300 miles to Portland, Maine, and back. Meanwhile Jaws, who'd left the island on August 16—early for an immature bird—had flown directly over Westport on his way to Providence. From there he headed farther inland to northern Connecticut, where he had spent the better part of the past month hunting on inland lakes.

What was Jaws doing out there on those lakes?

The short answer seemed to be *perfecting technique.* By leaving the roiling waters off the coast for the shallow, calmer lakes, he had found the perfect place to hone his craft. The basic skills he was using were innate: every bird gets essentially the same hunting kit of huge talons, long legs, strong gull-like wings, and the impulse to plunge into surf to spear fish. But what isn't innate is experience. Older ospreys, those that have survived a migration or two, can sometimes catch up to two thirds of what they dive for—sometimes, like Ol' Never Miss, even more. That is thanks to stored-up information, the bird equivalent of wisdom. They know that it means one thing when the water ripples a certain way or that they can lose a fish if they come down at too steep an angle or that it makes sense not to turn toward the sun. They also know how to play the odds: when it's best not to expend energy on a dive or when it's best to call it quits and move on to a new fishing hole.

These were the things Jaws was teaching himself during his

month-long crash course on the Connecticut lakes. He spent his days wheeling over the water, peering down for fish. He would pause, hover in the air, spot a fish—a pickerel, maybe—and anticipate its movements, still hovering. Then he would pull in his wings and transform himself into a fighter plane, stooping toward the water. This dive through the air was his first plunge, the splash into the water his second. He would strike the surface and immerse, reaching with those long white legs and stabbing with his talons. Often enough during his early attempts he came up empty. This wasn't all that surprising. Of all the tasks you can undertake on earth, both human and animal, this is one of the more spectacular and difficult, and even with your instincts prodding you, you don't just pick it right up.

The question of whether or not birds have emotions is one that can spark hours of debate in ornithological circles. No matter where you stand on this issue, anyone who has watched birds seriously will admit that they do have distinct personalities. Tasha, for instance, would soon prove herself to be a kind of impulsive plunger-inner, launching herself on long over-water crossings where she would either learn or die. Jaws, in contrast, was something of a perfectionist. He had clearly chosen a different approach for survival from the more impulsive Tasha, and only time and luck would tell which strategy would succeed. But if Jaws found himself eating a life-sustaining tilapia in Cuba a month from now, he would owe it in part to his training camp back in Connecticut.

For all the importance of preparation, randomness and raw luck are often the determining factors in migration. Only about three out of ten young birds from New England make it to South America and back. Already Elsie's young, Bunga, had succumbed. After his road trip to Maine, Bunga had circled back home, rested for a while, and then headed out over the water again. On August 27 he flew to the marshes on the Westport River, where I was heading, and spent a few days fishing and readying himself for the journey. By the last day in August he had made his way down the coast to Westerly, Rhode Island, and then flown over New London, Connecticut. But there the satellite signal stopped, which, according to Rob, suggested something dramatic like a collision with a car, since otherwise, even in death, the signal would have kept pulsing.

As I drove south, I knew the relative locations of all five radio-tagged birds. Bunga was presumed dead, and Jaws had finally left his lakes and started the trip south. Elsie, unaware that her only offspring had been killed, was already well under way, which wasn't unusual: adults, and particularly female adults, usually left earlier than the young birds. What *was* unusual, and quite individual, was the behavior of Bluebeard, who, despite one offshore venture, was turning out to be a homebody, showing few signs of leaving the nest. On his website Rob detailed the reasons for this: "Bluebeard is a truly devoted father. His young has apparently not figured out how to catch fish reliably. He heads off to hunt and returns wet but fishless. He then sits on his nest screaming for food, which Bluebeard is still bringing to him. It's not terribly late for the male to still be around the breeding grounds (some don't head south until early October)—but it is late for a young bird not to be catching its own food. This one may not have much of a future in the gene pool."

My particular interest in Tasha, the youngest of the fledglings, was simple: we'd begun our journeys on the same day. As I was racing around Cape Cod in search of nests, she was making her first flight across the water from the Vineyard, stopping along the Elizabeth Island chain and then flying over Falmouth and close to the center of Cape Cod, right where I'd been. While I was cursing and muttering about empty nests and an ospreyless day, she was soaring out over the backside of the Cape. Perhaps she'd dipped for a fish in a kettle pond, preferring that to the dark ocean water. Then she had headed home to rest up, her exploratory journey just a practice round, a dry run, to give her confidence and experience for the much longer trip ahead. It would be stretching it—lying, in fact—to say that Tasha was the bird I'd watched devouring the fish at Gray's Beach. For one thing, there was no tiny backpack on that bird; for another, by the time I got to that nest, Tasha was already back on the Vineyard. But like that bird, she was a young female readying for her first journey, and like that bird, she was about to undergo a trip into the unknown.

As I drove I wondered: what compels a bird to leave on a particular day? Is it something internal that matches the weather? Hormones triggered by the slant of the sun? The right proportion of sunlight to darkness? Or is it more random? Something as simple as the sun being out that morning and the wind feeling right?

After New Bedford, I drove south on Horseneck Road until I reached a spot near the mouth of the Westport River. There I pulled the car over and parked illegally by a dune. I threw my telescope over my shoulder and hiked over the dune, then down into a sandy valley marked by the charred remains of campfires and scatterings of broken glass. From the litter and coals it wasn't hard to imagine the ghosts of drunken townies dancing in the dunes.

Marsh elder and reddening glasswort, the color of bruised thumbs, grew near the edge of the tidal river. From where I stood, at river's edge, a quick scan with the telescope revealed over twenty osprey nesting platforms. DDT wasn't the only human threat the ospreys faced. Over the years development had all but wiped out ideal nesting sites, and those sites—the old dead trees, or live trees with room up top for nesting—were now few and far between. But humans giveth as well as taketh away. These platforms had been built in response to lost habitat. Ospreys have always been supremely adaptable to humans, sometimes nesting on channel markers and chimneys and buoys, and they took to these poles immediately, building their bulky nests on top of the manmade platforms.

No one had worked more fervently to build these platforms than Gil Fernandez, a schoolteacher and part-time dairy farmer who began erecting platforms along the Westport River in the late 1950s. One of the things he quickly discovered was that he could place the poles relatively close together. Unlike most raptors, ospreys are colonial nesters and don't mind having neighbors nearby. Now, over thirty years later, the Westport marsh was a virtual osprey mecca, and I could enjoy the results of Fernandez's vision. I scanned the marsh more slowly, about 180 degrees across the horizon, counting birds as I went. I saw a few gulls up in the osprey nests, several egrets nearby, and one ghostly blue heron flying low over the marsh. But mostly I saw ospreys, counting six spread out on twenty-one nests. There was a chance that the ospreys who sat in the nests were the nest's "owners," but there was a better chance, given the time of year, that migrating birds were just using the nests as rest stops or eating platforms.

Before I left, I trained my binoculars on two young ospreys who were soaring over the marsh. (Beginning birders often confuse gulls and ospreys, in part because of coloring, but also because of the fact that both birds have long, relatively narrow wings that bend in the middle. But while gulls' wings bend at the "elbow," osprey wings bend less symmetrically at the carpus, or "wrist.") At first I thought the birds were simply fishing, but then I noticed that they were rising up too high for that. They rode the air currents called thermals, bobbing up on the rising columns of air, up 100, then 200 feet, until they became specks even through my binoculars. They held their wings almost perfectly still as they rose, then floated for a while, adjusting to the winds slightly, before pulling in their wings and banking back down and rising again. Then they yoyoed up and down a few times while I watched. It almost looked like they were doing it just for the hell of it, just because they could, and maybe that was part of it. But it was also practice.

Like the young transmitter birds Tasha and Jaws, these juveniles were getting the hang of this flying thing, learning the subtleties. And one of those subtleties is rising on thermals and soaring, the preferred osprey mode of long-distance traveling. Soaring makes sense: you certainly don't want to *flap* all the way to South America. Better to rise on these hot columns of air, lifting up hundreds of feet, before pulling in your wings and gliding for a few miles. Much more efficient.

These particular birds weren't going anywhere today, so they just spiraled and banked back down, and by the time I was ready to leave the marsh, they were sitting lazily on the edges of two of the nests.

Before I headed back to the car, I put my binoculars down and tried to take in both the place and the moment. If you look closely enough, you can see the border between seasons, and the border between late summer and fall is a particularly fascinating one. Over the past few years I'd learned that by keeping my eyes open I could see animals practicing, just like the two young birds, everywhere in early fall. It's a sort of communal massing and preparation, nature's warmup act. You can observe it not just in osprey practice sessions but in the boils of fish and the staging of tree swallows, who gather by the thousands all through the Northeast and cyclone over streets and beaches and yards. A great sense of anticipation, as well as preparation, fills the air. As if the whole world is readying itself, poised for movement.

After Horseneck Beach, there is a stretch of beach homes that don't exactly bring to mind the nearby Breakers of Newport. A snob would hate this row of trailer homes, portable log cabins, and aluminum shacks that look like unhinged cabooses. But ospreys—packrats extraordinaire, who aren't afraid of patching their nests with aluminum foil or fishing line—would feel right at home.

Some of the trailers look as if they've taken root and grown foundations, and a quick glance tells you why they'd want to stay. If you turn away from the homes and toward the ocean, you have a spectacular view of Buzzards Bay, the water dark near the shore, with a vivid offshore streak of Caribbean green. This is the back way of looking at Martha's Vineyard and Nantucket, not the fancy front-door way, the classy way, but just as nice. It was also, I noted when I reached it, the direction from which Bluebeard—and likely the BBC as well—would soon be flying.

Right after the trailers, I saw a small shack with a sign that said AUDUBON HEADQUARTERS, and I spontaneously pulled into the clamshell driveway. It took knocking on a couple of doors before I got the right one, but finally a door opened and I was greeted by a woman wearing pink shorts, a blue T-shirt, and a big smile. She introduced herself as Gina Purtell. As I told her about my trip, and about the fact that I was in Westport to spend the night at Alan Poole's cabin, it slowly dawned on both of us that we had met before, during a dinner with Alan. Since ospreys had been the basis of Alan's and my friendship, we had frequently made it a point to dine osprey style, getting together over raw fish, and at one of these sushi gatherings Gina had joined us. Now we talked for a while, and before I left, she pointed out the window and said that Audubon himself had once stayed in the large house next door.

"He stayed with the Almay family in that big house, and he drew the whole time he was here," she said. "I always thought it would be neat if it turned out he drew his osprey here."

I thought it would be neat too, and said so before leaving. She wished me well, and I drove off daydreaming about Audubon drawing ospreys in Westport. I knew that Audubon, being Audubon, would have been shooting the birds as well as drawing them. But this didn't bother me as much as it does some people, who can't get their heads around the fact that the famous bird man was trigger-happy. While Audubon's way of becoming intimate with his birds was admittedly ugly and brutal, guns were the way of his time. Of course it was good that killing was no longer part of bird watching and that I wasn't packing heat along with my telescope. But I was still hunting, just without the killing part. And I liked it. Hunting, after all, brings with it an ancient encoded excitement. Since beginning my quest, I hadn't spent more than a second or two worrying about my things-to-do list or my unpaid electric bill or even the aching rotator cuff that had plagued me for months. It was exhilarating to simplify life into quest. How often in this scattered, compromised life do we get to focus on *one thing?* How often do we get to immerse ourselves fully?

Alan Poole, whose house I was now nearing, had for one brief period simplified his life to ospreys. Gil Fernandez's platforms had drawn Alan, a young biologist, to Westport, and it was here, beginning in 1974, that he had done his important early work, charting the recovery rate of the ospreys that began to breed again once DDT was banned. In those days his life was reduced to osprey terms: he spent all his time watching, studying, tagging, and tracking. He was learning things that no one had ever known about ospreys, and he was living in their midst, logging countless hours out in the spartina grass. I imagined him covered with mud and bug bites at the end of the day, falling asleep exhausted to find that ospreys had even infiltrated his dreams. I had always liked people who became obsessed, liked the way it seemed to enliven them and give a shine to their worlds. And if Alan was obsessed with all things osprey, it was not quite as reductive as it may sound at first. He found, as John Muir had, that when he picked up one thing, the whole rest of the universe was "hitched to it." Ospreys became his way of thinking about the world.

The osprey nest out on the water behind Alan's cottage stood empty, as did the cottage itself. Or almost empty. Alan was in Ithaca, New York, where he worked at the famous Cornell Lab on Sapsucker Woods Road. He'd generously agreed to let me stay at his small cabin in South Dartmouth, outside of Westport, perched in the woods along the water. But the house was not entirely deserted: Brian, a carpenter, stood up on a ladder, painting its exterior.

Alan had warned me that the cottage was being gutted and remodeled. Now Brian climbed down the ladder and we shook hands. He was an easygoing middle-aged man with a stoner's eyes and a white man's Afro like Jerry's, the dentist on the old *Bob Newhart Show*. He wore a soul patch, a white T-shirt, white painter's pants, and paint-spattered sneakers. He had a comfortable, slouching manner and spoke in a way that made you think he found the world pretty amusing.

"Alan was wrong," he said. "You can't stay here."

I expressed my concern, and he smiled.

"But you can stay at the *other* cabin. The *nice* cabin."

I'd always considered Alan's cabin pretty nice, tucked in the woods off a dirt road, with a view of the tidal creek, an osprey nest, and the ocean beyond. But now Brian led me down a grass path to a smaller cabin, a cabin that was almost all glass, right on the edge of a tidal creek that led to a body of water called Allens Pond and then the ocean beyond. This cabin was unfinished, propped up on cinderblocks, with an orange extension cord snaking in through one of the windows.

Inside, a large quilted bed covered more than half of the wood-floored space. A telescope pointed out the glass front doors, and I noticed a tattered copy of *Leaves of Grass* sitting on the night table. Large windows, as well as the glass doors, made you feel as if the indoors were outdoors or the outdoors in.

Brian pointed at all the windows. "You don't want to throw stones in this place," he said.

We stepped outside and walked down a little path until we stood at the edge of the marsh. Rash-red poison ivy surrounded the water like a row of flamboyant guards. Alan had described my quest to Brian, who now asked me how the trip was going so far. I told him about my plans to fly to Cuba and he nodded.

"That's a long way to travel," he said. "The longest trip I make these days is to King Lumber."

The woods were interlaced with paths, and we hiked up another, roughly following the winding orange extension cord, until we reached a huge rock. Protruding from the rock was Brian's own cabin, a low stone house that had obviously been inspired by the neighboring rock and that Brian called, appropriately enough, "the Stone House." He explained that he had built and repaired several cabins in these woods with the land's owner, a doctor named Rob Powel. Rob rented out some of the places and had his own guests stay in others. The glass cabin that I would be staying in was being built by Brian and Rob as a "place for contemplation."

Before we left the Stone House, I used the bathroom and discovered that it too was stone, with a stone sink and a slate bathtub. Once I reemerged from Brian's cave-house, we started walking back to Alan's cottage. I asked Brian how long he'd been living here.

"I've been working on these houses for a while," he said. "But I only moved into the Stone House a year ago. It's nice. No phone, no Internet, no TV."

When we reached Alan's, Brian said he had to get back to work and climbed up the ladder leaning against the house. I had started to walk up a path through the briars to retrieve my stuff from the rental car when he called out to me from his ladder.

"You know what I would do if I were stopping here for the night and I really cared about ospreys?" he asked.

I walked back toward him. I said I didn't know.

He cocked his head, Afro pointing skyward, and smiled. "I would probably visit Mr. Osprey himself. Gil Fernandez."

I told him the truth: I hadn't realized that Gil was still alive.

"Oh, he's alive, all right. For months now he's been bugging me to do some electrical work on his barn. He lives about a mile from here."

Things were starting to fall in my lap. I drove up the long road to Stone Barn Farm, passing fields of purple aster and Queen Anne's lace, and found Gil Fernandez, somewhat shrunken at ninety-three but hardy enough to be riding around cutting his huge lawn on a tractor mower. He was a little white-haired gnome in a baseball hat, hunched over and so intent on his work that he didn't notice me parking in his driveway. During the research for my first book on ospreys I had tried to interview Gil, but his wife, Josephine, had been very sick, and had since passed away.

As Gil circled the house on the slow-moving tractor, I walked around the other way to intercept him. I was nervous about startling him, for obvious reasons, but also somewhat nervous about simply marching onto his property. It's not only ospreys, after all, that can be territorial about their homes. For instance, I knew that Gil and Alan Poole no longer got along. Though I didn't know any of the details of their rift, I had heard that as Alan had risen like a young Michael Corleone of the osprey world, Gil had begun to bristle, perhaps feeling that Alan didn't acknowledge the debt he owed him and "his" birds. There had also been some vague conflict between them about how to trap birds for banding. Whatever the specifics, the rift was permanent. The two osprey lovers lived less than a mile apart but never spoke.

I finally decided to approach Gil from straight ahead, waving my arms as if in surrender. But head down and intent on the task at hand, he still didn't see me, and it looked for a moment like he was going to run me over. Just when I thought I'd have to jump out of the way, he slowed and pulled up beside me. I introduced myself, and he yanked off a work glove and shook my hand. He wore a little khaki coat over an explorer's shirt, and white pants and white socks above his sneakers. A proud prow of a nose jutted from his wrinkled face. One eye was swollen half closed, but the other shone intently. I'd heard he could sometimes be a bit sharp, but he was almost instantly welcoming.

"Nice to meet you," he said. "Any friend of the ospreys is a friend of mine."

One enjoyable thing about sharing an obsession with someone is that it eliminates the need for small talk. Without further ado, I asked him about his history with the birds. He was happy to reply, and before long I was getting the interview I'd hoped to get years earlier. We talked for over an hour, and the whole time he never got off his little tractor.

In a quiet but rich voice, Gil told me about how he had first grown interested in ospreys. He'd begun building osprey platforms back in the 1950s, when he noticed that the birds' numbers were dropping. He worried that raccoons, which were becoming more plentiful, were raiding the nests. "The birds accepted my platforms right away," he said. "And I never had any trouble with raccoons after that. What I did have trouble with was gulls."

I told him that I had just been over at the marsh and had observed several gulls sitting in the osprey nests.

"The ospreys hate that," he said with surprising vehemence. "Gulls use the nests to feed, bringing in their fish and, worse, their clams, leaving them in the nest. It's a real mess."

"Even for a sloppy bird like an osprey, that's a mess," I agreed.

I thought this was an innocent enough statement, but Gil looked offended by what I'd said. He rose up a little in the saddle of the tractor.

"Don't ever say they're a sloppy bird. They're not sloppy."

I tried to explain that I just meant they were sloppy in the construction of their nests, but he cut me off.

"They're not like gulls. They keep the insides of those nests in fine shape. Even the youngsters know enough to go to the edge of the nest to defecate. No, they are *not* sloppy birds."

Worried that I was getting off on the wrong foot, I shook my head. I hoped that my head-shaking signaled both agreement and contrition for my error.

"I admire the osprey," he said more quietly. "People ought to behave the way the ospreys do. You know, they are considerate of one another; they are dedicated to their family. I've had many cases of a male taking care of two females because the second one didn't have a mate. So if she was there in an adjoining territory, not too far away from his, he'd go over and help her build her nest, bring in material. He'd even mate with her, he'd bring in food for her and the youngsters, and he'd do double duty. And yet you can't say that he was a . . ."

"Bigamist?" I suggested.

"Yes, bigamist. Because he was faithful to his own family. Every night he spent the night right near his family, not near the other one. So it's amazing. I've learned so much from their behavior."

It occurred to me that a human male who did the same thing might get arrested, or, at the very least, would not exactly be regarded as a role model. But I decided to keep my mouth shut.

"I began banding birds in the late sixties," Gil continued. "One of my birds was found down near Iguazu Falls, in northeast Argentina. That's forty-five hundred miles, which was the record at the time. Still is, I think. I learned quite a lot from the banding, watching the same birds come back to the same nest. I studied one bird for over thirteen years, which helped me establish how long they live. He would come back to the nest every year on March twenty-fifth. You could set your calendar to it."

He told me he was further inspired in his work upon hearing a talk about ospreys by Dennis Puleston, the artist and naturalist, who had helped lead the fight against DDT in the 1960s down in Brookhaven, on Long Island. Dennis was the patron saint of ospreydom: a kindly, brilliant, inspiring activist, artist, and birder. I told Gil that I knew of Dennis and that though he had passed away, the next stop on my trip would be with his widow and children at the Puleston compound on Long Island.

"Well, you can tell all the Pulestons that I am full of admiration," he said. "Dennis was a great man."

I asked him if he still banded birds, and he shook his head. "You need to trap the birds to band them, and I soured on trapping long ago. Once a female bird got caught in a trap I'd put out and she flew off before I could get to her. She flew off with the trap, and I never saw that female again. After that I decided to stop trapping for good. I couldn't stand hurting the birds."

I described how Rob Bierregaard had trapped and wired the

Martha's Vineyard ospreys so he could outfit them with the satellite transmitter backpacks. I told him I had mixed feelings about the whole business.

"Well, the question is, what are they going to do with this information? What is it worth to know the routes of the birds if we don't stop destroying habitat near rivers and lakes and oceans? What is it worth if we don't do anything with this knowledge? The real question isn't how much does it all cost or what we can get. The real question, in the end, is how much an osprey is worth."

Before I left, I told him that I would also be visiting the famous raptor watch site Hawk Mountain. He pointed at the trees that umbrellaed over us.

"It's all connected," he said. "I got these trees as saplings from Hawk Mountain when I was there doing a slide show on ospreys." He shook his head as if marveling at something. "It seems my whole life has been intertwined with the birds," he said. "And for me, the intertwining has been such a pleasure. It's been lots of work, of course, but it's such a joy to watch the wonder of creation. And it's been fun just being around the birds. They have such fine habits. In many ways they're better than people, especially with the way civilization is heading now."

He added that he thought it was a fine thing I was doing, following the birds on their migration, something he wished he'd done himself. "In this torn world, I can't think of a better thing to do," he said. "I'd go with you if I wasn't so old."

That seemed a good note to end on, a kind of blessing for my trip from a gnarled old osprey wizard. I said thank you and apologized for taking him away from his work.

"Oh, I've enjoyed the rest," he said. "And the talk."

I'd walked halfway back to my car when he yelled out to me. "What time is it?"

"Ten past five," I called back.

He climbed down slowly off his tractor. "Quittin' time," he said.

Brian was taking a leak in the bushes when I pulled back up to the cabin. He smiled unselfconsciously, zipped up, waved, and asked me how Gil was.

I told him that we had talked about ospreys for over an hour.

"Well, that's one thing that old guy can do," he said. "He can sure talk about ospreys."

He suggested that I use one of Alan's kayaks before the sun set. Twenty minutes later I was floating down the tidal creek below Alan's empty osprey nest, paddling lazily as a marsh hawk glided over the long grass. Drawing close to the nest, I noticed a green sprig or fern hanging down from the brown branches. That meant that a bird had used the nest earlier that year.

My previous observations of ospreys had focused almost exclusively on their nests and nesting. The nesting season is about staying still, about incubation and patience. But migration is different. It's about movement, and at the moment that seemed infinitely more exciting and enlivening. And dangerous, of course, but that was part of it too. Travel is a precarious point in the lives of both humans and birds. But the reward makes it worth it. *To be in movement!* What could be better? Especially after a long period of immobility. Alfred North Whitehead wrote that art, and life, proceed in cycles of discipline and freedom. The season I spent at the nests had been the discipline, where I had learned to slow down and *see* and get to know the birds and their habits. And now came the exhilarating reward: the freedom of flight, the relief of no longer sitting still.

As I paddled back toward Alan's I received an unexpected gift, a sight I'd never seen before. Low in the spartina grass hunched a coyote, stalking a great blue heron. Streaks of fox-orange ran over the top of the coyote's head, and its tail swirled with blacks and reds and whites. Closing in on the heron, it crouched so low in the grass that all I could see was the white in its ears. Then a sudden burst of activity: a pounce, a moment of panicked fluttering, the huge bird flying off with a squawk. I followed the heron's flight for a moment, and when I looked back the coyote was gone, probably into the nearby woods.

Darkness was closing in as I paddled up to the bank behind Alan's house. Brian greeted me, helped me haul out the boat, and invited me over for a beer. We walked up to the Stone House, where we sat on lawn chairs on the patch of open grass that served as his front lawn. We drank the beer, ice-cold Wachusett IPAs, and ate tortilla chips from the bag—my dinner—and while we missed the actual moment of sunset, we did get to see its fiery coals reflected in the clouds, first as a blazing purple, then a duller blue. We sipped the beer and told each other about our lives, learning among other details that we both had once had girlfriends who went to Union College.

With darkness dragonflies arrived. Probably about forty of them, buzzing in and out of the trees that framed our view of the marsh. And then the bats came too, chasing the dragonflies. They danced a zigzagging dance of predator and prey, zipping overhead as I finished my beer and Brian smoked a cigarette. After a while longer, I thanked Brian and said goodnight, feeling my way back to my glass cabin by following the winding extension cord. I liked Brian: he was funny, and though he was a little deaf, he at least smiled as if he got my jokes. And I liked the way he lived, out here in the woods, building these brilliant cabins, these unseen masterpieces.

I took a leak in the poison ivy and climbed up into the cabin. The mattress was firm, the quilt was soft, and the bed had the number of pillows I required (minimum three: one for head, one between legs to ease my bad back, one clutched to stomach for reasons unknown). I flicked on the single small light and tried to read from the ragged copy of *Leaves of Grass*. Secretly I was hoping for something relevant to my own journey, maybe even a mention of an osprey, since Whitman, after all, was a Long Islander. I skipped around the pages, but the closest I got to an osprey was a goose, or rather a gander:

> *The wild gander leads his flock through the cool night*
> *Ya-honk he says and it sounds like an invitation.*

I scribbled the lines down in my journal. Then I flipped around some more. I can't remember what I read, one ecstatic song of procreation or another—"O vital self! O healthy body," or something like that—but after my long osprey day I was too tired to concentrate. I switched off the light and immediately fell asleep.

I slept well out there in the woods.

The next morning I woke at around 5:00 and lay in bed listening to crickets and an occasional duck, as well as an unearthly noise that I imagined to be the fox-red coyote killing something. By 5:30 the first insistent bird twittering rose from the marsh and the sky began its gradual lightening from black to dark blue. Since my bed pointed toward the water, I could watch the world lighten without rising, and there was no reason to get up until my craving for caffeine overwhelmed me. I climbed out into the cold and discovered some coffee, which I began grinding in the antique grinder by the sink. The grinding took forever and making the coffee was an elaborate operation, but it was worth it as I climbed back into bed, drank two cups, and lay there watching

the day come in. My brain buzzed awake with caffeine's resur-
rection, and I grew strangely fond of one tree branch that curled
in front of my window. It looked like a part of a great painting,
foregrounding the marsh, and I enjoyed watching the emerging
details of its thick-grooved bark.

Soon the marsh lit up in an olive-lime color and bands of
blue light and pink clouds alternated in the sky. I had a reserva-
tion on the eleven o'clock ferry to Long Island, and it was time
to pack up and leave. But after throwing my stuff in the car, I
walked down to the water for one last look around.

A pink line still ran through the sky, and the birds had taken
over the marsh. It was a heron time of day, and a great blue
hunted out by the osprey nest while dozens of other herons and
egrets stalked across the marsh. One egret flew right at me, with
that characteristic pulling-in of the bill and extension of legs
behind it, like a difficult yoga pose. From where I stood I could
see almost 360 degrees, and the sky soon filled with cormorants
and loons and a rattling kingfisher. There were humped lines of
migrating ducks and swallows migrating too, in their darting,
pulsing way. It was crazy bird action, with everyone going somewhere fast, but the morning's highlight was a young harrier, or
marsh hawk, scything over the grass. In the early light, the harrier, not quite osprey-sized but impressive enough, cruised over
the spartina grass on dark wings while its undersides shone an
almost molten red-orange. The contrast between the dark upper
wings and the way the sun hit it below made its colors as distinct
as an oriole's: dark back, white patch, blazing orange. And the
movement matched the color. I followed it with my binoculars
all the way across the marsh until it reached a high dune, and
then it began harvesting both sides of the dune, searching for
mice and voles. It worked back and forth from one side of the
dune to the other, flying low to the ground and then popping up.

There was a swinging motion to it—diving, then floating, diving, then floating—and it definitely was king of the marsh, scaring off other birds as it flew.

I pulled myself away from the birds. I had no idea how long the drive would take and couldn't miss the ferry. Brian wasn't up, but I scribbled a note of thanks on the back of a shingle and leaned it against his ladder. Then I was off.

It felt exhilarating to be on the move again, rejoining the migration. I passed Stone Barn Farm and thought about what Gil had said about living a life "intertwined with ospreys." That sounded good to me. If Gil had saved quite a few ospreys by choosing that life, he had also, to a lesser extent, saved himself. There is such a thing as selfish altruism, and sometimes it just comes down to picking the right obsession.

I wanted to get on the highway soon, but I couldn't bring myself to drive by the Westport River without getting a morning osprey fix. So I pulled over and ran out to the spot by the water where I'd stood the day before. Sure enough, there were the ospreys on and near the nests, standing guard, as if they'd never moved. The water had turned a winter blue, and before I left I watched one bird fly up toward the still rising sun, out for an early fishing expedition. That was enough for now. I ran back to the car and began my race toward the Long Island ferry.

Soon I was in Fall River, rattling over a rusty green bridge, a moldy Erector Set construction that didn't inspire much confidence. After Providence, near Warwick, I glanced out the window and saw a long line of ducks migrating south, roughly parallel to the highway. They were riding their own sort of highway, of course, and, like our human highways, theirs was a place of danger and accident. It occurred to me that if safety were their top priority, then animals would avoid migration at all costs. But safety is just one consideration. This is obviously true for humans too. For Americans, for instance, there is no place more dangerous than the road, but that hardly stops us from driving.

When I pulled over to fuel up at the next exit, I ended up chatting with a toothless man who was pumping gas over at the full-serve. He was the kind of guy who might have scared me in my new home in the South, but up here, closer to my own birthplace, I thought nothing of him. His accent was every bit as strange and garbled as that of the most hillbilly of hillbillies, but of course he was a New England hillbilly, which meant he was *my* hillbilly, and therefore somehow less threatening, less exotic, less frightening.

"Don't worry 'bout the ferry," he said in a mumbly voice. "You make the ferry. Plenty of time."

I felt secure in this information, enough so that I decided a little while later to squander that security by pulling off at the exit for Watch Hill. I vaguely remembered that there was a raptor watch site in the town, though it might have been just the name of the place that lured me in: *Watch Hill.* An insistent name, like a command. Before too long I found myself driving through an upscale oceanside community, big houses that were almost mansions, though old-fashioned mansions, not McMansions, which made the place somewhat nicer. I followed Bluff Avenue into the less upscale, more honky-tonk downtown, and I parked in a large lot near the water. This was osprey country, no doubt about it, and when I asked the first person I saw, he gestured out toward a spit of sand beyond the parking lot. "There are a couple of nests out on Map Hill Point," he said.

As I looked down at my watch, it occurred to me that perhaps I was intentionally cutting the ferry close, just for the adrenaline rush. I jogged across the lot anyway, and then up along a ridge of dunes where two osprey nests on poles stood near the end of the point. The nests were empty, but about 200 feet away, on top of the highest dune, a man in a baseball cap was looking out over the water with binoculars. Bingo. Even before I reached him, I knew I had my next informant.

It turned out that John Hammet came out to Map Hill every Saturday during the migration season, usually accompanied by a few other local birders.

"I don't know why the others didn't show today," he told me. "I've already seen one merlin, two sharp-shins, and a harrier."

I asked the obvious question.

"Oh yeah, of course. Seven ospreys so far."

He explained that the birds migrated over town and then flew south from Map Hill Point to Sandy Hill Point. The two points had once been connected, but the land had been breached during the hurricane of '38. From Sandy Hill the birds often flew directly to Long Island, though sometimes, depending on wind conditions, they shot south to Block Island.

In the birding world everyone always seems at least vaguely connected, so I wasn't that surprised when John told me that he had worked with a guy in Maine on the early studies of DDT in ospreys.

"We get a decent number of ospreys coming through here," he said. "And we get falcons too. But the real highlight here is the sharp-shinned hawks. We can get two hundred in a day."

I looked down at my watch. I had people expecting me at the Puleston compound on Long Island, and I was making myself late. But my osprey luck had been so good over the past twenty-four hours that I decided to stay.

It took less than ten minutes. The ones I spotted were flying a different route from most of the other hawks, coming more from the east than directly over town. I picked them out above the mast of a sailboat about halfway across the open water. They weren't gliding like the birds I'd watched practicing in Westport;

in fact they were working hard, flapping faster than any ospreys I'd ever seen except those treading air before a dive. They would pay the cost for this crossing in energy expended. Who knew what form that payment would take?

I thanked John and raced back to the car. Now I was really cutting it close, and I had only myself to thank. But I had seen two more birds and become at least a little familiar with yet another link in the invisible highway the ospreys flew down the coast. Anyway, I was playing with dealer's money. The BBC was still putzing around back on the Vineyard, and I'd already had a day jammed full of birds and luck. I was in movement, and I liked it. Was it stupid to think I could somehow link myself with the birds? Probably. I knew the ospreys were too busy to waste their time marveling to each other about the long distances that *I* was capable of traveling. But it didn't matter. While the ospreys hadn't shouted out Whitman's "*Ya-honk*," I was taking their invitation anyway.

Daring the ever-vigilant Connecticut cops, I sped toward the New London ferry. The past twenty-four hours had brimmed so full that I couldn't imagine life getting fuller. But it would. And though I didn't know it yet, the trip was about to take a turn for the strange.

CHAPTER THREE

STALKING THE
VIRTUAL OSPREY

I made the ferry. Just.

I locked the car on the bottom deck and took a backpack up top. Since I was on vacation and already had several osprey sightings to celebrate, I rationalized treating myself to a pre-noon beer on the top deck. Over the years I had come to believe that beer aided transcendence, and however dubious this conclusion was, I stuck to it. Gulls heckled us as we pulled out of New London harbor; the sun burned down hard on the sea. When I reached into my backpack for a notebook, I discovered that I'd turned into an unintentional klepto: there was the tattered copy of *Leaves of Grass*. Brian and Alan, and by extension the absent Rob, had been perfect hosts. And what had I done? I'd slept in their bed, ate their food, and then stolen their Whitman.

As the sun beat down I skimmed through the broken-spined book. When it came to the American Romantics, I had always been more of a Henry David Thoreau man. Since reading *Walden* in high school I had dreamed of a cabin in the woods and dedicated my life to being a writer. I'd somehow breezed over the parts Thoreau had written about voluntary poverty, but after two decades of living poor and going into debt, that point had been made well enough. The fall before, Nina, Hadley, and I had visited Walden Pond, and I had showed my three-month-old daughter Thoreau's cabin site. "That's where the man lived who ruined your daddy's life," I said. The closest Nina and I had ever

gotten to living our own Walden was on Cape Cod when we
squatted in the summer homes of the wealthy during the off-
season. But with the move south our concept of home had loosened even more. I certainly wasn't about to say of North Carolina
what I'd once said of Cape Cod: that I would stay there forever.

The reason I'd moved to North Carolina was to teach creative
writing, and a strange footnote to my new job was that I had
taken it without realizing that the school's mascot was none
other than the sea hawk, or, as it is more commonly known, the
osprey. During my very first week of teaching, a large statue of
the mascot had been sawed off at the legs and stolen from the
lawn in front of the student center, perhaps as a frat prank.
When the bird was rediscovered a few weeks later, I was invited
to the ceremony for the osprey's return.

I took some consolation in the fact that the migrating path of
real ospreys linked my old home and my new, and that I had been
able to carry my obsession along with me. But this was a feeble
justification for the move. The fact was that by leaving Cape
Cod, I, like the immature tagged ospreys Tasha and Jaws, had
launched myself into uncertainty. Like them, I had no idea what
was going to happen next.

For the next hour of my trip I lay on my back on a bench by
the ship's engines, skimming through the purloined *Leaves of
Grass*. I read and sipped warm beer while the sun burned my face
and the engines roared. After skipping around for a while I
found the famous passage that begins, "I think I could turn and
live with animals, they are so placid and self-contained." The
passage culminates:

> *I stand and look at them and long and long*
>
> *They do not sweat and whine about their condition,*
> *They do not lie awake in the dark and weep for their sins*

They do not make me sick discussing their duty to God…
They bring me tokens of myself, they evince them plainly in
their possession.

This passage's effect on me was momentarily inspiring but ultimately soporific. I managed to underline the phrase "tokens of myself" before dozing off. When I woke up a half-hour later, I was drooling and my beer bottle had rolled down the deck.

What I didn't know as I woke was that I wasn't the only one making the trip to Long Island. Earlier that morning Tasha had chosen a daring route for herself. Unlike Jaws, she did not spend weeks perfecting her technique but instead plunged right into this migration thing. After having made only one modest trip to Cape Cod, she suddenly decided that this was the day, leapt off her nest, and made a beeline south. She flew over the Elizabeth Islands and over Buzzards Bay, not bothering with a stop in Westport, keeping offshore and landing only briefly on Block Island, due south of my Watch Hill location. Even before she reached the Hamptons, it had been by far the longest trip of her young life, but she barely paused to fuel up on fish before continuing to the Bayshore area (which was just south of my own destination). It was the natural place to rest, with plenty of good fishing nearby, but the winds were with her and she felt the momentum of travel and didn't stop.

Tasha had no doubt been lifting on thermals like the young birds I'd watched in Westport. Thermals are spots—usually bare, treeless spots like beaches and parking lots—where heat rises from the earth. That heat can be ridden upward like an elevator, but how does a young bird like Tasha first "get" the idea of thermals? Instinct, of course, but that is too easy an answer. Pete Dunne, a writer who has ascended to ornithological superstardom, speculated that one way that juveniles might discover the phenomenon could be simple accident. Tasha might be fly-ing along when suddenly she feels a little lift under her wings and—*ah-ha!*—starts to get it. This elevator is going up, and luckily, she is on it. And so she rides it as high as she can, points herself in the right direction, tucks her wings slightly, and is off. The next time may not be quite so accidental, and according to Dunne she may even keep an eye out for "dust and rising debris in the air." And of course she will keep her eye out for other hawks, who have also been keeping their eyes out for thermals.

As the ferry neared Orient Point, a large hump of land became visible to the south. This was Gardiners Island, which early in the twentieth century was home to almost three hundred nests, the largest single osprey colony in the world. It was here that Dennis Puleston, whose house I was heading toward, studied ospreys. Puleston was a gentle man with multiple talents ranging from art to engineering. In the 1950s he began to notice a precip-itous drop in the reproduction rates of ospreys, and in less than twenty years 90 percent of the birds were gone. He took eggs from the nests and took them to his colleague and friend Charles Wurster, a chemist, who ran tests that determined that DDT was thinning the eggshells. It was this information about the birds, this discovery, that ended up saving them.

And saving humans, perhaps. Ospreys are an indicator spe-cies, and Puleston was fond of comparing them to canaries in a coal mine. Once again the sheer obviousness of ospreys played a big part. Just as the canaries dropped dead because of methane in the mines, warning the miners, so the ospreys' decline gave us our first hints that spraying this DDT stuff might not be the greatest idea for anyone. Ospreys weren't the only ones at the top of the food chain, and DDT, unbeknown to us, was also working its ugly magic inside human beings.

I disembarked from the ferry at Orient Point and headed west across Long Island on Route 25. As well as looking at the road, I glanced upward. The east end of Long Island is dotted with os- prey poles, and when I'd visited earlier that summer, dozens of birds had greeted me within minutes of my leaving the ferry. Now the skies were quieter, the nests empty, though I did see a young bird or two. Their feathers were checkered with a black- and-white pattern that my field guide poetically called "the white scalloped dorsal feather edgings." This pattern would be gone by the time the young birds settled down for their first win- ter in South America. So too the orange fire that glowed in their eyes, which would fade to a still vivid but less inflamed yellow.

Ospreys had done something I hadn't thought possible: they'd made me like Long Island. Before becoming familiar with the birds I'd regarded the place the way many people who don't know it do, as a snooty, slightly less urban extension of New York City. But studying ospreys had brought me into closer contact with the place and its people. Now I saw that its scrub forests and kettle ponds made it Cape Cod's geological sister, both places formed by the same retreating glacier. It was also home to many of the early osprey heroes, people like Dennis Puleston, Art Cooley, and Charles Wurster, who had created the Environmen- tal Defense Fund and fought for the banning of DDT with the blunt motto "Sue the Bastards!" A few years back I had visited the Mashomack Preserve, on Shelter Island, where I'd met the scientist Paul Spitzer, another of those early heroes. Spitzer had been the first to take osprey eggs from the Chesapeake Bay area, where less DDT was being sprayed, and place them in the then unproductive New England nests. The eggs took, and Northeast ospreys began to have some reproductive success at a crucial time.

I wasn't the safest driver on the road as I made my way across

Long Island. Though quick to grumble and curse when I see others using cell phones while driving, I reserve the right to do so myself, and in between looking up to inventory the nests, I kept glancing down at my phone. The BBC's satellite ospreys weren't the only animals being electronically tracked: there were three messages from my wife, each increasingly urgent. The last simply said, "Where are you? Where are you?" The reason I hadn't called back sooner was that I, like the birds, had recently had periods when my tracking device was off. The glass cabin down in Westport was out of cell phone range, which I explained to Nina when I got through. She was irritated but understood. It was freeing to be electronically untethered for a while. I had recently read that we can all be tracked through cell phones by GPS signals that are required for emergency and law enforcement reasons. As the BBC ospreys knew, there is precious little privacy left in the world. But even the birds had two-hour off-cycles on their radio transmitters, brief periods when Rob and "the Beeb" (which, in British style, he'd chummily started to call the BBC) didn't know where the ospreys were, allowing for at least a remnant of mystery.

Overall, Nina wasn't thrilled with the idea of being Penelope to my Odysseus, waiting patiently back on our island. But she understood that this was a once-in-a-lifetime chance and had even agreed to play the role of base commander, checking the Internet regularly to see where the BBC birds were. Now she gave me an update on the status and whereabouts of the ospreys. Bluebeard was still at his nest, helping his remedial fisherman of a son. Tasha, as best we could tell, was right above me.

After I hung up, I thought about how my trip was also a war game, and how my war, like any, involved a lot of spying. Spying and voyeurism made up a large part of not just my quest but of bird watching in general. The tools of the trade prove this. My binoculars were in my backpack, my telescope in the car. When

I watched the birds, I recorded what I saw on a microcassette recorder or took notes in a journal, with little left unobserved. The birds, if they had regarded me at all, would only have regarded me as what I was: a kind of stalker.

You could argue that the fact that ospreys are so easy to watch has something to do with their popularity. An osprey isn't considered quite as sexy as an eagle or a falcon. So what's the fuss? Well, while those other birds might nest on a craggy mountain ledge, ospreys can just as easily plop down in your backyard. You don't even have to be a birdwatcher to notice them, particularly if you live near the water during the warm months. A scientist friend once suggested that if you overlaid global maps of human populations with ones of osprey populations, you would come up with an almost exact fit, since both groups cluster around water. What distinguishes ospreys from other raptors isn't just their distinctive brown-and-white markings; adhesive, reversible talons; and derring-do dives. It is their general transparency, their unconscious obliviousness to human beings. They make voyeurism easy.

During my earlier seasons at the nests I had watched the birds daily, observing them during their most intimate rituals, like the fish dance, a dramatic lifting and falling flight that signals courtship. I saw everything: the male offering fish to the female in early spring, indicating fealty as a mate; the same male bringing sticks and then gently placing them by the female; and, eventually, their offspring being born. And I'd gone even further than that. Through a telescope, no less, I had watched them copulating, noting on my tape recorder that while the buildup to sex was elaborate, the act itself was blunt. I had even gone as far as to time it once on my watch. Six seconds.

I did all this, I claimed, because I wanted to have some deeper connection to the birds, and of course a connection to the animal in me, "a token of myself" as Whitman wrote. But did the birds want a connection to me? I seriously doubted it. In fact, they were not shy birds, and they let me know that they weren't so crazy about all the spying. Though they eventually habituated themselves to my presence near the nests, during my first weeks out on the marsh they would greet my arrival with high-pitched warning cries—*kew, kew, kew*—and circling flight. Later I wondered: could my tramping so close have endangered them? Could those moments when the female was not incubating have made the difference in whether she would produce offspring or not? It was certainly possible.

Of course, Rob Bierregaard and the BBC had taken it a few steps further. Even before tying the little backpacks on the poor birds, like readying anxious second-graders for camp, they had climbed up the poles and captured the birds, stuffing them in bags and putting hoods over their heads. Indulge in anthropomorphizing for a minute and imagine what the birds must have felt. After being kidnapped and released, they would find themselves dazed and then, perhaps, briefly exhilarated. "Whew, that was a close call," they would think, and go about their business. But what about the funny strap across their chest and that strange wire arcing off their back? And what about the feeling, subtle at first, that they were being *watched?* Once they began to migrate, that feeling would be exacerbated. It would play out as a kind of *Goodfellas* scene, with the bird constantly glancing back at the plane or van that was following it. Or maybe another movie analogy worked better. It wasn't hard to imagine a poor osprey thinking, like Butch and Sundance, "Who *are* those guys?"

I pulled up to Dennis Puleston's home in Brookhaven ten minutes late. Dennis had died a couple of years before, and after his death a camera was placed just above one of the osprey nests on his property as a tribute. The camera was attached to the platform and pointed down into the nest, displaying streaming footage of osprey home life on the Internet. The website that showed this footage had spawned a group of devoted, even fanatic followers who observed the ospreys round the clock throughout the nesting season, rooting for them as their eggs hatched and they raised their chicks. They watched ospreys 24/7.

My contact with these virtual birders had come about when they started to use my book on the birds as their basic text, calling it "Osprey 101." (They used Alan Poole's more comprehensive and scientific book as Osprey 201.) One of the strange things about this group was that while they had watched hundreds maybe thousands, of hours of footage of this one nest, they had never been to the Puleston home, the actual place where the nest was. Like Batman's Batcave, its location had not been disclosed, but for my visit, Betty Puleston, Dennis's widow, made a most generous offer. She invited the entire group out to her farm to meet me and see the nest.

Most of the website watchers had already assembled by the time I got there. Betty was a white-haired, chain-smoking eighty-seven-year-old with a raspy voice and a strong laugh. She shook my hand heartily in front of the cedar-shingle dairy barn that housed the command center for osprey operations. She wore long khaki shorts and a T-shirt that sported what looked to me like a picture of the four Beatles rowing a kayak through outer space. Right away you got the sense that while she had put up with her husband's bird activities and still enjoyed the posthumous glow of his ornithological celebrity, she wasn't exactly a birder herself. She smiled and pointed a cigarette at the couple dozen people gathered near a telescope by the side of the barn. "It's quite a group you've got here," she said.

She was right about that. A burly mustached guy wearing a

USA shirt stood next to a proper-looking Long Island matron, who stood next to a short, wiry, ponytailed guy named Tim, who stood next to a man in a wheelchair who introduced himself as Mickey. It wasn't just the group's apparent eclecticism that was remarkable. There was a communal shyness, people tentatively shaking hands, as if they'd never met before.

Which, I soon realized, they hadn't. Though they all posted their comments on the website and had gotten to know each other well through their virtual personas, most of them had never met in person. After I figured this out, it was fun to watch as they began to recognize each other, putting two and two together, matching the actual person in front of them with his or her online alter ego. It was like watching a whole bunch of online daters meet. They gathered in two spots, around the telescope and around a table with wine and crackers off to the side of the barn. Gradually the talk and laughter grew louder.

I joined the small group milling around the telescope. The Puleston land was beautiful, sloping gently down from the barn toward a reedy marsh and the mouth of the Carmen's River. The telescope pointed over a fence to a field of conservation land abutting Betty's property, where the nest with the camera stood. Like my nests at home, this one was empty, but the blue sky was full of birds migrating out over the water.

While I took in my surroundings, a silver-haired woman named Cecilia Wheeler came up and said hello. We'd met at an osprey talk I'd given earlier that summer on Long Island, and from the first moment I liked her—she emanated a kind and serene air. She introduced me to Celeste Molinari, who seemed to be the group's unofficial cocaptain, along with Cecilia, and to Tom Throwe, who kept the camera and website working, and Dave Shore, who was the group's chief birder and who posted the osprey footage on the website. As we stood there, Cecilia and

Celeste told me about how they had first gotten hooked on the website.

"It's a strange thing," Celeste said. "I've tried to turn other people on to the site and they get bored with it. They say it's like watching paint dry. But I think it's fascinating. I mean, I've never been into chat rooms or anything like that. But this is *drama.* Like a good TV show. You get hooked on the plot and can't stop watching. The early nest-building, the egg-laying, the birth of the chicks, the first flight. I keep the computer on while I'm drinking coffee or having breakfast. It's got so I can recognize the different calls of the different fledglings without looking."

She spoke about the birds with a contagious enthusiasm, and Cecilia nodded in agreement.

"When we first started watching, we really didn't know much," Cecilia said. "Dave was the only one who really knew about birds. As I started getting more into it, I began reading everything I could about ospreys. And then I suddenly realized that we were seeing things that were not in the books. For instance, the camera's sensitive enough to pick them up at night. And sometimes when I can't sleep I'll watch the birds. I realized they barely slept. During nesting they keep moving all night long. They only sleep in five-minute stretches."

I mentioned that I'd never read this fact anywhere in the literature.

"Yes," she said, nodding vigorously, "That's just it. I think we're beginning to discover things. New things."

I nodded. Ornithology is one of the few fields in which amateurs still make large contributions, and as I talked to these people, it became clear that they probably did know things that scientists didn't know. It made sense that the most compulsive watchers would see things that Gil Fernandez and Dennis Puleston and even Alan Poole had never seen, since scientists had always watched nests from the outside and from below, through telescopes. But this group had watched the nest as if they were inside it, living right next to the birds, a kind of *Real World* with ospreys.

Over the next twenty minutes Celeste and Cecilia told me as much about osprey nesting habits as I'd ever read or heard anywhere. Soon we'd drawn a crowd and everyone was chiming in. John, the guy in the USA shirt, told me about the incubation of the eggs in early spring. After the eggs were laid, in April or early May, the ospreys spent the next six weeks incubating them, and it had always been assumed that the bulk of that work fell to the female.

"The male pretty much split the incubation duties with the female. Fifty-fifty," John said. "In fact, he hated to get off. She would show up for her turn and he just wouldn't budge. He was like a slug."

"She would nudge him and kick him," Cecilia said.

John nodded. "Yeah, she would bring branches in and put them on his back to get him to move."

Someone else pointed out that once the chicks were born, the male wanted no part of sitting on the nest. The female did all the sitting with the young and he brought almost all the fish.

"Once in a while she would fly off and he would guard the nest," Celeste said. "But for the most part he would fork over the fish and she would cut the meat for the kids."

Soon everyone was talking at once and I was being hit with osprey facts from all directions. Someone said that the male would sometimes bring back as many as seven fish a day, a much higher number than any I'd ever read, and someone else said that the camera's microphone was able to pick up the sound of the female ripping fish apart, and then someone described the day that the female had defended the nest from another osprey by lying on her back and kicking up at the intruder. Finally Mickey mentioned that these ospreys had a sweet tooth for goldfish and koi. "One day they ate three in a row," he said. "We always wondered where the hell they got them all."

I scribbled down notes as fast as I could, my head spinning from facts and wine. But people kept spouting osprey tidbits, and it became a little much. After a while I decided to sneak over to the side of the barn to write all of it down clearly. These people were sweet and generous, but they were also like a classroom of overeager third-graders, all raising their hands at once, wildly excited about sharing their pent-up knowledge. My appearance had served as the occasion for pulling the cork on the champagne bottle of osprey facts, and now it was all bubbling out.

There was also a basic contradiction about this group. With the exception of Dave Shore, they seemed to be terrible birders. Every now and then someone would point up at a far-off gull and yell out, "There's an osprey!" Of course, this happened because they knew the birds only at the nest, from close up, on a computer screen. This forced me to play the slightly uncomfortable role of expert again, correcting them and pointing out and naming actual birds.

I grabbed another glass of wine and some crackers and turned the corner of the barn, and there was Betty, cigarette in hand, leaning against the barn's corner like a tough kid in junior high school. Earlier I'd heard one of the osprey people ask her if she would ever try to quit smoking. "I started smoking when I was thirteen and I'm eighty-seven now," she'd said. "I don't really see any reason to stop, do you?"

She asked me if I'd like a short tour of the grounds, and I said I would.

Beyond the barn, the Puleston compound was made up of a

series of low houses that Betty and her daughters and sons-in-law occupied. Another occupant was George C. Stoney, a former Fulbright fellow and professor of film at NYU, whom we came upon near the horse barn. I didn't know exactly what George's role in the household was and certainly wasn't going to ask. He was a dapper and sharp-minded little man, and after we'd talked awhile, he asked me where I taught.

"UNC," I said. This was a strange moment of vanity for me, one I'd never had before (and have not repeated). UNC is shorthand for the University of North Carolina at Chapel Hill. Since no one in the North has ever heard of the school where I actually teach—the University of North Carolina at Wilmington, or UNC*W*—I decided to leave off the *W* to impress.

"Oh, I graduated from UNC in 1937," he said.

Knowing I'd be caught in my lie, I immediately admitted to the *W*. He nodded and smiled, and then described a piece he'd written about Thomas Wolfe's years at Chapel Hill. While he told his story I did a little math. If he'd graduated in 1937, he had to be close to ninety.

Betty walked me back to the dairy barn. When we got there, she slid open the side door. "You'll want to look in here," she said. "Mission control."

She left me alone in a small room that housed a large TV screen, a computer, and equipment for filming the nest. It was an odd juxtaposition of old barn and new gizmos, and you could see the nest itself through a single window with chipped white paint on its frame. The room also held Dennis Puleston's extensive bird library and a caricature of Dennis that someone had painted. In the painting Dennis stands on a small glacier with penguins by his side and puffins and terns flying overhead. As I marveled at all the equipment for watching the birds, it occurred to me that as voyeurs, the BBC and I had met our match in this crowd. Not just tags and satellites but TV cameras and microphones. Celeste had said that they watched the ospreys like a soap opera on TV, and that was true. But if I preferred mucking around with actual birds, it was hard to argue with the results of the Puleston group. By watching their virtual birds, they, more than almost any human beings in the world, had become intimate with ospreys. Maybe theirs was simply an amped-up version of my telescope: a technology that let them enter directly into the lives of the birds.

When I left the barn, I found that the whole gang was now gathered around the picnic table that held the wine, cheese, and crackers. They sat on benches around the table and on the ground as they ate and drank. Someone had brought a bowl of raspberries, and as I joined them, we passed the fruit around. It was a delightful early fall day, and the group's shyness had disappeared. As we drank and ate and talked passionately about ospreys, I felt as if I had found my lost tribe.

Soon the conversation turned to the summer's most dramatic—and gruesome—event. If the televised osprey show was a little like *The Real World*, it also had more than a dash or two of *Survivor*. This was the second year the camera had been on the nest, and for two years in a row now the osprey runt had starved or been killed by its siblings. I had witnessed something similar at one of my nests on Cape Cod, a brutal object lesson in sibling rivalry. In a nest of four chicks, a couple of chicks have the disadvantage of having been born later—sometimes almost a week later—and therefore being smaller and less developed. This makes it harder for them to fight for food, which makes it harder to grow, which makes it harder still to fight for food. Sometimes this vicious cycle ends in death. What I had witnessed was ugly enough: the number-three chick essentially pecking the number-four chick to death. But the camera had allowed the Puleston group a more intimate look at murder in the nest.

I sat on the edge of the picnic table, drinking my wine, while different members of the group, led by Celeste and Cecilia, tried to describe the experience of watching the nestling deaths from up close.

"The first year it caught us by surprise," said Celeste. "We had been ooh-and-ahing over how lovely the birds were and weren't expecting something gruesome like that. That first year it was a rainy spring and the fishing was tough, so there wasn't as much food as there was this year. Every meal meant the smallest chick would be pecked into submission. There were some hopeful signs at first. Sometimes when the others were done eating the mother would carry the fish over to the smallest bird and rip off chunks for it. But as the days went by and the fishing stayed bad, the little bird grew weaker and weaker. It would just lie there near the end rather than competing for food."

Cecilia agreed. "Some of us couldn't watch near the end. It got so vicious. And you kept wanting the mother to interfere. But she never would. One morning I looked at the screen and the chick was just gone. We never found out what happened."

Some members suggested that the experience had been good for the group, toughening them up—that they had learned the cruel calculus of evolution: for osprey parents, three healthy chicks beats four not-so-healthy.

Tim, the wiry guy with the ponytail, was one such proponent. From the beginning the adult birds had been called Dennis and Betty, after the Pulestons, but he had argued for not naming the chicks. "Essentially, I don't see the birds as having emotion toward each other. Maybe in more domesticated birds, maybe that goes on. But with diurnal and nocturnal raptors, I see them all as just powerful, killing, surviving beasts of the wild. We give them cute names and stuff. But I wasn't into that. With what happened to the runt you got to see them for what they are."

When the same scene was repeated the second year, the

group was ready and battle-hardened. But while they could stomach the runt's death, what they saw *after* the death shook even the hardier veterans.

What they saw was this: the smallest bird, too famished and exhausted to move, was smothered lying under the other chicks. Some members of the group described the mother's reaction to the dead chick as "remorseful" and said that she had let out a little wail, though others refuted this. Whatever the case, the mother almost immediately went to work digging the runt body out from the pig pile of the other nestlings. She clutched the limp body in her talons and lifted it and flew off the nest. From the point of view of the camera, and the watchers, she then disappeared from sight—offstage, as it were. But after a few minutes she was back, the carcass still in her talons. If she had ever had a twinge of remorse about her offspring's death, it was now gone. She treated her dead chick just as she would a fish. It wasn't a fish, of course, but it provided what a fish did: energy—energy to aid the growth and survival of the other nestlings. So she tore into the dead runt's sides with her bill, ripped off chunks of flesh and feathers, and then doled them out to her three living chicks, who had already lined up for the meal, fighting for position. And who eagerly gulped down chunks of their sibling.

"We care about the birds," said Cecilia. "We miss them when the season's over and celebrate their return in March. But after the cannibalism we had fewer illusions about the birds. Maybe it's just that we have a less soft appreciation for them now."

I thought again of how amateurs contribute to ornithology. The secret is time: time committed, time spent simply watching, time at the nest, whether the nest is real or virtual. When I began to study ospreys, I read that cannibalism, though common among other raptor broods, was rare among ospreys because of their diet of fish. But now the Puleston Web group, by staring at their screens and watching their osprey video game, had witnessed perhaps the most dramatic example of osprey cannibalism ever seen, proving it was otherwise.

The day was winding down. It was past four, and a few people started to say their goodbyes. Betty had long since wandered off. You got the feeling that three hours was more than enough time to spend with a bunch of osprey freaks.

We all bustled about, piling up plastic cups and plates.

"You know, I get a lot out of watching," Celeste said to me while we cleaned. "It's an escape from everything, all the problems in your life, all the tension. It's like instead of just going to sleep, you sit and watch this other world. And sometimes you become part of it."

"It's an escape," Cecilia agreed. "But it's also like visiting with friends."

I had one more thing I wanted to ask them before we broke up. I remembered my conversation with Gil Fernandez about how clean ospreys were. I asked the group about the neatness of the nest. Who would know better?

"Oh, it's pretty messy," Tim said. "Sticks and fish crud strewn everywhere. For the most part they try to crap over the side, but they don't always. The microphone's so good that you can even hear them crap. It's not like a stork's nest that's all white with dung. But it sure ain't neat."

Celeste laughed and shook her head. "He's right," she said. "And you know you've been watching too long when you can tell they're gonna go before they do."

I helped the others neaten up, tossing the trash and leaving the crackers and wine for Betty and her family. I hugged Celeste and Cecilia goodbye and promised to send e-mail reports of my trip to Cuba. Then we dipped into the house to thank Betty.

I was already on my way back to the car when George C. Stoney appeared from around the side of the barn. He called out to me and I walked over to where he stood.

"Where are you staying tonight?" he asked.

"I might call a friend up in Stony Brook," I said. "Or I might just grab a hotel."

George looked at me and smiled. He wore a pleasant but satisfied expression, like a genie ready to grant a wish.

"I was thinking that you might enjoy spending the night in Dennis's marsh shack," he said.

It was my turn to smile. "I might enjoy that," I said. "I *would* enjoy that."

He patted me lightly on the shoulder.

The next thing I knew I was gathering my journal, backpack, and sleeping bag from the car. George and Betty insisted that I also take the wine and leftover raspberries and crackers. An abundance of gifts was being heaped on me, and the gift-giving continued when Betty's daughter Jen Clement came out of one of the houses with a print of an osprey from a painting that Dennis had done. She handed it to me rolled up in a scroll.

My arms full, I walked down the sloping lawn with George, past the lake and canoe and into an opening in the tall phragmites reeds. The reeds stood at least 14 feet high, and the path we followed was out of view of Betty's house and the barn and most everything else. The marsh grew spongy below our feet as we walked down the short path to where a tiny cabin stood on stilts above the marsh.

George held out his arm as if introducing me to a friend. "Here's your humble abode," he said.

I thanked him, and he left me alone outside my new home. My third cabin in three nights. Like the other two, it was Walden-sized, though if anything it was smaller and certainly more primitive than the first two. It stood all by itself, tucked amid the tall phragmites and encircled by eastern red cedars. I climbed up the front stairs and stood on the top step looking around. Poison ivy grew almost as high as the reeds, and grape leaves crawled up from below the cabin. A deck jutted off the cabin's backside, and from the deck I had a view of the water, which was pretty much the only thing I could see beyond the surrounding vegetation.

Inside, the marsh shack was even less fancy: a flat wooden bed, a long window over the bed that looked out on the water, one wooden chair, a bedside table with a candle in a candlestick, windows with heavy screens. There were no sheets, and bug carcasses and cobwebs littered the floor and bed. In other words, perfect. I rolled out my bag and unfurled Dennis's osprey print, which I set up on the bedside table, leaning it against the wall. Then I took the wine and crackers and the chair, as well as my journal and binoculars, and headed out to the back deck for an early dinner.

An osprey platform stood like a flagpole right next to the shack, just 20 feet off to my right. This platform, unlike the one that held the website celebrity ospreys, was old-fashioned. Platform building had become widespread after DDT, but humans had been making homes for ospreys since at least the 1800s. Those early platforms, like this one, often consisted of a tall pole with a wagon wheel on top. Though a few starter sticks sat scattered on top of the wheel, it had obviously gone unused during the past season. It occurred to me that this might be a potential future home for the website fledglings.

Sitting there, 10 feet above the marsh on that rickety deck, I felt perfectly at home. I took a large glug of wine. A green heron landed on the marsh only a few yards away, and a catbird shot out from one of the windowsills above my head. I proceeded to get pleasantly drunk while the setting sun reflected strange purples in the clouds over the water and migrating birds flew over the back of the shack. It was an experience you might have called Whitmanesque even without my handy reading material, which I now retrieved from my backpack. Over the next hour I took turns watching birds through the binoculars and reading snatches of the poems. By the time I got to "Song of the Open Road," I felt like doing some singing myself. I read:

> *You but arrive at the city to which you were destin'd, you hardly settle yourself to satisfaction before you are call'd by an irresistible call to depart...*

I remembered that ornithologists have a specific word for Whitman's "irresistible call to depart." They call it *Zugunruhe,* a German word for the restlessness birds feel before they migrate. Similar to the stomping of nervous deer, it is the general unease, the bristling, of a creature about to embark on a journey.

As I read on, I felt suddenly lucky that it was *Leaves of Grass* and not *Walden* that I'd found (and then stolen) back at the glass cabin. For one thing, Whitman was a cheerier traveling companion than Thoreau. For another, I no longer believed in a cabin in the woods. Or, to put it another way, who wanted just one cabin at Walden, permanently anchored to just one place, when you could have what I'd had over the past three days, a series of Waldens? This was better. So many possible Waldens. Cabin after cabin. Waldens on the fly.

The initial idea for my trip had been to commune with birds, but now, in my rush of sunset- and alcohol-aided euphoria, I saw that even more than that, it was about communing with bird people. I'd loved meeting the Web group that afternoon, especially Celeste and Cecilia, but this was even better. After all, this was the place where Dennis Puleston had come to draw and observe his birds. During my research for my first osprey book, I had just missed meeting Dennis and regretted it. But I was learning that now, even though he was dead, there were still ways to get to know him. Before I'd headed to the cabin, Betty had handed me a printout of the tributes from Dennis's memorial service. In it I was reminded that Dennis was a designer of the DUKW, the amphibious vehicle used during World War II (now better known as a tour bus/boat in Boston and other cities), and that he had been "decorated by President Truman and honored by *Time* magazine." He had also been an adventurer who sailed around the world and an artist who painted all of the nesting bird species on Long Island. Art Cooley, his fellow founding member of the Environmental Defense Fund, who had fought beside him to ban DDT, remembered him as a teacher full of humor and patience, a quiet man, though still capable of singing the crudest of sea shanties.

Even more than Gil Fernandez, Dennis Puleston had led a life intertwined with birds. And now here I was, fortunate to be in one of the places where he had done that intertwining. The marsh shack was really just a slightly larger bird blind, which of course was no accident. If you simply sat still in this place, you could see the world swirling around you. The insects were active now, and swallows jagged after them, zigging like the bats I'd watched in Westport. As more and more of the swallows poured over my roof, I turned back to the tribute for Dennis and read that one of the burdens of his later life was that his son, also named Dennis, had been killed by lightning on top of a mountain in Mexico. I tried to imagine Dennis's loss but couldn't get my mind around it. I put the paper down and thought of my daughter back in North Carolina, of the joy she had brought me but also the new sense of being deeply vulnerable. During her first year I'd been struck daily by the fact of her creatureliness, and by the fact that this squirming little apelike animal, barely 2 feet high, had somehow been allowed to live in the same house with us.

I watched the crepuscular show of the birds. The swallows seemed perfectly adapted to catching bugs but less so to the rigors of migration. Did they flit and shoot about when they covered long distances? They didn't have the osprey luxury of lifting on thermals and soaring for miles. How much raw energy did their indirect, zigzagging journeys require? As I wondered, geese *ya-honked* overhead and ducks crossed the sky like a line of cursive. Though the sun was setting behind me, its reflection built up in the purple clouds and in a single line of orange above the purple-headed phragmites.

Once the sunlight died entirely, I retreated inside and lit a candle. I was growing fairly rank from not showering for three days, but that too seemed right, and I happily climbed into bed. Eventually the candle flickered out in a puddle of its own wax. All night long water trickled in and out of the tidal creeks, intermingling with my dreams, and somewhere behind the reeds the halyards of boats dinged on masts. At one point I woke to the screech of an owl and at another to the garbled cry of something being killed below the shack. It took a while to get back to sleep after that, so I just stared out the nearly room-length window, which perfectly framed the Big Dipper and a sliver of moon. I finally dozed off but woke again before daylight and had mushy raspberries for breakfast as the sun rose over the marsh in imperceptible humpings of light. By six the geese and ducks were moving across the sky, the roosters crowing.

Then I became what I had mocked. Like High Priest Beaver Chippings, I decided a ceremony was in order. "You shall be treated to the ironical smiles of those who remain behind" was how Whitman put it. Fuck the ironical smiles—even my own. I retrieved the osprey skull and wing bone from my backpack and took them out to the deck. After a brief nod to the sunrise, I tossed the skull out toward Dennis's osprey pole. But it was so light that it floated up in the air, barely making it halfway to the pole. The wing bone was a little heavier, and I threw it harder, like a football. It arced up into the air, and when it came down, it hit the pole right below the metal sheet that was meant to keep raccoons from climbing. Not a very artful dawn ceremony, but something.

After carrying my sleeping bag and empty wine bottle and other belongings across the dewy lawn, I had a second breakfast, of oatmeal, with George and Betty. Betty suggested that I start my day off with a swim and led me through the house to a long room made up almost entirely of glass. The room held a narrow, 30-foot indoor pool, and she explained that she swam laps naked every morning. "It's how I stay young," she said.

"Do you smoke while you do it?" I asked.

"No, it gets the cigarette wet," she said with a wink.

She was one of the few people I'd met who could actually pull off a wink. She left me alone and I did a few laps, though I kept my boxers on. It was already time to leave: the plan was to head through New York and west across New Jersey and to get to Hawk Mountain, Pennsylvania, by the afternoon so I could watch migrating ospreys from the mountaintop. But when I got out of the pool and went to say goodbye, Betty told me that Dave Shore had called and asked if I'd like to take a canoe trip on the Carmen's River. The mouth of the river was adjacent to the marsh shack and the Puleston property, and the river itself wove through thousands of acres of the Wertheim National Wildlife Refuge, land that Dennis had fought to conserve. How could I say no?

We paddled for a couple of hours. Dave was a fine guide, humble and apologetic about his birding skills, though they were superior to mine. At one point we saw a young female osprey hovering and then diving into the creek. We missed the dive itself because of the high marsh grass, but then Dave said, "I think I know where she's going." We paddled up and down a few side canals until we came out below the crook of a large tree with flaming red leaves, where, sure enough, the osprey, its subtly striped tail hanging over the edge for balance, was tearing apart its meal.

On the way back Dave told me how he had first gotten into birding. Dennis Puleston had taken him out with his dad and patiently explained the names of birds to him.

"You never saw Dennis lose his temper," he said. "The first time I went birding with him, I didn't even own binoculars, but every bird Dennis saw, he would hand over the binoculars to me and say, 'Look at that. That's what it is,' in a kind voice, as if we were peers. He was a name-giver."

I thanked Dave for the great morning but told him I had to get going. Hawk Mountain was waiting, and I felt Whitman's irresistible urge to depart. Before I left, Jen Clement let me use her computer to locate the BBC birds. Bluebeard was still at home on Martha's Vineyard, feeding his remedial child. But Tasha had shot directly over us during the party the previous afternoon, flying right over the Carmen's River and straight to the west end of Long Island before finally crossing the Hudson and spending the night in northern New Jersey.

I had to make one final stop before I followed Tasha off Long Island and over the river to Jersey. My wife had asked me to drop in and say hi to the mother of an old childhood friend somewhere in the Brookhaven area. I didn't have the address, so I asked Jen Clement if she knew of a Kate Ince. Of course, the way things were going, she more than knew her.

"She's an old friend," Jen said. "She lives less than a mile from here. Just pull out of our road and count four dirt roads down on your left."

I followed the directions, and soon I was sitting with Kate in her backyard garden. She was a delightful woman, somewhere in her fifties, and she offered me a glass of lemonade. We drank from tall cold glasses next to a small goldfish pond as I told her about the gathering the day before. I pointed my glass toward the fish and mentioned that one of the things that the Web group had discovered was just how much of their ospreys' diet was made up of goldfish and koi. I also told her that the group had wondered where all these pet fish came from.

"Oh, I can tell you that," Kate said. "Those are *my* fish they eat."

I asked her what she meant. The tiny pond obviously couldn't support a nest full of hungry birds.

"Oh, this is just a feeder pond," she said. "My ex-husband and I built an artificial pond less than a mile from here. We stocked it with goldfish and koi. We used to watch ospreys dive down out of the sky and fly away with our fish in their claws. The fish shone like jewels, like orange flames in the sky."

I tried to picture it. To an osprey, a pond stocked with goldfish—slow, tame, fat, delicious goldfish—would have looked like a perfect buffet.

As I drove off, I reminded myself to send an e-mail to Mickey and the rest of the group. I had inadvertently solved one of their mysteries and could now tell them just where the hell all those goldfish had come from.

CHAPTER FOUR

HAWK MOUNTAIN

There was one downside to all my osprey good luck. During many of my past nature adventures I had had as a companion a large, hairy, Sasquatch-like man named Mark Honerkamp. Hones, as his friends call him, is a great eater and drinker as well as a serious nature enthusiast, and I'd promised to call him to report on the trip. Hones can be a skeptic, however, and I knew he would be suspicious of my wild string of good osprey luck—not just the wacky group on Long Island and the cabins I'd stayed in, but also my solving of the goldfish mystery and the many birds I'd seen. In fact, the two of us had coined a term for people who consistently exaggerated their nature stories. We called it *Kathleening*, after our friend Kathleen, who was sure to see a bear or bald eagle or whale whenever she stepped off the sidewalk. "Are you sure it was a cougar you saw, or are you just Kathleening?" we would ask each other. Anyone who saw amazing sights reliably became, by this logic, unreliable. So: I had to find a way to tell Hones all my stories so far without coming off as a nature fake. I didn't want to pull a Kathleen.

Of course, nature fakery has a storied history. One of the most famous examples is the controversy surrounding the writer Edward Thompson Seton early in the twentieth century. He was accused by Teddy Roosevelt and John Burroughs of Kathleening, but also of sentimentalizing the inner lives of animals, of anthropomorphizing. Describing the emotional life of animals remains a sticky issue to this day. How to describe something we can only ever know from the outside, despite the leaps of intuition and the observations of science? But isn't it somewhat random—and unscientific—to make the blanket assumption that animals don't have complex emotional lives? The word *anthropomorphizing*, which means imparting human qualities to animals, is itself part of the problem. It stacks the deck, assuming that to give animals thoughts or emotions is to give them *human* qualities, which itself is a prejudiced assumption. That is, it assumes right off that we humans have cornered the market on emotion. The two extremes are equally problematic: on the one hand a kind of Disneyfied natural world full of sad bunnies and joyful robins, on the other a scientific view of animal automatons guided solely by blind instinct.

The evolution of the Long Island group's thinking was interesting in that it mirrored the general movement of environmental thought from the anthropocentric to the biocentric, or life-centered. They had toughened up, leaving behind their early "cute" view of ospreys while starting to see the birds as the ruthless creatures they can sometimes be. But it wasn't that simple. They hadn't come over to an entirely scientific viewpoint, and they still recognized that the birds had distinct personalities and that, as well as exhibiting "cruel" indifference, they were capable of things easily recognizable as affection, loyalty, and concern. To try to peel apart what guided these "nobler" actions, as well as the more brutal ones, was to delve into a nearly impossible hairsplitting in the world of instinct and individuality.

One thing seemed clear. Science can complete only part of the puzzle. The best observers, both scientists and amateurs, combine disciplined observation with a willingness to follow occasional leaps of intuition. I certainly counted Alan Poole and Dennis Puleston among this elite group. As for my own studies, what interests me most is something a little different. I am intrigued by the points where human beings and birds interact, where their lives overlap or, as Gil Fernandez put it, "intertwine." As interesting as it is to speculate on why a white-breasted nuthatch crawls down a tree to feed while a brown creeper crawls up, it is equally fascinating, to me at least, to wonder how a human mind—Audubon's, maybe, or David Sibley's or Dennis Puleston's or Alan Poole's—is transformed by spending so much time among birds.

My destination that afternoon, Hawk Mountain, is one of the world's most intense points of interaction between human and avian. Watch sites are spots where people gather to observe and count the migration of birds, and my next two stops, Hawk Mountain and Cape May, New Jersey, epitomized the alternate choices, for both me and the ospreys, for the route south. If the migratory flyway is a kind of sky river, then these are two of the main branches. The ospreys that take the inland route, by Hawk Mountain, fly along the Kittatinny Ridge, part of the greater Appalachian spine, riding the updrafts that naturally rise when the wind hits the mountains. The birds that choose the coastal route, by Cape May, ride the offshore breezes and lift on thermals, and often cross large bodies of water on their trip. Ospreys, being ospreys, more frequently choose the coastal route. But I wanted to see both.

Maybe I was secretly hoping for a bad, or at least mediocre, osprey day to balance things out before I had to call Hones. I wasn't going to get it.

That morning, as I'd driven through New York and west across New Jersey, I'd called Keith Bildstein, the director of conservation science at Hawk Mountain. Keith had agreed to meet me at four at a spot on the mountainside called the South Look-

out. Since it was already four when I hit the base of Hawk
Mountain, I sped up the steep, winding road as fast as the Pontiac would go. At the top I parked, threw my backpack over my
shoulder, and began to run up the path to the lookout.

The South Lookout is only a couple of hundred yards up the
trail. It faces out over a great bowl of trees, a lowland between
ridges known locally as the Kettle. An impressive line of sandstone chunks called the River of Rocks runs through the land below. If you look straight out over the trees and over the River of
Rocks, you can see another mountain, part of an earthquake-
broken ridge that raptors and other birds usually follow while
flying over Hawk Mountain.

As I approached the lookout, Keith was talking with an older
couple who were visiting from New Jersey, pointing out some
broad-winged hawks that were migrating over a landmark called
the East Rocks. I'd never met Keith, but I recognized his face
from pictures I'd seen on the Hawk Mountain website. His cre-
dentials are impressive, and the picture that had been posted
made him look somewhat intimidating—and mildly foppish,
with a thin gray mustache like that of the sports writer Frank
Deford. But in person his clothes were plain, his face engaging,
and the mustache less foppish than regular-guy. My plan had
been to approach the great hawk expert deferentially and see if I
could arrange a short interview on migration, but that plan soon
went out the window. We shook hands and I said something
about not wanting to take up too much of his time.

"That's too bad," he said. "I was hoping you could stay with
us for a couple of days."

It was late in the afternoon by migration standards, and most
of the birders had already packed it in. Only a half-dozen people remained at the South Lookout, staring out from the rocks
through their binoculars. Keith introduced me to those who

were left as an "osprey expert," which made me feel instantly self-conscious.

"I'm afraid I'll have to apologize in advance," Keith said. "It's been a decent day for broadwings, but we've had very few ospreys."

He said this as if he were being a bad host, personally responsible for the lack of birds. But I told him not to worry and began, perhaps overenthusiastically, to share the details of my trip so far.

"So you've become a kind of osprey magnet," he said.

"Kind of," I admitted. "And if things get really desperate, I can always do my naked osprey-summoning dance."

"Let's hope it doesn't come to that," he said.

There is an interesting rhythm to the sort of hawk watching that takes place at watch sites. Bursts of conversation alternate with periods of silence while people stare through their binoculars in search of migrating birds. The South Lookout is the lowest and most easily accessible in a series of overlooks that lead higher up the mountain, culminating in the magnificent North Lookout. The North Lookout is like a black-diamond ski slope, where the experts congregate, while the South Lookout is a blue circle, the bunny slope where newcomers and beginners hang out.

But even at the South Lookout there is a constant implied competitiveness—who will see the bird or birds first?—and for some a pressure to perform. Of course Keith was so relaxed and accomplished that this barely fazed him. On the other hand, despite and in part because of my recently conferred title of "osprey expert," I was a bundle of nerves. I did manage to see a half-dozen beautiful cedar waxwings—after Keith pointed them out—that were fluttering over the gulf between the two mountain ranges, but even here on the bunny slope the lingo was beyond me. People called out things like "Accipiter over Number

Two!" and I would nod and point my binoculars in roughly the same direction as everyone else.

Maybe it was the fact that I didn't yet know the landmarks, or even the direction I was supposed to be looking, that led to my big sighting. Whatever the case, I couldn't have been there more than seven minutes before I saw four black-and-white birds off to the east, near landmarks I would later learn were Donat Mountain and the town of Bethlehem. *Hones isn't going to believe this one,* was my first thought. But I didn't say anything out loud. There is a self-consciousness to hawk watching: you don't want to make silly mistakes and call something too soon, exposing yourself as a rookie or, worse, a poseur. Later Keith would tell me that even the hotshots up at the North Lookout pause until they are confident in their diagnoses, though it is of course a much shorter pause. Beginners often have the opposite problem, waiting too long and therefore not getting credit for the sighting.

After a minute or two I was pretty sure I was seeing what I was seeing, but it also seemed unlikely, given the day-long osprey drought. I waited as long as I could before finally suggesting to Keith that he might want to look down near the east end of the ridge.

He trained his binoculars on the ridge and almost simultaneously laughed. "You've got your ospreys," he said.

The birds were over a mile away, but we could see them clearly as they rose above the mist. Keith called out to the group: "We've got four ospreys rising on an updraft over the Donat."

The binoculars all turned that way, and someone let out a little cheer. I felt the old lucky gambler's excitement rising in me.

"That's a pretty good sighting," Keith said. "The most we ever get here is about six in a group. They must have followed you here."

What I saw next was a classic example of migratory raptor behavior, a lesson in why these birds were following the mountains in the first place. The four ospreys began to soar upward in a manner similar to that of the juveniles I'd watched above the Westport marsh. Of course, in this case they were rising not on thermals but on the updrafts the mountains created. As they lifted, they barely moved a wingtip, rising easily on their crooked wings. Though the wings are actually dark brown, the impression from a distance was of black-and-white patterns, a black-and-white that remained distinct while the ospreys rose. Unlike the Westport ospreys, however, they didn't then come swooping lazily back down. This was no practice run; they weren't doing this for kicks. After they had lifted almost out of sight, becoming tiny specks above the clouds, they made their move. They pulled their wings in tight, tucking like falcons, and then they shot southward. As they pulled in their wings, they sped up. They held their tucks, looking roughly like the Bat signal shining over Gotham, and their speed increased. You can read about updrafts and soaring migration in books and can nod and say "Uh-huh," but to see it like this you suddenly understand *why* they are doing it. It's a free ride south, and a high-speed ride too. Barely moving their wings, the ospreys started shooting over the forest and then over a landmark to our south called Owls Head.

"They're by the small tattered cloud," Keith called out. "The first one's going through it now."

As the birds shot over, all our heads turned. The first one flew out of sight, gliding fast over the mountains to the south. And then the next one went through the clouds, wings pulled in in the same manner, and then the next, and the next.

When they were gone, Keith turned to me with a smile and patted my shoulder. "That was the sight of the day," he said.

I didn't know if he was just being nice, but it didn't matter. For me it had been the sight of the day, and more: a kind of primer on osprey migratory behavior. Now I had seen with my own eyes the advantages of rising and gliding.

A couple of other people from our group packed it in after the ospreys flew out of sight, and I considered joining them. In fact, I had to stifle a wild impulse to say goodbye to Hawk Mountain immediately and follow those four birds south, jumping in my car and cutting across hill and dale. Or at least heading on to my next stop, since I knew I wasn't going to see anything like that at Hawk Mountain again, even if I stayed a week. It was a gambler's impulse, to keep rolling, but an opposite gambler's impulse worked against the first: to stay at the hot table.

I followed the second impulse, but as usual, it didn't prove fruitful, at least as far as the birds went. Over the next hour we saw little other than turkey vultures. It wasn't unpleasant, though, and for me there was kind of almost postcoital bliss in knowing I had already seen what I'd come to see. Certainly my performance anxiety was gone. By five o'clock only four of us were lounging on the rocks, occasionally raising our binoculars to our eyes. At one point Keith called out, "Gas hawk over the East Rocks" and I lifted my glasses. But it was just an inside hawk-watching joke: *gas hawk* was their name for airplanes.

Not long after, Keith got a call on his cell phone. The one snippet of his conversation I overheard was this: "Did you get the carcass that came in on Friday?" When Keith hung up, he explained that the sanctuary's interns were using a deer carcass to lure turkey vultures so that they could place satellite transmitters on them.

After a while longer Keith and I started gathering up our stuff. Though I'd originally planned on grabbing a hotel room, the sight of the ospreys and Keith's easygoing manner emboldened me. I told him about the three cabins that I'd stayed in over the past three nights and asked if they had anything like that on the Hawk Mountain property.

"I was planning on putting you up in the Acopian Center,

our biological field station," he said. "But if you want to try a primitive place, we might have something for you."

It was quickly becoming obvious that one of Keith's salient traits was generosity. We walked together to his car, a white Land Rover, and he drove me down the mountainside a bit and then pulled over by the woods. The light was fading as we walked a few hundred yards down a trail to something that Keith called "an Adirondack shelter." A shelter it was, with no front wall and just a platform of wood for a bed, making my previous accommodations look luxurious. While I wanted to keep my cabin streak alive, I hadn't showered in four days and wasn't sure that I was up for this.

"I don't know," I said out loud.

"You're welcome to stay here," Keith said. "But I had hoped you would stay as our guest at the visiting scientists' quarters in the Acopian Center. There's a kitchen where you can make coffee, a bedroom, a shower, a private hawk-watching platform, a bird library, and a TV. No one's there right now, so you'd have the whole place to yourself."

I thought about it for a second. It was almost dark.

"That sounds nice," I said.

My days of cabin living were over.

Keith drove me to the Acopian Center to show me my quarters, which were every bit as grand as he'd described. After I'd tossed my stuff on one of the beds, I headed back out to the living area, where he waited. He pulled two beers out of an industrial-sized fridge: Yuenglings, from the brewery just up the road. We drank them as we walked up a trail behind the building to what he called "my private watch site." The trail wound through an old Christmas tree farm, and long grass spotted with goldenrod and oxeye daisies soaked our shoes. A couple of hundred yards later, we came upon a gray deck jutting from the side of a hill, over-looking some train tracks and the Little Schuylkill River.

"You can come up here in the morning with your coffee," he said. "I've seen ospreys traveling through this valley in the mountains and have seen them land on the trees here and dive in the river."

I nodded happily. I had expected to come begging and maybe get a twenty-minute interview with the famous raptor expert. Instead I was being treated like a visiting dignitary, with my own private room and my own private osprey viewing platform to which I could bring my coffee. And Keith wasn't done: he now insisted on taking me out to dinner. As we walked back to the car, he tipped his beer can toward the sun, which was dropping over the ridge like a big orange ball.

"Not bad," he said.

"Not bad," I agreed.

We walked across the parking lot and climbed into his Land Rover. As we were pulling out of the Acopian Center, a truck drove up beside us and Keith rolled down his window. It was the interns, who were heading out to place the deer carcass up on the mountainside to draw in the turkey vultures, which would be rigged up with telemetry devices similar to those on the BBC ospreys. As we drove off, I asked Keith how he felt about satellite telemetry.

"For me, it's a necessary part of the job," he said. "We learn a lot from it. It allows us to individualize a long-distance move-ment of a bird. Instead of saying 'Raptors travel an average of eight hours a day and fly about two hundred miles,' we get to see an actual route of an individual. But what I'm interested in is an-imal behavior—watching animals, learning things. That's what natural history really is. I love to watch birds, and for me under-standing birds comes from *watching* birds, and deep understand-ing comes from watching birds for long periods of time."

I described the website group from Long Island and how they, though not scientists or even exceptional birdwatchers by traditional standards, had learned new things by putting in their time observing their computer screens.

"Sure, they're watching. In a different way, they're watching too." He shook his head. "With traditional radio telemetry, before the satellite stuff, you had to drive around with antennas sticking out of your car, driving onto people's property, looking like spies. My interns and grad students get pulled over by the cops all the time when they're doing telemetry. It's kind of suspicious-looking. Most of the time you're not really seeing the animals. The information's good, but I'd rather have someone else get it.

"Personally, I like to use telemetry as part of a larger view of the birds, but for me telemetry alone is not as satisfying, because I'm not watching the birds. It's not any less important, but from a selfish standpoint, the most satisfying day for me is coming back in after having studied a bird or watching a large number of migrants for eight hours. I'd much rather do that than pore over the results of satellite telemetry. In the end, the most important thing is to ask the right questions. Getting the answers is very tool-dependent, but asking the right questions is the essence. If you don't ask the right questions, it really doesn't matter if you're using technology or not. And confusing high tech with sophisticated science is, I think, a mistake a lot of people are making these days."

The whole time Keith had been delivering this low-key lecture, he had been driving at around 120 mph along the narrow, hilly road. In contrast to his mellow voice, the Land Rover bombed up and down the winding Pennsylvania hills. This would have been scary enough if we'd been alone on those roads. But what heightened my fear was the fact that a half a dozen eighteen-wheelers had been bombing toward us, going about the

same speed in the opposite direction. Over the next two days I
would learn that this was the local custom, and I thought that in
this way, at least, small-town Pennsylvania shared something
with small-town France and Italy.

I mentioned this to Keith as we pulled off the hilly speedway
onto the main road of a little town called McKeansburg.

"Yup, and there's another way it's like Europe, too. Each of
these little towns has only a few buildings, but each town has its
own inn with a bar."

That was where the similarities ended, however. The ambi-
ence of the McKeansburg Hotel Bar and Restaurant was more
rough-and-tumble Pennsylvania than fancy Europe. We sat
at a high table next to the crowded bar and ordered two more
Yuenglings. Up on the TV the Eagles were beating the Giants.
Then a highlight clip of Michael Vick and the Falcons flashed
on the screen, and I noted that two of the three teams we'd just
seen had been named after raptors.

"You don't get many teams called the Pigeons," Keith said.
"Raptors are the sex symbols of the bird world."

I mentioned that there was even a team in the NFL that
had ospreys on its helmets, though probably only a handful of
Seattle fans or players knew the real name of the bird they were
rooting for.

We drank our Yuenglings and ate prime rib for dinner. Between bites I said that I thought it was funny that Keith had
called me an expert, and we began to talk about the inherent
modesty and bumbling that go with watching nature. We agreed
that no matter how much you learn, you keep getting thrown by
new discoveries.

"For the beginner this is almost overwhelming," he said.
"What are the names of those trees, those plants, those birds? It's
like they've come into the world anew and know nothing."

I suggested that the amateur naturalist's greatest asset might be not being afraid of looking like an idiot.

"If you are the sort who is afraid of looking foolish, you never get anywhere," he agreed. "It's almost as if the most important urge is the first one—to ask questions, to risk looking silly, to accept being a bumbler."

I took what he said as permission to ask a question about something that had been bugging me. I had been following the osprey migration but still felt almost entirely unversed in the intricacies, or even the fundamentals, of migration itself. Every time I picked up a book on the subject, the language was so dense and scientific that I felt repelled and then, not long after, sleepy.

"Speaking of idiots," I said, "let's pretend I'm an idiot for a minute."

"Okay," Keith agreed.

"How about you describe the basics of raptor migration for me? In layman's terms—remember, I'm an idiot—and in less than five minutes. Can you do that?"

He finished a beer and thought for a second. "Sure," he said. "Ready?"

I looked at my watch. "Ready."

"Well, assuming you are a relatively smart idiot, you might think that birds migrate because of the weather, right?"

I nodded.

"Well, that's not the case. Migration is *food*-driven, not weather-driven. Weather is just a factor in affecting food availability. Ospreys, for instance, established their migration patterns by following fish."

That made sense. It was hunger that drove them on. Hunger that made staying still impossible.

"Like the ospreys returning to Cape Cod in March," I said.

"Right when the herring are migrating into the local streams and the ice is melting on the ponds."

"That's exactly right. So birds follow their food. But there's another reason that birds migrate. They are predisposed to migration because their manner of transportation is one of the most effective ways of moving, not only over long distances but over long distances in short periods of time. So they can move from one good place to another good place and they can do it *fast*. And those good places can be quite far apart. There really aren't any other land-based organisms built for that, except for some insects that are remarkably like raptors—dragonflies, for instance—which use winds to help them disperse themselves. But birds in general, and raptors in particular, are predisposed to migration. Raptors are the only large predatory vertebrates that can move truly long distances, because they sort of cheat the typical trophic pyramid when they're migrating. Other birds have to store up on food and fat for energy. But most of the energy that a raptor uses to get from point A to point B doesn't go through it physiologically and isn't metabolic energy. It's solar energy in the form of updrafts and in the form of thermals. In other words, they don't have to hunt to get that energy. It comes right from the sun. If they didn't have that—if they couldn't get most of their energy from the sun, directly from the sun, without its going up a food chain—they wouldn't be able to make those long-distance journeys."

These were the same concepts I had read about, dull-eyed, but the way Keith put them, they now seemed like common sense.

I told him that until just recently I had been using the word *updraft* as a synonym for *thermal*, and he explained the nuances. There are two kinds of updrafts, thermal updrafts and mountain updrafts, the latter occurring along the mountain ridges, like the Kittatinny Ridge. In the simplest terms, mountain updrafts occur when horizontally moving winds hit the vertical sloping mountains and are deflected upward, like a ski jump. That is the jump the birds ride.

In contrast, a thermal updraft, or "thermal" for short, occurs when heat rises off the earth, and the birds use these for lift. This is solar energy at its most basic and effective, and it's one of the obvious reasons hawks migrate during the day. As I'd learned, the best places for thermals are generally open, like fields and parking lots. You don't get solar energy rising off trees because the plants have already used that energy. "It can only be used once," said Keith. That is why the bare plains of Mexico are geographically perfect for soaring birds, with heat rising from the land like steam from a pot.

"If you look at a raptor, you'll see they're built to soar," he continued. "Soaring is a hunting behavior as well as a mode of travel. Ospreys, for example, spend a lot of time looking for their prey during the breeding season by being up over bodies of water, and they need to do that in an efficient and effective way. They're not flapping all the time. The kind of flight that they depend on so heavily to feed effectively predisposes them to this notion of being able to fly long distances. What you saw this afternoon was a kind of textbook case of how raptors travel."

To describe the perfect osprey flight plan, Keith twirled his finger upward in whoop-de-doo fashion until it rose above his head, then flattened his palm and let it glide down and forward over the table. "That's the ideal pattern, all the way south," he said.

It sounded good, but I still wasn't entirely sold. "But isn't just looking for a thermal a lot of work? Isn't there a lot of energy expended in the looking? How long can they glide like that?"

"Anywhere from maybe a half a kilometer to fifteen to twenty kilometers, depending upon how strong the thermal is."

"And if the wind's right, too."

"And if the wind's right. Gliding and getting that wind at

your back. That brings us to the concept of thermal highways, areas where thermals, updrafts of hot air, are more predictable and act as concentrating mechanisms for raptors, for ospreys. What migration allows an osprey to do is to pick the best place to breed as well as a super place to overwinter. They really don't have to compromise, because they're capable of having the best of both worlds. Fish often migrate too, up and down the coast, and that is a huge factor. Ospreys can only hunt for fish close to the surface, and so ospreys are sort of bound by the migration of particular kinds of fish. As you mentioned, the spring herring runs are an example of how nature times out almost perfectly."

Keith took a sip of his beer. "Am I out of time?" he asked.

I looked down at my watch. "You did it in just under five," I said.

We finished our beers. I still had a lot of unanswered questions about migration, but at least a picture was beginning to form. Thousands, likely hundreds of thousands of years ago, ospreys began to make these journeys from their winter to their summer homes, in part to find food but in part simply because they could. They had gradually learned the best routes, following the updrafts and thermals, the rivers of wind, soaring rather than flapping, drawing energy from the sun, conserving their own energy. That was enough for now.

When the bill came, Keith's generosity continued. He insisted on buying my meal, since I was a "visiting scientist." I liked the sound of that, even if it wasn't true. Keith also said that he hoped that I would spend at least two nights on Hawk Mountain. I had thought about taking off the next morning and chasing the birds down to Cape May, which was, after all, the more common route for ospreys. But it was hard to say no to such a welcoming host.

It was great to be able to shower in the morning, and I felt like a king as I approached my own private coffee machine. But I found that no matter how I tried and no matter how desperately I wanted it to work, I couldn't make the machine spit forth its life-giving black juice. I circled it warily, like my mother with the answering machine, slapped it with the flat of my hand, and flipped the on-off switch repeatedly, but nothing happened. Finally I gave up and headed over to my hawk-watching platform, caffeineless and cranky. Dawn comes late to the Acopian Center, since the sun has to climb over Hawk Mountain. The day was hazy and drizzly, but I made myself stay at the gray platform. I was half hoping for an osprey to scream down into the Schuylkill River and catch a fish right in front of me, but I was also aware of what that would do to my credibility with Hones. A few songbirds I couldn't identify passed by, and a few cedar waxwings too, but the haze made the river hard to see.

When I walked back to the main building at the Acopian Center, it wasn't quite seven, but Keith's white Land Rover was already there. I headed into his office and he said hello and motioned for me to wait a second while he finished talking to the grad students and interns who were conducting the turkey vulture study. He spoke to the interns in the same calm, informed, and easy way he'd spoken to me about migration at the bar. Obviously Keith's gift was to make people feel comfortable, no matter how much or little they knew.

He came over to shake my hand, and when I told him of my trials with the coffee machine, he used the same patient tone to describe the workings of the machine, explaining that you had to fill it up with water and wait.

Then I saw the light and said, "Oh, so you have to wait for it to warm in the back."

"That's exactly right," he repeated. As soon as he said those words, I realized he'd said the same phrase to me after several of my birding comments the night before. And I imagined him repeating the phrase to students and interns as well. It had a nice ring to it, the kind of thing a student, or anyone really, likes to hear. *That's exactly right.*

We agreed to meet up at the South Lookout in early afternoon, and he offered to let me fill my cup at the office coffee machine until I had worked out the complexities of my own. I spent the morning on my private viewing platform, drinking coffee and filling Hones in on my trip so far in as understated a fashion as I could manage. It was a pleasant way to pass the time, occasionally looking down at birds through my binoculars and at one point sliding down the steep bank for a baptismal dip in the Little Schuylkill. I enjoyed being at Hawk Mountain and enjoyed my accommodations and enjoyed my host. But by late morning I felt something nagging at me, and it didn't take long to figure out what it was. I had an itch. Noon was closing in, and for the first time since leaving Cape Cod I'd had an ospreyless morning.

I decided to head up the mountain to the North Lookout in the hope of killing two birds with one stone, so to speak: I wanted to get a taste of what life was like among the top hawk watchers while maybe seeing another migrating osprey. When I arrived at the North Lookout, I was expecting the hushed, tense air of a gunfight, but if it was a gunfight, it was a pretty casual one. People reclined in different spots on the jutting rock field, boulders of various sizes made of Tuscarora sandstone broken apart by an ice age glacier. The hawk watchers sat on the scattered rocks, wearing shorts and T-shirts, some leaning back in little folding birder chairs, and they all had their binoculars pointed at the range to the north. If the hawk watchers up here were gunslingers, quick-draw artists who had great eyes and quick minds, then binoculars were the gun of choice. You didn't find a lot of telescopes at the North Lookout. Yes, Greg, the chief counter that day, had a scope to get a better look at birds, but that was usually after the bird had already been spotted. Telescopes were too unwieldy for that first sighting. The guns that these slingers slung were fancy thousand-dollar binoculars like the Austrian-made Swarovskis or the German Zeisses and Leicas.

Keith had suggested that I introduce myself to Greg, who stood behind his scope in the center of the rocks, but I preferred playing the spy at first, sitting quietly, seeing what there was to see, and listening. Another reason I was quiet at first was that I was catching my breath. The thing about the North Lookout is that you actually have to hike to get there. All the views at Hawk Mountain are spectacular, jagged rock lookouts peering down at a bowl of forest and across at mountain ridges, but this is more so. From here you can really see eye-to-eye with the birds.

There wasn't a lot of talk. Every now and then someone would call out something like "Sharpie over Number Three" or "Broadwing over Donat" followed by some *hmms* and short comments like "Yes, it's lifting into the clouds." I gradually figured out that the peaks across the valley from us were numbered and that the local landmarks, even down to certain uniquely shaped trees, provided a common language for the watchers. (In fact, one of these landmarks, the lowland known locally as the Kettle —first named *der kessel,* a local Pennsylvania German term meaning "a hollow enclosed by hills"—had been the origin for the word *kettling* to describe the way raptors circle and lift in flocks, since hawks often rise above the Kettle in just this way.) I was in over my head, but at least I knew enough to keep my mouth shut when several turkey vultures lifted up over the ridge, their great *V* shapes tottering unsteadily. It would be the greatest faux pas to call out a sighting of a lowly turkey vulture with this crowd. But while the vultures were ignored, not so the other birds coming over the ridge. These were named while they were barely specks in the sky, and once again I just pretended to point my binoculars where everyone else was pointing them, nodding my head and mumbling, "Hmmm . . . yes." I did witness one spectacular sight, however, when a broad-winged hawk sped into a long stoop and went crashing into the bushes, presumably to surprise its lunch.

All over the world people gather at watch sites like Hawk Mountain to observe the migration of raptors in the fall and, to a lesser extent, in the spring, when the birds are not as concentrated. Over dinner the night before Keith had tried to summarize the appeal of watch sites for me. Birds of prey are generally secretive, and are spread out during the breeding season and even during much of the wintering period. It is difficult to see large numbers of individual hawks and eagles, and often difficult to see them close up even when you do see them. But a good watch site is a place of concentration during migration, a bottleneck that puts a large number of people and a large number of birds together in a way that doesn't distract the birds and that allows the people to see them up close. Because of this, birders learn to identify birds quickly. If you see a thousand broadwings go over in the course of one day, you can develop identification skills that you wouldn't be able to develop at a less concentrated point even over a span of years.

Hawk Mountain is the oldest official raptor migration watch site in the world, though of course people had been watching birds from such sites for centuries before they became "official." In earlier years people didn't just watch: long before humans started to come to places like this to count hawks, they came here to kill them. No one can be sure whether Native Americans ever shot arrows at hawks from this mountainside, but there is photographic evidence of the slaughter in the early twentieth century. Pictures on the walls of the Hawk Mountain Visitor Center reveal the mountain's legacy: thousands of limp hawks and eagles and ospreys lying in humped piles of feathers. The birds were easy picking, since they were funneled toward the shooters along their ancient routes. The shooters waited for them at places like the North Lookout. Those pulling the triggers might not have known about updrafts or even had any idea where these birds were heading, but they sure knew that this place was a bottleneck for the birds. And therefore a convenient place to kill them and rid the skies of pests.

It's hard to imagine our way back in time and put ourselves in the hunters' shoes, as hawks have now been elevated from pest to symbol of magnificence. "I'd rather kill a man than a hawk," Robinson Jeffers wrote famously. But while Jeffers, looking out from his Hawk Tower on a bluff above Big Sur, might have felt that way, his early-twentieth-century contemporaries did not. Hawks and eagles were killed for the same reasons wolves and coyotes were: they were seen as a threat to livestock, specifically poultry, and therefore had to be eliminated. It was, as always, us or them.

Although the guns were long gone, it seemed to me that what I was now watching at the North Lookout wasn't that far from hunting. Not senseless slaughter but good hunting—a quiet stalking. I thought again that one of the pleasures of this sort of hunting is the complete absorption in the task, a task encoded in humans from our beginnings. What the guy with the flip-flops and baggy hat and fancy Austrian binoculars was doing really wasn't all that far from stalking a wildebeest. The skills of the hunter—to be stealthy and watchful in nature, not to miss a thing—were also the skills of the hawk watcher. While the people on the North Lookout were not murdering birds and would have been appalled by the thought, they were experiencing a kind of poised intensity that humans first learned stalking prey. It was, I thought, a pretty good way to channel human nature. Not to deny our genetic, animal selves, not to make false claims for human calm and passivity, but to *use* those aggressive impulses, to nudge them toward finer, less violent purposes.

The night before, on the drive home from McKeansburg, Keith had talked about the kind of hunting that most interested him. He had been driven since he was a kid to figure out the mystery of why animals did what they did. Though he enjoyed teaching and working with the interns, nothing was better than solving mysteries in the field. He was a slightly different kind of hunter from most of the people I was observing at the North Lookout. He was hunting for answers, while they were hunting for sightings and for numbers.

I'd asked Keith about the difference between hawk watchers and other kinds of birdwatchers.

"There are birdwatchers, and there are hawk watchers who are birdwatchers," he said. "But hawk watchers per se are cut from something of a different cloth. It's a kind of competitive birding that is different from the competitive birding that most people think of when they think of 'twitchers,' the kind of birders who are building life lists. This really isn't about lists. The hawk-watching competition is often about first identification. Taking that pepper speck that's floating off in the distance and being able to taxonomize it before anyone else does. And the remarkable thing about this is that there's a built-in check, because the bird almost always comes into full view, where its identity is revealed to all. So you can't just say, 'That's a broadwing out there' and then the bird disappears and you get away with it. That doesn't typically happen. The bird comes up closer and can be transmogrified into a Cooper's hawk."

Keith had some reservations about the degree of specialization hawk watching led to. He told me a story to illustrate how one part of a birder's mind might grow while another part might atrophy. A few years ago there'd been a guy up at the North Lookout who could identify anything from miles off. He could tell a redtail from a sharp-shinned hawk (or "sharpie") when it was still the smallest speck. One day while driving home from the mountain the guy found a dead hawk on the side of the road. He put it in a bag and took it to Keith at his home. "It's a sharpie," the guy said, handing it over. But from his years in the field, Keith could tell right away, just by the heft of the bag, that there was no way it was a sharp-shinned hawk. It was clearly a much bigger and heavier bird, and when he opened the bag, he found it was one of the most common of American raptors, a broad-winged hawk. "This guy could tell hawks apart from miles away but not in his own hands," Keith said.

This reminded him of a scene in *Butch Cassidy and the Sundance Kid*, when Butch and Sundance are hired in a mine in South America and the boss says, "Can you shoot?" The boss puts a can on the ground and Sundance can't hit it, so Butch throws it in the air and Sundance peppers it with holes. Just like Sundance, the hawk watchers prefer their targets on the move.

At the North Lookout, I quickly tired of playing spy and walked over to Greg to introduce myself. He was a nice young guy with a shaggy black beard and mustache, big binoculars hanging around his neck. He stood in the center of the rock field behind the Swarovski scope that he used to confirm sightings. We talked for a while, and I learned that he was about to head off to start his doctorate in West Virginia. Something to do with warblers.

I told him that I was having trouble spotting some of the birds that the others were seeing.

"Birds are hard to watch, you know," he said with a smile. "They just keep movin,' you know?"

I revealed my purpose in being there. Why fuck around? I was there to bag an osprey.

"I usually require twenty-four hours for requests," he said.

I looked out over the green bowl to the northern ridge. "You don't want me to get shut out," I warned him. "It would reflect poorly on Hawk Mountain."

Greg alerted the group to my quest. Far from being snobs about it, the gunslingers all seemed eager to help. A couple made jokes on the order of Greg's, about how they didn't do requests. I didn't mention anything about being an osprey magnet this time, but my luck held. At that point in the day they had seen a dozen or so ospreys, so it was likely I would see one if I was patient. As it turned out, no patience was required. In a little less than four minutes after Greg yelled out to the group, someone spotted an osprey migrating over Number Three. There was a light spattering of applause, and Greg trained his scope on it and let me have a look. It was a large female, stroking through the air in a manner that was at first quite different from that of yesterday's gliders. But then, just like the foursome of the day before, she pulled her wings into what ornithologists call a "flex glide" and picked up speed. I watched as she came closer and jetted directly over our heads. Her white belly shone.

"How's that for service?" Greg asked once the osprey had passed out of sight.

"I'll tell Keith you did your job well," I said.

And with that I said my goodbyes. I suspected there was probably some mild disdain for my twenty-minute stay among the hawk watchers, most of whom had been sitting there patiently since nine or ten in the morning and would probably be there until four or five that evening. But for today at least, mine was a hit-and-run approach. I was acting like a different sort of competitive birder, closer to what Keith had called a twitcher, a birder who sees a bird and checks it off on his list before running on to the next bird (though not really, since I was only after my single species). Anyway, I didn't feel like explaining myself to anyone, and the truth was, no one was asking for explanations. The gunslingers seemed genuinely happy, and not a little proud, to have provided me with what I was looking for so quickly.

I hiked back down the trail to the South Lookout, where Keith was holding court, just as he had when I'd arrived the day before. He smiled when I told him about my experience at the North Lookout.

"You see, they're not so scary," he said. "It's usually a good mix. Migration watch sites generally attract top hawk watchers, but they also attract novices. And the people with a lot of knowledge are usually willing to share it."

We passed the afternoon sitting on the rocks and lazily looking out through our binoculars. Near us two of the Hawk Mountain interns, young women from Argentina and Spain, carried on a nonstop, high-speed discussion in Spanish, their voices a trickling, lisping river in the background. They barely paused for breath, but their chatter wasn't annoying, more soothing really. I mentioned that I liked the rhythm of the place, the pulsing of talk with silence, though it was never completely silent, thanks to the gas hawks.

Keith told me about one day when it really had been silent. He had gone up to the South Lookout on the day after September 11 to get away from the world. "The most striking thing about that day was the quiet. It was incredible, because there were no planes in the air. And it's not until you sit at the North Lookout when there's nothing in the sky but the birds that you realize how noisy the sky usually is. It was a clear blue day when the towers came down, and it was clear blue the next day, and it was painful being up there. It was so silent. Unbelievably eerie."

Talking about September 11 led to talking about how government restrictions have affected the worldwide birding community. Migratory birds cross borders, but that has been getting harder for people to do. I mentioned my own troubles trying to find a legal way to follow the ospreys through Cuba. The whole time I'd been making my plans to get to Cuba, the U.S. government had been tightening its restrictions on travel to the island. Tourist travel was now forbidden, and a permit was required for travel related to work, which in my case meant journalism or research. The problem was that these permits could take up to six months to process, which meant I would miss the migration. The other problem was that outside of my e-mail exchanges with Freddy Santana, I had made no real plans and hadn't the foggiest notion of how to get there, where to stay, or how to see birds while I was there.

Keith expressed sympathy. Then he pointed out at the panoramic view from the South Lookout and described La Gran Piedra, the Cuban watch site he had visited with Freddy Santana.

"Imagine a huge rock jutting up from a mountaintop higher than this one," he said. "And instead of looking out at Allentown and Bethlehem, you have the Caribbean right over there and the rainforest right below. And of course Guantánamo Bay back behind you to the east."

Keith put down his binoculars and grew animated as he told the story of how Freddy Santana had first gotten in touch with him. He called from Cuba about a dead osprey he had recovered that had originally been banded at Hawk Mountain. One thing led to another, and the next thing they knew, Freddy was Hawk Mountain's first Cuban intern. When Freddy got back home, he began searching in earnest for the osprey highway that led through his country, scouting for potential watch sites. He decided that the best spot to see the largest number of birds was La Gran Piedra, and in the fall of 2001, Mark Martell, whose satellite tracking had first revealed the density of the Cuban route, flew with Keith to Santiago to watch the birds from Freddy's site.

"To me, that's science at its best," Keith said. "When you can bring in a guy who has put satellite units on more ospreys than anyone else in the world and hook him up with a person who's been studying their visual migration in the temperate zone for some time, and then you introduce the tropical connection, an individual on his home turf who can put us right underneath these birds."

Before we left the lookout, Keith told me one more story about his trip to Cuba. One day he and Mark Martell were looking for ospreys from the top of La Gran Piedra when the ground began to shake. "I think the rock just moved," Mark said to Keith. And then suddenly the world below started to do a little jig, all of it—the rainforest and the Caribbean and the city of Santiago—dancing along with the rock. It took a second to understand that they were in the middle of the earthquake, and they didn't know whether to try to scramble down the side of the rock or just to lie low. On instinct they crouched to the ground and held on to the huge, no-longer-stable rock while the mountains shook.

The next morning I got up early and took another dip in the Schuylkill, then headed over to the office at seven to say goodbye to Keith. Of migration, Alan Poole had written: "It is the ospreys' internal clock and subtle changes in the flow of hormones that no doubt generate the necessary restlessness." I don't know if the increasingly autumnal sun was affecting my hormones, but I too felt the migratory unrest of *Zugunruhe*. I itched to get back on the road, but first Keith had promised me that we would try to call Freddy Santana at his home in Santiago. At that very hour Hurricane Ivan was battering Havana, but Keith had followed the weather reports closely and said that Santiago had not been hit. We tried Freddy's home number for half an hour, but the lines were down and we couldn't get through.

Despite this failure, I left Hawk Mountain with both Freddy Santana's number in my pocket and the growing conviction that I would get down to La Gran Piedra to see the sky fill with ospreys. I still had no concrete plans, just a vague romantic notion of following the birds. But something had begun to change while I talked to Keith the day before. The effect of our coversation up at the South Lookout was to light a fire in me. As I drove away from Hawk Mountain, I still didn't have any tickets or plans for the Cuba trip. But for the first time, I knew I was really going to go.

CHAPTER FIVE

YOUNG GUNS
AND OLD PROS

Admittedly, I'm obsessive. But I don't think I'm so different from most human beings in this respect. We all have our objects. Now I was heading to one of the few places in the country, and in the world, where my bird-focused behavior would not seem at all peculiar, where it was quite likely that the local postman had a handy pair of Swarovskis and the grocer had spent the weekend chasing hoary redpolls through the thickets. Cape May, New Jersey, situated perfectly where land ends and water begins at the southern tip of the Jersey coast—a location that guarantees that almost all coastal migrants are funneled through—has one of the most intense concentrations of both birds and birders in the world. There are visiting birders and there are everyday backyard birders and there are smiling superstar birders like local legend Pete Dunn and there are hungry young unknown birders like the ones I would soon meet. Not only that, every subsect of the birding world is well represented, from hawk watchers to scientists to tour guides to artists to cranks. One of this last group was a local newspaper writer who went by the name of "the Osprey Man." He claimed to have telepathic communication, and called himself "a conduit for the Great Osprey."

The drive to Cape May was a poetic one, despite the drizzle, and in the course of a couple of hours I crossed the Walt Whitman Bridge outside Philly and saw a sign for Corson's Inlet State Park. The Whitman was a good omen and Corson's even better, since it is the name of one of my favorite poems by A. R. Ammons. Ammons was a poet of movement and randomness and accident, and in that way I thought him the perfect poet for migration, with all its risks and unpredictability. Appropriately, the walk I took at Corson's Inlet was through a wild maze of underbrush and dunes, and I got lost twice. At one point thousands of tree swallows spiraled above me, their white bellies flashing as they filled the air with squeaky-wheel cries.

Soon I was back on the road. At 2:29 I saw the day's first osprey, peering down over the edge of a nest on top of a huge electrical tower, the highest nest I'd ever seen. I thought of making a U-turn to look at it through the scope but decided to press on. The land narrowed, and the southern tip of Jersey became a single thumblike nub jutting out into the water. It was this fact of geography that led to there being so many birds and birders here: the birds follow the coast as far as they can, until finally, at Cape May, they run out of land. Then they have to either double back and make a long detour or get up the nerve to make the jump and fly across Delaware Bay toward Lewes, Delaware, a water crossing of about 20 miles.

One of the birds making the coastal trip was Tasha, who had beaten me to Cape May by a day after her night spent in northern New Jersey. Many birds pause for a while in Cape May, in part to gear themselves up for the water crossing, and this leads to a great massing of birds in the area. As Rob Bierregaard put it on his website, the birds in Cape May wait "for the right winds and migratory restlessness to overcome the fear of heading out over open water." But Tasha, as was her wont, didn't wait. She was proving herself a true seabird and, having already tested herself by flying straight from Cape Cod to Block Island to Long Island, was showing little fear of crossing open water. Consequently I just missed her, and by the time I drove over the bridge onto the Cape May Peninsula, she had already launched herself out over Delaware Bay. After that crossing she would stay over land for a few hours, following the Delmarva Peninsula (so named because it incorporates land from three states: Delaware, Maryland, and Virginia). Then, again showing her characteristic boldness, she would attempt another late-day crossing, flying over the Chesapeake Bay before dark and spending the night just south of Norfolk, Virginia. Her watery route had the advantage of affording her many opportunities to fish as she went. No doubt she plunged into the shallows and flew off with fish to nibble on as she migrated. Keith Bildstein called this "taking lunch to go."

Keith had pointed out that one of the benefits of telemetry is in seeing how individual migrations are, depending on the personality of the bird. Jaws was once again proving just that. After nearly a month of fattening up and honing his fishing skills on the lakes of Connecticut, he had taken off about the time I left Hawk Mountain, crossing Long Island Sound to the island itself, where he would spend the night. Meanwhile, Elsie's migration had involved some backtracking. After reaching New Jersey she boomeranged north again, camping out east of the Hudson River in Westchester County. As Rob Bierregaard wrote, "She probably ran into a hurricane—and had second thoughts about this whole migration thing." After a couple days of lying low, she had pushed off, reaching Cape May by September 11 (the day I spent with the Puleston group on Long Island) and continuing on to her present location on the Potomac, outside the Washington Beltway. Finally there was Bluebeard, who was still at home dealing with his problem child, perhaps getting ready to give up on the kid as fall rains threatened the Vineyard.

So with the exception of Bluebeard, the robobirds were on the move. As I neared Cape May, I decided to call Rob Bierregaard to get a few more details on their locations. Rob had initially responded to my project with great enthusiasm, and with the kind of generous sharing of information that I was finding so common in the birding world. But after Tanya, the BBC producer, gave me the electronic brushoff in early September, he began to dry up as a source as well, and for a while my e-mails weren't being returned quite as eagerly. But now Rob was starting to crack. When I called, he was friendly and forthcoming, and to my surprise he filled me in on the BBC's first couple of days. I will admit to a small tingle of pleasure when he let me know that the crew hadn't yet managed to film any of the satellite birds. In fact, as he went on, I began to understand that the whole operation had a somewhat different flavor from what I'd first imagined. For one thing, Animal Planet was one of the show's cosponsors, and since this was a channel whose programs my one-year-old liked to watch, it suddenly became harder to imbue the project with sinister KGB-like qualities.

The BBC show would be called *Amazing Journeys* and was set up so that the audience would follow Steve Leonard, the star—or "presenter," as the Brits called it—as he embarked on a quest similar to mine, traveling down the coast in a van and interviewing people along the way as he followed the birds. After his emergence as the star of *Vets School*, Steve had followed up with another reality show called *Vets in Practice*. In fact, his career seemed like the veterinary equivalent of *The Truman Show*. As the BBC press office put it, "From his very first day of work, including his first diagnosis as a new graduate, Steve had lived with cameras following his day-to-day life." In other words, Steve knew a little bit about how the radio-tagged ospreys felt. He had eventually quit his vet practice and become a full-time TV star, and judging by the titles, his shows had been increasingly dramatic. These included *Vets in the Wild, Extreme Animals,* and the subtly named *Ultimate Killers,* a quest to find dangerous animals.

Because of his obviously busy schedule, Steve Leonard hadn't been available to narrate the osprey migration until September 10. Since adult female ospreys tend to leave earlier than the young and the males—they must be understandably sick of nest life after months sitting around tending chicks—Rob Bierregaard had decided to band mostly males and young birds. In short, because the BBC would start late, it needed birds that started late as well. But most of the tagged birds, perhaps not craving fame and attention, had impolitely taken off before the BBC landed. That gave the camera crew nothing to film except poor Bluebeard, run ragged trying to feed his slow-learning kid. Since the birds were gone, the BBC resorted to doing interviews with human beings on Martha's Vineyard. One of those interviews had been with Gus Ben David, who had played a role on Martha's Vineyard similar to the one Gil Fernandez played in Westport, building platforms and helping shepherd the ospreys' return. Gus was a born showman, and after the interview he'd mentioned that a friend of his had a single-prop plane called the *Red Baron* that the BBC might consider using. The BBC producer liked the idea. She decided to film Steve Leonard landing at the Vineyard airport with Gus's friend at the wheel, as if the two were a couple of barnstormers who had just made an unlikely transatlantic journey chasing birds.

It just so happened that Rob Bierregaard was hanging around at the airport when they landed, and it just so happened that the cameras caught him shaking hands with Steve as he climbed out of the plane (Steve no doubt jauntily throwing his scarf over his shoulder). While the cameras were still rolling, Rob smiled and told Steve the story of how the Vineyard birds had been caught and how the telemetry devices had been attached. The next day, before the crew left to follow the birds, the BBC staged another airport scene. This time Rob stood on the runway waving goodbye as the intrepid Steve flew off over the water toward Westport. One of the last things that Rob shouted to Steve—in front of the cameras, of course—was this: "When you get down to Cape May, make sure you bump into my friend Mark Martell!"

I have nothing against a little staging. Writers manipulate events too, and one of the reasons my own quest felt so electric— and one of the reasons I was doing some of the things I was do- ing—was the fact that I knew I was eventually going to write about it. For instance, that morning I'd dived into the Schuylkill River in part because I liked the bracing feel of the cold water. But another part of my mind thought it would make good copy, and I had half an eye on the romantic picture I could create of the dashing birdman hero. I'd be lying if I said I didn't some- times think of how things would appear on the page later. There is an old saw about how writers have to choose between their writing and "life," but I have always thought this wrongheaded. For me, the level of self-consciousness actually added extra ex- citement to my quest.

But when it came to stagecraft, I had nothing on the BBC. Yes, Mark Martell was going to be in Cape May to "bump into" Steve Leonard. But that wasn't because Mark happened to be out getting doughnuts and coffee on the streets of his hometown in southern Jersey. In fact, at that very moment he was driving down the Garden State Parkway, only a couple of hours behind me. He was coming to Cape May from Newark Airport, where he had been flown in by the BBC from his home in Minnesota so that he could bump into Steve when the BBC team arrived the next day.

When I got to Cape May, I headed right to the hawk-watch plat- form near the lighthouse. I'd only been to the town once before, but as I navigated fairly easily through the streets, I thought of something Alan Poole had once said to me. "We have all these fancy theories about how birds navigate, and they may all be true," he said. "But we shouldn't forget the commonsense fact that birds can look down and pick out landmarks, just like you and me."

In fact, as Alan had pointed out, birds can pick out landmarks a lot better than you and me, since they are doing so from the air, with the world below laid out like a map. For a four-month-old bird to fly south to a place it's never been before, prompted by instinct, is a mysterious thing. But when it returns, particularly in subsequent years but even during its first return, it can simply look down at Cape Cod, for instance, and think something like *Oh, yeah, I remember that big hook.* In a similar manner, with only a couple of wrong turns, I made my way to the lighthouse and the platform.

If Cape May is a birding epicenter, then the platform is one of its epi-epicenters, a two-level wooden deck facing northeast, with the Atlantic off to the right and Delaware Bay directly behind. The deck bustled with serious birders absorbed in the business of watching birds sweep by as they migrated.

It was birding heaven, really, though when I got there I didn't feel entirely heavenly. In fact, I felt a growing purposelessness. While I thought it was silly of the BBC to import Mark Martell from Minnesota, I was also a little jealous. It wasn't just that they had money and resources. It was simpler than that: they had a plan. They had come down to Cape May months before and scouted out the location and then had scripted a series of encounters with the locals. Meanwhile, I was planless, no more sure of what I was going to do next than the juvenile ospreys. So far I had relied on spontaneous decisions and had been lucky, but my stay at Hawk Mountain had gone on too long, and my rental car was due back in North Carolina in less than two days. I'd

called the company to see about extending my lease for an extra
day but had been told that an extra day would cost me as much
as the previous week had. There was no logic for this or reason
given. The woman on the phone spoke in a sweet voice, but
the gist of what she said was "We're screwing you just because
we can."

My nerves were frayed. I really had no idea what I was going
to do in Cape May, other than watch a few more migrating ospreys. It wasn't that there weren't any interesting bird people to
talk to; if anything, the problem was the opposite. Cape May
was so stocked with ornithological experts that I didn't know
where to start. Keith Bildstein had scribbled down a bunch of
names for me, and on the way into Cape May I had called one of
those contacts, Mark Garland. Mark worked at the Bird Observatory and promised to meet me at the hawk-watch platform.
When I got there, I found about a dozen people up on the platform, all armed with binoculars, and I walked up to a guy standing next to a large Swarovski scope and clicking off the birds
he saw with a handheld metal counter. He obviously had the
same job that Greg had had at the North Lookout, and introduced himself as Cameron. I asked him if Mark was there,
and he pointed to a bearded, middle-aged man standing on the
lower deck.

Mark was a fine birder, and quickly proved this as we stood
on the platform. He had a low-key, easygoing manner, and since
I was at a loss about what to do, I asked him if he had any sug-
gestions for how I should spend my time at Cape May. He said
it really depended on what I wanted to get out of it, which was
logical enough. I shrugged and thought about it some more.

"Well, I was kind of interested in the way the birders at
Hawk Mountain were like gunslingers," I said finally. "Who
would you say are the best birders in town?"

He rattled off a list of names that included Michael O'Brien, Chris Vogel, Richard Crossley, and Pete Dunn.

I was a little surprised by the last name on his list. In my prejudice, I had assumed that Dunn was too handsome and popular to actually be any good. I mentioned something like this to Mark, figuring he would like nothing more than to dish out some dirt about the current poster boy of the birding world. I couldn't have been more wrong.

"Oh, no, I work for Pete and he's a great guy, and a great guy to work for. He was out here at the platform this morning for a while, helping people out. He's a great storyteller. And he knows his birds."

We talked for a while more, but then Mark said he had to get back to the office to work. He let on that that work included, among other things, preparing for the members of the BBC crew, whom he would be showing around tomorrow.

Before he left the platform he gestured back at Cameron. "If you're looking for a gunslinger, that kid can spot birds with the very best of them," he said quietly. "That's the thing about this place. You have all these renowned birders, but then you have the young kids who come in hungry and can give anyone a run for their money."

After Mark left, I walked to the upper platform and stood next to Cameron, where I could both watch birds and watch him watch birds. I asked him how he had come to Cape May, and he explained that he was one of several interns chosen each year to live in town and work at the various bird-watching platforms for the Cape May Bird Observatory. I told him about my osprey quest, and he said that the people on the platform had already seen quite a few ospreys and he was sure that I'd see a few more if I stuck around for a little while. The kid had a low-key manner and didn't emote much—he wasn't a Keith Bildstein kind of teacher, at least not yet—but he could call out a merlin before I could even see it on the horizon.

The merlins, small, aggressive falcons capable of preying on larger birds, flew with strong sharp beats over the marsh, moving fast, no-nonsense, in a kind of hard pumping flight. They had varied coloring, including a metallic blue back, but looked mostly black in flight. We saw a couple of kestrels too, lighter-colored falcons with slimmer wings.

"Which is more of a badass bird?" I asked Cameron. "A kestrel or a merlin?"

He looked at me as if I had asked which color was darker, black or white. Clearly, I had revealed my birding ignorance.

"Oh, a merlin. No question."

"Because kestrels are pretty impressive in their own way," I said defensively.

"Oh, kestrels are *pretty*, true, but in terms of just having attitude and hunting through the sky, there's nothing like a merlin. I've seen them diving down and taking pokes at great black-backed gulls and pigeons. These are birds a merlin could never catch, but it just wants to hit them to let them know who's boss. They'll attack anything."

I watched side by side with Cameron for a while, trying to see the birds after he called them out. Though I wasn't even close to being in his league, my level of sophistication had grown somewhat over the past few days. Now when I saw a turkey vulture, for instance, I would dismiss it almost immediately (with some fanfare), and I finally understood what the pros meant when they said that TVs (as they called the vultures) flew with a rocking motion. I saw how you could begin to identify other birds in a like manner, through their details but more through a kind of gestalt. I mentioned this to Cameron.

"With those merlins, for instance, is there a specific thing you're looking for that identifies them, or is it the whole bird?"

"It's everything, basically. It's a real quick take. Merlins give a distinctive impression. Compare them with sharp-shins, for example. A merlin is a little bit shorter-winged, and it's about an inch smaller in both length and width and wingspread, but it weighs twice as much. In a wind, a kestrel flutters. Merlins have got so much more mass and so much more muscle. And they have so much more power to their flight. They're more angular. Kestrels trim their wings. The wingtips just kind of curve and make a real smooth curve, and merlins are just straight triangles and bulk."

Another intern who had been helping people on the lower platform overheard our conversation and came up to join us. He was a personable, outgoing man in his early twenties named Jason Starfire.

"We have a word for what you're talking about," he said after introducing himself. "We call it *giss*."

"Giss?"

"I think it's an old military term. It's an acronym for 'general impression shape and size.' That's how you identify stuff after you get good. It's not any one thing. You just kind of get a feel—maybe the tail is a little shorter, but all kinds of other things are coming into play too. It's just your general impression initially. From far away you don't have time to look for small details."

A third intern joined us, a young woman named Jess with a bashful but radiant smile, who could have passed for sixteen but who knew her birds cold. From the way she leaned toward Cameron I gathered that they were dating, and I soon learned that her pleasant, youthful features hid a competitive streak and a birding eye that were every bit as intense as his (and that her life list of species was actually the longest of the interns'). After we said hello, I asked her when she had started birding seriously.

"I was nine," she said. "Then in sixth grade my science

teacher noticed that I had an interest. He took me out on a one-day count, and it's just gone from there."

Cameron had been a year older, ten, when he started, and Jason, the late bloomer, had been fourteen. Internships at Cape May are extremely competitive, and the three of them had applied and won their positions. But while they came from different parts of the country, they'd gotten to know each other many years before.

"Cameron's from Texas," Jason said. "I was living in Seattle. Jessie's from New York. But we all knew each other before we even met. One day I read a post on the Internet and I thought, 'Who's this Cameron guy?' "

"I met all my best birding friends through the Internet," said Jess. "I don't even know if I would have survived my teenage years without it, because you think you're the only serious young birder out there, and then you get on the Internet and realize, 'Oh, other people are interested in this. I guess I'm not such a freak after all.' And since there really aren't that many young people who are hardcore birders, you all kind of get to know each other."

Soon after they met online, the three virtual friends met in person. Jess and Cameron entered a one-day birding competition called a Big Day, during which teams of four birders try to identify as many species as they can within a twenty-four-hour period. Jason and Cameron met at a competition along the Texas coast and began traveling together, bird watching from the back of another friend's pickup while surviving on one Subway sub a day.

The whole time we'd been talking Cameron had barely put down his binoculars, and now he told me that an osprey was coming in along the shore. I kept following the osprey while the others turned to the next round of approaching birds. The interns were there in part to encourage and teach other birders on the hawk-watch platform, but their main job was to count migrating birds. This required determining which birds were migrating and which were local residents or just hanging around. One of the more obvious ways to do this was to see if the birds continued over the platform and then launched themselves out over Delaware Bay. The osprey I was watching, a large male with particularly distinct black-and-white coloring, didn't hesitate for a second. Like Tasha, this bird was a bold water-crosser, and he flew straight out over the bay without so much as a pause or a change in direction. Ospreys, of course, are less likely to balk at water than the other birds counted here.

When things were going well on the hawk-watch platform, it had the feel of a successful cocktail party, with strangers interacting and calling across the deck to each other, everyone doing something he or she truly enjoyed with like-minded people. Cameron might have had the superior eye, but I noticed that Jason, gregarious and funny, had a way of making the birders on the deck feel comfortable and making sure that everyone who wanted to be involved was. One way I had begun to think of migration was as an exercise in exuberance, in raw lift, and that was the quality that Jason brought to the platform.

I pointed across the marsh to the spot where most of the migrating birds first flew into sight. A dilapidated single-room shack that looked ready to collapse into the marsh stood on the edge of the phragmites. I told Jason about my string of cabin living over the first three days of my trip and asked, "What do you think the chances are that I could stay in that shack tonight?"

"I don't even know how you'd get out there without sinking into the muck," Jason said. "But I have a better idea. You should come spend the night with us in the intern house."

I thought about it for a second. Why not? It made perfect

sense. In Cape May the natural thing to do would be to seek out the famous, the celebrity birders, the bigwigs. But here was the next generation, the young guns, the up-and-comers.

"If you're serious, I'd like that," I said. "I'd like that a lot."

An hour later I was walking in the front door of a tall, rundown Victorian home on Columbia Ave with a cold case of Sierra Nevada Pale Ale in my arms. A pot of pasta was on the stove, and the place had the feel of an off-campus college apartment, though this particular apartment spilled over with telescopes and binoculars and feathers and bird bones and field guides. Jason and I plopped down on the ratty striped couch, and soon Jess and Cameron had pulled up chairs and joined us. For a couple of hours we drank beer and talked birds, while several other interns drifted in and out of the house. These other young people, most also in their early twenties, were all birders except for Gail, who was there to study the movement of butterflies, a lightweight and fluttery migration even more miraculous, and preposterous, than that of birds.

The living room and the group of kids felt familiar to me, and it didn't take very long to pinpoint why. In a way you could have substituted any passionate and somewhat obscure pursuit for birding. All over the country similar groups in similar apartments were following communal passions. For instance, when I was in my early twenties I played Ultimate Frisbee as fervently as these folks searched for birds. My teammates and I tended to rent group houses just like this one, warrens all over the city of Boston, where we lived on couscous and cheap beer. While this group spent most of their waking hours learning about birds, we had spent ours throwing and catching a plastic toy. Even though we'd passed our days doing something most people found strange and incomprehensible, we had been very ambitious within our own realm. Likewise, this group burned with ambition. A bunch of homemade CDs lay scattered on the table; I picked up one that turned out to be a recording of the calls of flycatchers and bobolinks. "We use it to test each other at night," Jason said.

I wondered aloud what the career track was for their sort of birder. What did they eventually want to do, or be, in the bird world?

"Well, I've kind of come up with my own term for what I want to be," Jason said. "A field ornithologist. Someone who studies birds out in the field."

Jess nodded as if in agreement, but Cameron folded his arms and leaned back in his chair. "I don't like the word *ornithologist*," he said. "I'm a bird bum."

Jason made his case, saying that ornithology was what they did, after all—studying birds in the field—but Cameron kept his arms folded and shook his head.

"I don't have much respect for scientists. I was in the field last summer with this guy, a big famous professor. I won't tell you his name, but he just embarrassed himself in the field. His expertise was in southwestern birds and he was doing some specialty collecting, but he didn't know many of the calls. I'd hear it and say, 'There's a Brewer's sparrow,' and he'd say, 'That's not a Brewer's sparrow.' And then he'd actually shoot it, and once he had it in his hand he would say, 'Well, I guess it is a Brewer's sparrow.'"

"Shoot it?" I asked. "I didn't know that that was still done."

"It's done, but very, very quietly. And a lot."

Cameron shook his head again. He played the James Dean role in this crowd, having dropped out of college to pursue birding full-time. He had figured that the way to follow his passion was to spend the fall and spring months in places where the birds congregated, like Cape May, instead of at a university.

"The best birders I know don't have Ph.D.'s," he said. "I understood I was taking a risk by not going to college, but birding is something I love to do. I've learned ten times more by going this route."

Cameron's real ambition was to lead bird tours, like Pete Dunne or the English birder Richard Crossley. *That* would be a good life. Day after day out in the field with the birds. I mentioned a line from a Robert Frost poem about uniting your avocation and vocation. Making work play, it seemed to me, was one of the best things you could do on earth. (I would later learn that Jason's father had taken this to its extreme, working as a professional poker player in Vegas for forty years.)

It was the most passionate of the birders, the most obsessed, who drew the most praise from the interns. Michael O'Brien, for instance, had a standing order to anyone in town to call him and wake him in the middle of the night if they heard songbirds.

"Michael is one of the top two or three birders in the country," Jason said. "But no one outside of the birding world has heard of him, because he doesn't publish that much."

It was inevitable that David Sibley's name would come up, since before his famous field guide came out, he had been an almost archetypal bird bum, running around without any money, with torn sneakers and empty pockets, spending all his time out in the field drawing and watching birds, looking like he wasn't ever going to publish anything. Until, of course, the quiet bird bum became a millionaire and a celebrity, writing the first field guide to crack the *New York Times* bestseller list. It was Sibley's early disregard for traditional rewards, living poor and birding hard, that appealed to Cameron and the rest of the interns. Of course, if a little fame and cash were thrown in later, then all the better.

Empty beer bottles filled the table like chess pieces by the time we turned to our dinner of pasta and salad. After we ate, Jess played the birdcall CDs for Jason, who had just started as an intern two weeks before and was new to the area and its birds.

A low *ssss* sound upslurred on the tape.

"A yellow-bellied flycatcher?"

"Nope. An Acadian fly," said Cameron.

"Damn."

They went on like this for a good while, testing each other, until we said goodnight. I crashed in the living room, but the fold-out bed was too saggy for my middle-aged back, so I moved the bottles aside and dragged the mattress onto the floor. I was almost asleep when Jason popped his head back into the room.

"You should come out to the dike with us in the morning," he said. "It's the best place to watch songbirds. We head out at six."

I said I'd love to. Then I fell into a deep, beery sleep on the interns' floor.

Though the hawk-watch platform was the raptor lover's shrine, for warbler freaks there was no place like the dike at Higbee Beach. It was there that Michael O'Brien counted birds in the middle of the night and came back again at sunrise to count the early-morning movements out across the Delaware Bay. And it was there that I followed the interns at dawn, despite the drizzle and drear light. The dike faced the woods, though if you walked north a bit along its ridge you could also observe shorebirds out on the sand flats. To get on top of the dike you had to scramble up a steep path. By the time I arrived the interns were all there, as was a short, solid-looking birder named Vince. This morning Vince was substituting for Michael O'Brien (off to give a bird talk at the Smithsonian). Vince's job was to count songbirds that had finally screwed up the courage to fly over the bay, and to try not to recount them when they chickened out and doubled back.

For warblers, ending up at Higbee Beach was often the result of a grand navigational mistake, of following land until land ended and then, trapped, massing and trying to get up their nerve to cross water.

Even in the dim light Cameron was in good form, and I listened as he and Vince named bird after bird, then debated the identification of a couple of rarities. Soon we were joined by three young Swedish guys, all blond and tall, who had come to the United States just to visit Cape May. They were hardcore, outfitted with the fanciest binoculars and equipment, but since they weren't on their home turf they glanced down at their copy of the Sibley guide and deferred to the locals, asking occasional questions of Vince, Cameron, Jason, and Jess.

I noticed that Cameron and Jess touched each other and whispered a lot, in the usual manner of young couples. But it wasn't sweet nothings that they were whispering in each other's ears. Keith Bildstein had explained that even the best of the birding gunslingers had a moment of doubt, of waiting, before identifying a bird out loud. At that moment there was usually a quick dialogue in the birder's head, but Cameron and Jess, as a couple, had the advantage of being able to have that dialogue out loud with each other. In that moment they quickly debated, brainstormed, concluded, confirmed. And *then* called out the name of the bird.

Vince had a gruff, funny manner and playfully disagreed with some of the interns' calls. "Cameron's good," he admitted to me. "Sometimes he'll be right and I'll be wrong. That's just the way it is. I'm not afraid to make mistakes."

He wasn't quite as generous when another birder, a white-haired older man, arrived and began walking toward the dike from below. "Not *that* guy," he said, shaking his head.

I asked about *that* guy and he told me that he was a "one-upper." "Every bird you see, he's seen two. If you spot a bar-tailed godwit, he'll tell you about the time he saw three back in Rhode Island."

Vince clammed up as the one-upper and his friend ascended the dike. A wild gurgling whoop came from the woods, a sound I would have thought more fitting in the tropical rainforest. The Swedish guys and I looked at each other and then at Vince.

"American crow," he said.

I assumed he was teasing, some kind of birding joke I didn't get. But then a loud *caw, caw, caw* came from the same patch of woods.

"See?" Vince said.

I tried to scribble down a phonetic approximation of the crow's earlier sound in my notebook. I had lived in America and known crows my whole life and had had no idea they were capable of such a whooping jungle call.

Not long after the crow's gurgle another small group arrived. Cameron explained that it was a birding tour group of the sort he had told me about the night before, led by none other than Richard Crossley.

The rain started to come down in earnest but seemed beside the point when one of the Swedes spotted a Baird's sandpiper on the tidal flat. This was big news. Soon Richard's group had headed down to see the sandpiper, Vince and our group had followed them, and the one-upper had followed us. Everyone was pointing and nodding and Richard Crossley had already earned his money, but when I took my turn at the scope, all I could see was one drab wet bird amid a dozen other drab wet birds. I wasn't even sure I was seeing the right bird, but of course I nodded enthusiastically and pretended to be impressed. Then Mr. One-Upper took his turn at the scope and, after mouthing some mild appreciation for the sight, said, "It's just too bad that you folks didn't get to see yesterday's Baird. We saw it from quite a bit closer than this."

Vince rolled his eyes. He looked as if he weren't going to say anything for a second, but he couldn't quite hold his tongue. "Well, this is *today's* bird," he said gruffly.

"It's nice, I suppose, if you didn't see yesterday's bird."

"It's nice even if you did see yesterday's bird," Vince snapped. "It's a nice sight. Just try to enjoy it."

Jason, Jess, and Cameron were already walking away, and while I was curious to see if two grown men would come to blows over a sandpiper, it was time to get down off the dike. The rain was pelting us, and after I caught up with the interns I decided to say my goodbyes. Jason expressed disappointment that he wouldn't get to witness a confrontation between me and the BBC crew, which would be arriving in just a few hours. Before I left, I made him promise he would do everything he could to undermine the BBC's efforts.

"Maybe you could throw some tacks in the road in front of their van," I suggested.

"I'll do something," he promised. "Maybe just misidentify some birds for them. Tell them a merlin is an osprey."

Then he gave me one of his cards. It read: "Jason Starfire, Avian Consultant."

"What about field ornithologist?" I asked.

"I hadn't thought of that at the time. That'll be on my next card."

Now I faced a choice similar to that of the migrating birds. I could double back up the peninsula and head north on the parkway to the Jersey Turnpike before hooking around south into Delaware. Or I could take the direct route, the osprey route, and catch the ferry across the Delaware Bay from Cape May to

Lewes. Despite the weather, there really wasn't much of a choice, and with the rain drumming my roof, I headed over to the ferry terminal.

As it turned out, I'd missed the early ferry and had to take the one o'clock. With a couple of hours to kill, I pulled the piece of paper Keith Bildstein had given me out of my pocket. There were several names of birders on the list, but the one that intrigued me most was Paul Kerlinger. I'd bought his book, *How Birds Migrate*, at the Hawk Mountain Visitors' Center, and it contained a particularly lucid description of raptor migration. The interns had warned me that Kerlinger had a reputation as being somewhat cranky, but when I dialed his number he picked up, and when I asked about dropping by he said sure. He invited me to come over and have a cup of "strong coffee" on his porch.

Soon I was doing just that. I didn't have the BBC's resources, but accident was once again turning out to be a fine tour guide. And while I hadn't flown Kerlinger in from Minnesota, I now, through sheer luck, was able to talk to one of the country's leading migration experts. There was a problem, however. Paul Kerlinger wasn't interested in talking about migration. A tall, wiry man with granny glasses and a thin mustache, he spent almost my whole visit monologuing about windmills. Like Don Quixote before him, windmills were his obsession, though not tilting at them so much as building them.

As we sat on the porch and sipped our coffee, he explained that he had been vilified within the bird community for his role as science adviser to wind farm projects, the erection of tall wind machines that would provide alternative energy but that were unsightly to those who didn't want to see them anywhere near their homes.

"The fucking environmentalists hate me now," he said. "They think I want to kill birds. But the wind machines don't kill damn birds. Look where all the bad press is coming from. It's put out by the coal companies, among others. They make me look like a shill for the wind industry."

One of his gripes with environmentalists in general was that they were too pure, too above dirtying themselves with anything practical. He was one of the first to do economic models for birders, for instance, and show how birding brought millions of dollars to different towns and communities.

"Birding is an eight-billion-dollar industry," he said. "Bigger than hunting and fishing combined. So when you try to convince a place to put land aside, you have to emphasize the economic benefits. That's what they listen to. I developed economic models that show how keeping fields as fields and not condos, or keeping a forest a forest and not an onion field, can economically benefit a community by making it a popular birding destination. But the money argument, which might make perfect sense to the local chamber of commerce, sometimes won't fly with the fucking environmentalists themselves. It may be more 'pure' to argue for a rare species or the purity of the forest. But these things don't work. I'm not saying that environmentalists should *only* use the economic argument. Just that it's a tool."

He spoke with an intensity that gathered in his wrinkled brow. After his second cup of coffee, after I'd finally nudged him away from talking about wind power and economics, he told me a little about the early days of the Cape May birding community, in the early 1980s, when he and Pete Dunn had been two of the first to recognize the potential of the place and transform it into the birding center it is today. They were both great birders, but while Pete Dunn went on to become the public face of Cape May, Kerlinger was more of a behind-the-scenes guy. As he carried on, I began to see him as Pete Dunn's darker, perhaps more intellectual doppelganger.

Suddenly he turned that intensity toward me. "I've been reading a scientific paper that suggests that ospreys migrate across the Caribbean at night. What do you make of that?"

Again I was being treated like the expert I wasn't. I looked out at the rain dripping off the trees in his front yard, scrunched up my face as if thinking profoundly, and changed the subject.

As I drove away, I thought about the contrast between the person and the words on the page. In person Kerlinger was an edgy monologuist, but his voice in his books was lucid and reasonable. He also swore a lot less in his books.

Between the coffee and his intensity, talking with Kerlinger had been like doing a stint inside a Dostoyevsky novella, and I was relieved to get away. I still had time to kill, however, and drove over to the Northwood Center, which was part bookstore and part observatory headquarters. To my surprise, Cameron, Jess, and Jason were there, and when I saw that the store had my osprey book in stock, I bought them all copies and signed the books for them. As the woman behind the register waited for my credit card to go through, I noticed that farther down the counter another cashier was helping a man buy binoculars. On second glance I realized that there, discussing the virtues and flaws of various binocs, was Pete Dunn. He was helping a beginning birder buy his first glasses. I went over and shook his hand and reminded him that we'd once done a talk together. In my head I had created an image of him as the aloof birding diva, but he was nothing but friendly.

The interns and I said our second round of goodbyes and then I headed for the one o'clock ferry. I'd known them less than twenty-four hours, but I felt a good deal of affection for Cameron, Jess, and Jason. They were a small band of hunters, with birds as their quarry, and birding would connect them to many other things in the world. For instance, not once had they mentioned environmental concerns, but as habitat destruction impinged on *their* birds, they might take up that fight, as other birders had before. But for now joy was more important, and more interesting, than activism. Watching them watch birds, I couldn't help but feel they fit perfectly in their environment. There is a German word, *funktionslust,* which means "pleasure taken in what one can do best." No doubt ospreys experience *funktionslust* when they soar. And no doubt the young interns felt it when they birded: a sheer animal pleasure in what they did best.

By taking the ferry I was also taking the approximate route of most northeastern ospreys. Of the birds that Martell, and later Bierregaard, had tagged, a whopping percentage, well over 90, flew south along the coast. This was the route Tasha had taken, and close to the route of Elsie, who had flown across the bay just to my north. Given that I was following this well-traveled osprey route, you might think I was poised on the bow of the ferry, binoculars at the ready. But I was tired and wet, and the rain was still pouring down, so I spent the first half of the trip sleeping in my car. As we approached Delaware, I went up on deck and took a few casual looks for birds, spying a dozen or so soaked gulls but no ospreys. After we landed in Lewes, I pulled off the ferry and soon managed to get lost in a forever stretch of strip-mall hell. If I was hoping for quaint seaside towns, I'd come to the wrong place. Gradually, after I passed Bootsie's Barbecue and the Sea Esta Motel, the strip malls gave way to farmland. I spent a long tired afternoon crossing the Delmarva Peninsula, and by the time I reached Virginia, my fourth state of the afternoon, a jittery exhaustion had come over me. I cranked the radio to an oldies station as I drove through Modest Town, Accomac, Locustville, and Birdsnest, and finally pulled over at a sign for the Great Machipongo Clam Shack.

The shack was right on Highway 13. At first glance it looked like the kind of place where your clams would be served up by a crusty, shriveled old-timer, the sort of character who would dole out helpings of folksy wisdom along with the slaw. But the guy behind the counter was a Tom Selleck look-alike whose five o'clock shadow seemed the result more of style than of neglect. As had become my standard practice, I gave him a summary of my osprey trip so far and said I hoped to find a bird or two before sunset.

He thought about it for a second. "The place you should go is Kiptopeke State Park," he said. "Just stay on 13 until you see a kayak shop on your right. Take a right there. And if you want to rent a boat, just stop in. They're cool guys and they stay late. They're probably smoking doobs out by the shop."

Apparently my facial hair and scraggly, unshowered look made him assume I wasn't the type to be offended by the sight of people smoking marijuana (he was right, of course).

On the way out I noticed one sign on the door: WE'RE RURAL, NOT STUPID. Another sign read EAT AND DRIVE, and I tried to take its advice, jamming crabmeat and crackers into my mouth as I sped south on Route 13. I passed a Tom Jode–style truck towing another truck with an old rope, and then I came to the kayak shop (though I didn't see any "doobs" being smoked). I took a right and pulled into Kiptopeke State Park, almost hitting a beautiful white egret.

The park was deserted except for two fishermen, one human and the other avian. An old man hunched over his rod out near the end of a pier, while the other fisherman, its brown-black mask and wings shining, was attempting to catch fish the old-fashioned way, by diving directly into the water. It wasn't terribly surprising to see an osprey here, since the Chesapeake Bay is, despite recent environmental woes, still the largest and most productive estuary in the United States, yielding over 200 million pounds of seafood annually. In fact, the bay is home to the largest concentration of ospreys in the world. It was from nests on this bay that Paul Spitzer, and later Gil Fernandez, had taken healthy eggs for the depleted northeastern nests. The Chesapeake had helped save the New England ospreys.

The fact that the sight wasn't surprising didn't make it any less exhilarating. It was 6:25 P.M., and to that point, the only osprey I'd seen all day had been a drenched one flying by the dike at Higbee. Now I walked along the beach, with the bay to my left and woods to my right, and watched the bird patrol up and down the same beach, looking for one last meal before the sun dropped into the water. Backlit by the sun, it seemed to have a nimbus or aureole beaming out around its head, and I noted that the head itself was particularly dark, almost black, hooded like a hangman's. The osprey peered down into water that had taken on a late-day color, a kind of metallic blue stained by the pink shreds of the dropping sun.

Though I hated to leave the bird and the sunset, there was a walkway heading into the woods called Osprey Overlook Trail. How could I resist? The wooden ramp sloped up from the beach over a kind of swampland, and as I followed it into the wooded uplands, I felt something like hope rise in my chest. Yes, development was chewing up habitat and the overall picture was grim. But here I was traveling down the eastern seaboard, the most populated part of the country, and again and again I had stumbled upon wild places and wild moments. It might not be wilderness, but it was wildness. And despite all the development and pollution, it was still here, a still wild America.

When I got back to the beach, the osprey was hovering and hunting, but the sun had dipped behind a low cloud right above the horizon line and I knew the bird would have to give up soon. The cloud was huge and continent-shaped, the sun behind it coloring its fringes a blazing orange. A couple of hundred yards offshore an old battleship stood in silhouette, grass growing from its pockmarked, bombed-out deck.

I had the beach to myself, so I stripped off my clothes and waded into the bay. I thought I would plunge right in, but the water proved surprisingly shallow and continued that way for almost 100 feet. After wading out to where it finally came up to my waist, I dove into the dark water. The osprey was out of sight, either having called it quits or having become invisible in the dusk. My rental car was due back at noon the next day, and this leg of my trip was almost over, and I still had absolutely no idea how I was going to get to Cuba. I'd also blown my chance at having a close encounter with the BBC in Cape May. But at the moment I didn't really care. It was enough to be floating in the salty Chesapeake, knowing there was a black-hooded osprey somewhere up above in the gloaming.

CHAPTER SIX

FISHING THE SKY

Travel is excitement, travel is opportunity, travel is expansion of one's territory. Might one unscientific reason for osprey migration be the sheer fun of it? This sounds silly at first, until you factor novelty and *funkstionlust* into your definitions of fun.

But then there is the other side: travel is stress, travel is danger, travel is the weak point in the lives of all animals.

If my trip had had its moments of Whitmanesque exultation, then that exultation was now laced with edginess. My swim in the Chesapeake had momentarily lifted me, but it was getting dark and I felt a nervous exhaustion coming on. The osprey I'd watched probably wouldn't be crossing the Chesapeake at night but instead would sleep in a tree in these coastal woods. I didn't have that luxury. I headed up onto the Chesapeake Bay Bridge and tunnel, a long series of high bridges and underground passages. Headlights flashed everywhere, and I was momentarily gripped by the thought that I would veer off the elevated road and end up deep in the bay, never getting home to Nina and Hadley. There is a momentum to travel, when you feel like you can drive forever and get anywhere and that you are capable of doing things you can't imagine before you start. But there is also a point where that momentum begins to fray.

I found the sight of other late-day migrants reassuring. Lines of flying eider ducks and scoters humped along, up and down, roughly parallel to the bridge. But even more impressive than my avian companions was the bridge itself, which to my mind seemed nearly miraculous. Just who had built this thing? Who had thought that spanning miles of water—and then going *below* the water—was possible? Human beings, sure, but not human beings like me. The feat was beyond the ken of my clan. The best my people could do would be a big log over a stream. This had been built by a different tribe, part man, part beaver.

On the other side of the bridge I had a decision to make. The middle of my trip across the Delmarva Peninsula had been spent yelling at some poor woman at the rental car company. Couldn't she just extend my deadline a little? *No,* was the answer. Worse, I had to return the car to Raleigh, two hours' drive from my own house, near where my sister lived, because it had been cheaper to return the one-way rental there than to my smaller town. The car was due at noon, at which point the absurd overcharges would start kicking in. My first plan was to drive late into the night back to my home on Wrightsville Beach, get a couple hours' sleep with my wife and daughter, wake up early, and head to Raleigh to return the car. (The last time I'd called home on the cell phone, Hadley had kept saying, "Da-dee, Da-dee," and my wife swore that her first real sentence was "When Da-dee home?") Though it would require a marathon drive, the idea of heading home made a sort of wired sense, and maybe I could ride my jiggly momentum all the way there.

But another idea prevailed. I was in southern Virginia now, heading toward the Carolina line, less than two hours from the Outer Banks. My college roommate, Jon, had recently moved to the Outer Banks and was living with his family in a town called Nags Head. I hadn't talked to him in about six months, and it was already dinnertime and he had three small kids, but I dialed his number anyway. After we said hello and caught up, I began to tell him about my trip, aware that a kind of lunatic excitement was leaking into my voice. Jon wasn't fazed, having heard the same frothing tone plenty of times back in college. After I'd gone on awhile, he interrupted me.

"It sounds good, Dave, it all sounds good," he said. "But where are you right now?"

I told him.

"Then you should come here. We'll get you food, a nice bed. Maybe Beth can make her margaritas."

By going east onto the Outer Banks I would be taking myself at least an hour, maybe two, out of the way. But why not? I wasn't usually the type to say, "It will all work out," but on this trip it had all worked out, and quite well, with only serendipity as my guide.

I said to Jon, "Just talk to Beth about it. Talk to Beth and see if it's all right and call me back."

It turned out it was okay with Beth, or at least Jon lied to me and pretended it was. Soon I was on the road to the Outer Banks, passing a church and then a billboard that read "God allows U-turns." Next came a bunch of shops that sold pools and hammocks and another billboard that read "Carolina Charm," which was kind of sad, since that charm now too often consisted of crappy overdeveloped roads like this one filled with billboards and strip malls. But what redeemed the place, and gave it real charm, was my drive over the Wright Memorial Bridge. Even in the dark I could make out the bulky, organic clumps above many of the bridge stanchions and recognize them for what they were: osprey nests.

Another nest sat on a pole above the canal right behind Jon's house. Jon and Beth fed me, and sure enough, after the kids went to bed the margaritas appeared. Soon I was telling my friends the story of my trip so far. Beth's father, Russ, who was something of an amateur birder, joined us in the living room. They all got caught up in the story, or at least the spectacle of this unshaven guy waving his arms around telling the story, but when I started to describe the virtual birders on Long Island, Jon again interrupted me.

"Let's see if we can find those birds," he said. He walked over to the other side of the room and flicked on the computer. A quick Google search and we were inside the nest with the Long Island birds. I had never before seen what the Puleston group saw, and I immediately understood their addiction. As Cecilia and Celeste had promised, the camera puts you right in the nest with the birds, part of their life, and you can hear every scratch and screech and shit. Then Jon clicked on the link that had the disclaimer about the death of the runt. The four of us watched the mother tear apart her young and dole it out to the other three birds.

"This is fucking unbelievable," he said. "No wonder they got hooked."

I slept in a guest bedroom over the garage and woke early. Jon had said to make myself at home, so I took my coffee and binoculars out to the hot tub on the porch and examined the empty osprey nest in the early-morning light. These birds had left the month before, but gulls often used the nest to perch on, and Jon later sent me a picture of a pair of bald eagles that used the nest in winter.

Before I left, Jon and I checked the computer again, this time looking for the current location of the BBC birds. It turned out that Rob Bierregaard had done some updating while we slept. Bluebeard still hadn't budged, but the other robobirds were on the move. Elsie had left the Potomac area and flown down to Fayetteville, North Carolina, and then on to Charleston, South Carolina. Jaws had cut down through New Jersey and reached the northernmost point of the Delaware Bay just as I was getting on the ferry, but that was the last signal Rob had received and he feared that Jaws was dead.

Then there was Tasha. She had crossed the Chesapeake about four hours before I had. Like me, she had then had a decision to make: she could keep pushing south through the last hours of the afternoon or stop for the night, tempted by food and rest. She chose, as I did, to take a break. And though she didn't get to drink margaritas, she couldn't have picked a better place to stop. The waters of Albemarle Sound were wonderful osprey habitat, and she had probably spent the end of the day fishing and then resting in the trees.

Russ joined Jon and me by the computer, and he laughed when he saw the spot where Tasha had spent the night. He got out a large, detailed map of North Carolina, and we compared it to the map Rob Bierregaard had posted on the screen. It wasn't hard to count the number of bays and estuaries, and we pinpointed Tasha's location at the northern end of the Perquimans River, just south of the small town of Hertford. This meant that while our little group had been slurping down our margaritas, Tasha had settled down virtually next door. I had given up on following the satellite birds, but now they seemed to be following me: Tasha had spent the night less than 15 miles away.

After I said goodbye to Beth and Russ and the kids, Jon pulled me aside. The night before we'd talked late, just as in college, and I'd expressed both fairly wild excitement and keen anxiety about my trip to Cuba. How would I get there and how would I pay for it? Now Jon put his arm on my shoulder and spoke in a quiet Dad-ish way: "If you need any financial help with this, please let me know." He had grown wealthy through investments and had always been willing to back my cockamamie schemes. I thanked him profusely and drove off.

Promising to get my rate down, Jon also called the rental

car company. But despite his haggling, the company wouldn't budge. Its representatives were tough bastards, and Jon told me that it would cost thirty dollars an hour for every hour I was late. I would have been lucky to get the car back in time even with no detours, but then, around Elizabeth City, I felt the old osprey lust rising. I knew I was passing near where Tasha had decided to sleep, the closest I'd been yet to one of the satellite ospreys. How could I not take a look around?

There was water nearby, lots of it, and fields full of what I, transplanted northerner that I was, first took to be pretty white flowers, until gradually it dawned on me it was cotton. I pulled off at Old Neck Road in Perquimans and then into a driveway next to the cotton fields. At the end of the driveway a big guy worked on an enormous green cotton-picker twice the height of a large dumptruck. I said hello, and he said something in an accent I could barely decipher. When I told him about my search, he pointed me down the road, but I found no landing or place to gain access to the river. Finally I pulled up in front of a big house where two guys were working on a dock out back. I talked to one of the workers, Dave Rue, and when I told him about my plight, he gazed out at the river for a second before replying.

"Shit, man," he said. "There been shitloads of boats out on the river this morning. It's kinda strange. I wonder if they're looking for the same fuckin' bird."

This made me nervous and I said so, then wondered aloud how I might get hold of a boat.

"Easy enough," he said. "Head over to the fuckin' marina and talk to my brother Robert. He's the fuckin' dockmaster there."

I thanked him and left. This was the real South, thick with humidity and accents, which made me a little uncomfortable. But if I was out of place here, the BBC would be more so. I imagined the crew making its way through downtown Hertford: "Pardon me, old chap, but have you seen a fish hawk this morning?" Of course, money transcended language, and for all I knew the BBC might have been out on the river right then and there, filming Tasha as I drove by.

I wasn't really about to rent a boat. For one thing, I couldn't afford it, and I would never even have considered the possibility if I hadn't seen the osprey nest as I drove over the bridge into Hertford. It came up right before the billboard that proclaimed the town to be "The Home of Jim 'Catfish' Hunter." Even a quick glance told me the nest was a beauty, so as soon as I crossed the bridge I pulled a U-ey and parked on the nest side of the road. A truck barreled by and the Pontiac vibrated in the rush, but I got out anyway and sneaked onto the bridge for a better look. Most of the nests I'd seen on my trip so far had been on platforms, but this was the real deal: a perfect cup of intertwined branches that seemed to grow out of the top of a gnarled eastern red cedar. Another truck roared by and nearly blew me off the bridge, but I stood there for a while, admiring the nest the way you would a great painting.

Back in the car, I drove for less than twenty seconds before seeing a huge bird circling above. As I pulled over at a Citgo station, I felt the old familiar hunter's buzz overtaking me. Yep, it was an osprey, dead overhead, a big, beautiful bird soaring in lazy circles right over the Citgo self-serve and the car wash. I knew it was unlikely, or maybe impossible, but I couldn't help but wonder: was it Tasha? Through my binoculars I watched it soar for a while, its head dark like that of the bird I'd seen on the Chesapeake, but I couldn't make out from below whether it wore a backpack with jutting wires. When it flew off I got in my car, but instead of heading back to the highway, I found myself following the directions that Dave Rue had given me to the fuckin' marina.

It turned out the marina was inside a gated community

called Albemarle Plantation, so I had to stop and talk to the guard at the gate. But I just followed Dave's instructions and told the guard that I was there to rent a boat from Robert Rue, and he waved me in. It took a while to find the marina. It was 10:54 when I did, and I was supposed to return the car in Raleigh, a three-hour drive, by noon. I figured I was screwed either way, and walked out onto the dock.

There were lots of boats but few people. A small cottage stood on stilts, with a sign that read DOCKMASTER'S OFFICE, but I didn't find Robert until I got out to the far end of the dock, where he was steam-washing the dock surface with two other guys. Robert had slightly less of a taste for profanity than his brother and had made a few more trips to the dentist. He put the hose down and nodded when I called out his name over the din of the steam hose. At first he said flatly that he didn't rent boats, in a tone that sounded more like "Get the hell out of here." But then I described what I was up to, and I could see him warming up a little. Finally I hit on just the right phrase to sell him on the idea. "It's kind of like that show *The Amazing Race*," I said. "But with birds."

He nodded and smiled. I told him the British might already be out on the water. "Those fuckers might be on my bird already," I said for emphasis.

He spat into the water, and his previously scowling lips lifted in a slight smile. I knew I had him. He couldn't let a bunch of limeys beat an American. And of course it didn't hurt that I had inferred that the whole thing would be on TV.

"You see that yellow boat back by the office?" he said.

I nodded.

"That's John's boat. He'll find your bird if it's here. His number's right on the side of the boat. He'll help you beat them fuckers."

I thanked him and walked back to the yellow boat to scribble down the phone number. But my cell phone was out of juice. I looked back at Robert—he was a couple of hundred yards away, down at the end of the dock, and had turned the hose back on. After another quick glance, I decided to risk climbing up the steep steps into his office. From there I used his phone to dial the number.

A man with a Long Island accent, not a southern drawl, answered the phone. John had retired to the South a dozen or so years back and now made his living on the Albemarle Sound with his boat. I told him my story, reusing the line about *The Amazing Race.*

"So you want to rent a boat?" he said.

"Kinda rent," I said.

"How much kinda?"

I asked the going rate, which was a hundred dollars an hour, and I told him I could afford about half that. Thirty-five minutes later he met me at the dock. In the meantime I'd gathered up my scope and backpack and bought a six-pack of Corona at the Plantation provisions store. John was a scraggly-toothed, white-haired man with a ruddy face and an open smile. He didn't waste much time with pleasantries, and before I knew it I was untying the lines and jumping onto the bow of his boat.

A loud cricket hum filled the air as we puttered away from the dock. Spanish moss hung low, the trees and plants seeming to droop from the heat, and you knew you weren't in the North anymore. You could see how an osprey would want to stop here to hunt and rest, how the birds would be forgiven if they briefly mistook this for their ultimate migratory goal: the tropics. Cypress trees grew along the water's edge—perfect nesting territory. I counted thirteen turtles sunning on one half-submerged log.

Once we were well free of the dock, John pushed down the throttle. "Let's find you a bird," he yelled.

To get to the Perquimans River, where Tasha had spent the night, we had to head down the Yeopim River and out into Albemarle Sound. The anxiety I'd felt the night before vanished as we sped across the bay: I was back in the hunt. It was a pity we were tracking Tasha, not Jaws, since I now had my very own Quint (which I suppose made me Hooper). Although we weren't looking to harpoon any great whites, searching for the satellite bird gave our trip purpose, and John took to it immediately. I cracked a Corona while he spread the maps I'd printed out back at Jon's over the steering console. His only gripe was that I didn't have an exact GPS location, so we couldn't track it with his radar.

"We may not find her right away, but if the British are on these waters, we'll find them."

He was right; we could see for miles. I scanned the sky with my binoculars. Occasionally John stopped the boat and joined me, both of us glassing the horizon.

"I like this," he said. "It's kind of like fishing the sky."

We passed a peninsula called Harvey's Neck, a huge spread of land that John said belonged to the CIA. "It's a CIA training camp. Don't use your binoculars when we go past. And damn well don't use your telescope. They'd be on us in a second."

I entertained the thought of poor Tasha, already one of the most spied-upon birds in history—already tracked by satellite, for god's sake—spending the night under surveillance by the CIA.

Over the next hour our excitement began to wear off. Sky fishing turned out to be almost as boring as the real thing sometimes is. We hadn't seen any birds, and John, perhaps feeling sheepish, suggested that we pull over at the dock in his backyard, which was nearby. He said there were bald eagles in the trees

near his house, and after docking we hiked into the swamp. We
didn't find the eagles, and when John warned me about chiggers,
I thought it best to get back to our primary quest. It took another
half-hour and another beer to putter up the west bank of the
Perquimans River, but though we saw osprey nests in the crooks
of trees and on buoys, and though we saw lots of shapes in the
trees that at first looked like ospreys, we didn't see any actual
birds. As we neared the bridge that I'd driven over earlier, I
scanned the beautiful nest in the eastern red cedar tree, but it remained empty.

By the time we headed back up the east bank we had already
been out on the water for two hours. My trick of using beer as an
antidote to the anxious end-of-the-trip feeling could last only as
long as the six-pack. Already I'd asked John twice to slow down
so I could urinate off the bow. As the day lengthened, our inter-
actions became decidedly less jolly, and I noticed that we were
starting to say things to each other that teammates say during a
losing effort.

"Well, it's been good just to be out here," I said.

"Yup, it's been fun to look, even if we don't see anything."

"A good day," I repeated.

But it wouldn't have been a good day, not really, if we had not
seen what we saw as we were getting ready to turn back. An osprey, of course, and not just any osprey. An immature female,
like Tasha, feeding on the branch of a cedar snag, occasionally
lifting her white head to stare out over the river. The fish she held
shone orange, like the goldfish on Long Island, though John
wasn't sure what kind it was. We drifted in close, but the bird's
back was to me and I couldn't see any sign of a transmitter or
wire. I climbed up on the roof of the boat and tried to center the
bird in the scope, but the boat was too unstable. John nudged the
throttle and we pushed even closer, until we were 30 feet from

the snag. The osprey took a break from its meal and looked up to let out its high-pitched warning *kews*. Now John was excited too. We didn't say anything, but we were both thinking the same thing: Could this be my bird? Had we found the proverbial needle in the haystack? Had my good luck just become *extraordinary* luck? Why not?

John cut the engine and drifted even closer. The bird took turns between ripping chunks of fish and warning us. As it leaned forward to rip the fish, I thought I saw a hump near its primary feathers. It could have been . . . But then, as we drifted very close, it became clear that what I first thought was a backpack was just the shadow and a knot on the tree. Finally I confirmed this bad news through the binoculars. The bird was an immature female, all right, and it was no doubt migrating, but it wasn't wearing a backpack.

"Damn," I said to John.

"Damn," he agreed.

But we had seen a bird up close and had buzzed with the pursuit of our quarry, and that was enough. We both felt better, and our earlier camaraderie returned. John even suggested we look farther east, in another bay, free of charge, but I told him I had to get back. Three hours had now passed, and I would be lucky to get to Raleigh by nightfall, when I would have to fork over an extra two hundred dollars I didn't have.

We sped back across the bay and were halfway home when a pontoon boat came racing toward us. John handed me a life vest. "Put this on," he said as he pulled on his own. "They may board us."

We slowed and watched as the coast guard approached: a small boat filled with large men. They might just as easily have been Hollywood actors playing coast guard roles, and they all could have stood in for various members of the Village People. They wore police-style vests with no sleeves, revealing large bi-

ceps, and sported holsters with guns on their hips. It was scary
to think of these young men having so much power. We passed
ten uneasy minutes as John made small talk with them and they
eyed his boat. They knew him pretty well, but he'd told me as
they approached that that hadn't stopped them from boarding
him twice in the past six months. They were particularly curious
about what I was doing.

"He's looking for ospreys out here," John said. "Seen any?"

I explained myself further, using the *Amazing Race* line one
more time. Reality TV apparently had great cachet, even with
the authorities, and they started nodding their heads as if it all
suddenly made great sense. Why not have a reality show about
an obscure bird? They pushed off and bombed away in search of
their next victim.

As we passed Harvey's Neck, I saw another osprey from a
good distance away. It was making the crossing over Albemarle
Sound toward River Neck and the Alligator River. A helicopter buzzed through the sky after the bird, and I wondered who
it belonged to. The CIA? The coast guard? The BBC? John
suggested that it could just be a regular helicopter, without any
mysterious connotations, and I nodded. Yes, that made sense.
No need for conspiracy theories. I watched the lone osprey fly
across the bay with long rowing strokes as we headed back to
the opposite shore. I learned later that this was the same crossing that Tasha had made earlier that afternoon, while John and
I searched for her. Always an impulsive flier, she had gotten an
early jump and flown south to her next stop, in Pamlico Sound.

Already mildly hung over, nerves jangling, covered with salt and
sweat, unshaven and with hair uncombed, I was a wreck by the
time I reached the rental car office. The moment of my approach
couldn't have been a happy one for the pert young woman behind
the desk. As well as taking a four-hour detour, I'd managed to

get off at the wrong exit and become lost in downtown Raleigh. I was saved only by the kindness of strangers. At a red light, I pulled up to another car and asked a woman for directions to the airport. She gave me the directions but then saw something desperate in my eye and took pity and simply said, "Follow me." Her young daughter was in the car with her and she was clearly going miles out of her way, but she drove me right up to the airport exit before beeping and pointing. I wanted to jump out of the car and give her a kiss of thanks, but knowing that this might be taken the wrong way, I settled for waving goodbye.

The rental car girl felt no such pity. At least at first. Her nametag said "Cindy," and Cindy clicked ferociously on her keyboard for twenty minutes or so before handing me my bill. It was even worse than I'd imagined. Somehow I'd managed to exceed the point in time when I was merely paying an extra thirty dollars an hour and now I was being charged for a full extra day, which, according to arbitrary rental car logic, cost more than the entire rest of my seven-day trip. It was like returning a video or DVD late, but on an enormous scale: the amount I owed was staggering. Usually I would have spoken to the young woman in a deep voice, trying to assert my professorial authority. But after the intensity of the week, I just wanted to dissolve into a puddle. I began to babble about not being able to pay. Cindy just stared at me, her spunky smile fading when I refused to respond or even move. She grew uncomfortable; she wasn't trained for this. What did she think of this man, who had to be her father's age, who appeared ready to break into tears?

"I can't pay this bill," I said again.

Cindy just looked at me, no doubt waiting for me just to do the normal thing and give in and fork over my credit card. I stared back and said nothing.

"I'll see what I can do," she said finally. Once more she

clicked away on her keyboard, entering god knows what facts and figures. After another long wait, a new version of bill came chattering out of the printer. She tore it off and handed it to me. It was still outrageous but not quite as devastating, only a couple of hundred more than I'd agreed to pay. Now I did give in and hand over my card.

But my nightmare wasn't over. I've found that the final legs of trips are the hardest, and in this case it would cause me more raw stress to get from Raleigh back home than it had taken to get from Cape Cod to Carolina. Apparently I'd used up all my luck earlier in the trip. No buses or trains ran to the coast, and when I'd called Nina earlier, she'd said that she couldn't meet me as planned because Hadley was sick. Finally my sister's husband said he would pick me up at the curb of the rental place, where I stood with all my belongings, including my sleeping bag and telescope and scattered bird books and Dennis Puleston's osprey painting. The first pulsing rains of Hurricane Ivan began as I waited for him, and that night at my sister's the weather turned severe. Since there was no other way to get home, my sister took me to a cheap local rental car place in the morning, but that company wouldn't accept my debit card. There was no alternative. I had to get home to see Nina and Hadley. And so it was back to the airport and the same rental company as the day before.

Cindy wasn't there, but an equally pert young woman told me that it would cost me a hundred dollars to make the two-hour drive and drop off the car near my house. Without complaint I forked over my card. I unpacked my belongings from the back of my sister's car and piled them into the rental. Then I hugged my sister goodbye and hauled my sorry ass home.

Blinding rain slowed the trip. It was the sort of rain where you really are taking a grave risk by driving at all. When I finally got home, I kissed my wife and daughter and collapsed into a long, happy nap. Ulysses had ceased wandering the known world and had slain the suitors (or at least argued with the rental car people) and was now back on his home island in the arms of his family.

I imagined I would spend the better part of the weekend sleeping, but I imagined wrong. When I awoke, I immediately noticed something strange: strong winds slammed against our windows and buffeted our walls, just like on the night I had left, only stronger. Ivan, the third hurricane in three weeks, was storming up the coast, and by night the local authorities had issued a tornado watch. The pier near our house was the one where the Weather Channel people always filmed when hurricanes threatened the Atlantic coast, but even for us this was an extreme week. Rain lashed and lightning burned across the sky; the wind blew in bursts that exceeded those of the hurricane that had hit us earlier in the year.

I could only imagine how the birds were faring. It turned out that Tasha was also spending the night on a barrier island, north of me on the Pamlico Sound, a terribly exposed location that would have left her in the midst of the wind no matter how she tried to hunker down. The next day, when her radio was no longer functioning, Rob feared the worst. What had it been like for Tasha and the other juvenile birds to be hit with winds so strong that to try to fly meant being blown about like a scrap of paper? The birds had nothing to compare it to and might have been forgiven if they had begun to wonder about the evolutionary logic of migrating during hurricane season. Of course they had no way of knowing that they had picked an extraordinary year to be born in, at least in terms of wind. Having watched ospreys out on the marshes on Cape Cod during nor'easters, I tried to imagine how Tasha would respond to the storm. Though ospreys look large, their hollow bones give them little ballast, and most actually weigh less than four pounds. Tasha would try to flatten herself in a futile effort to avoid the winds, feathers blowing back over her, eyes squinting. This was a better fate than that of those birds caught in the air or, worst of all, over the sea. If that's how the dice rolled, it was all over.

Even inside our house, my wife and I crouched together around our daughter and debated whether to head down to the ground-level garage (the island houses have no cellars). Of the birds, only Elsie continued to move during the storm, probably because Ivan was to her north and west. She gradually worked her way down from Charleston through South Carolina and Georgia, tiptoeing, as it were, along the edge of the storm.

The winds died the next day, and I spent the rest of the weekend making up time with my family. Hadley seemed to have inherited some dominant bird-chasing gene and charged at gulls on the beach, squealing in delight when they scattered and flew off in front of her. Offshore, the pelicans followed their bills like divining rods and hit the water with great awkward splashes, and the gannets, another spectacular diving bird, had come south from Canada for their winter visit.

On Sunday the winds completely reversed themselves from two days before, blowing hard, but not violently hard, from the north—the kind of winds that would nicely fill a sail, or a pair of wings. *These,* I thought, *are osprey winds.* Sure enough, the birds took advantage of, or, in Rob's phrase, "hitched rides on," the northerly winds. Having fought against the wind for so long, they must have instinctively known that this was their big chance, and first Tasha—her radio working again—and then a suddenly resurrected Jaws, whose signal had miraculously reappeared, flew out over the Atlantic, using the land near Bald Head Island, just to my south, as a kind of launch pad for their long flight to Florida, skipping South Carolina and Georgia entirely.

It must have been with something like hope—or, to use the biological equivalent, so as not to appear to be anthropomorphizing, some sensation of physical lift—that Tasha greeted those
northerly winds. The day before she would have crept cautiously
from her hiding place in the woods along the marsh, heading out
to fish after a sleepless night. But now, after gathering herself for
a day, she would have felt the tailwinds rustling her primary
feathers and playing through her scapulars. In that moment she
would also have understood that the winds had shifted completely around and that although they were strong, they were no
longer fierce. Even for a first-year bird with very little experience, something had to tell her that this was very good news.

We are warned not to impose emotions on the birds we
watch, but the story of those few days tells us something of the
very physical nature of both our language and our lives. What
Tasha had been suffering from, at least in a geographical sense,
was depression. The storm had laid her low and kept her there,
the winds pressing her down into the spartina grass. It wasn't just
that she wasn't able to migrate; the winds also made hunting, and
therefore eating, impossible. She was famished and exhausted.
But with Sunday's winds her slump was over, and she quite literally felt uplifted. We are not allowed to say that her response
was an exuberant or joyous one, but we can say that what she did
next was an almost perfect physical manifestation of what humans think of when we think of exuberance and joy. She sprang
into action.

The first order of business that morning was catching a fish
in the now calmer waters, eating it, and transubstantiating its
energy into her own. Then, with the tailwinds lifting her, she
sailed out over the barrier islands and sea oats, above the hordes

of gulls and awkwardly diving pelicans, pointing her black bill south. She rode a gust of wind up to an altitude where she could simply spread her wings and let the wind fill them like sails. After days of battling the wind, it now was her ally, and she sailed southward at speeds well over 40 miles per hour. In one morning she took down more miles than she had in the past week.

At Bald Head Island she probably dived into the shallows for a midday meal. Below were egrets and herons, and deer trails cut across the lime-green marshgrass like a knife blade through bread—a dull knife blade, though, not cutting but indenting. Tasha couldn't have "known" in any sense that this island was the easternmost point of land until Fort Lauderdale, in southern Florida. But while she didn't have MapQuest or a GPS system, on some level she must have understood that it was imperative to fuel up and ready herself for what was becoming her signature move: a long over-water passage. She started that afternoon and flew through the night, sailing on winds coming down from Canada. Bald Head was a jumping-off point, a launching pad for many birds that didn't feel like detouring inland and instead headed straight across what Rob Bierregaard called "the Bay of Georgia." She must have felt the encoded pleasure that all animals, including *Homo sapiens,* feel in taking down miles, in pushing it farther and farther. The sheer momentum of the thing would have built inside her.

I wonder at what point that momentum began to wane and exhaustion set in. Were the last hours before landfall miserable, ragged ones? Did the fact that this was her first trip—that she had no idea when land would finally appear—make it even more miserable? Or is that pushing the human comparison too far? Perhaps, but wouldn't there have been a sense of relief, the bird equivalent of a sigh, when she finally saw land? Or was it a more

stoic response, an instinctive need to get to shallow water and
fish and replenish the lost energy—just another box to check off
on the survival to-do list?

The next morning Tasha found her way to Lake Okeechobee, in south-central Florida, where gangs of other ospreys
let her know she was on the right migratory track. Only hours
after she arrived, another young osprey appeared on the shores of
the lake, having made a similarly impressive journey. Following
Tasha on the heels of the high-pressure system and the perfect
warm winds blowing down from New England, Jaws left a day
later, barely beating the next hurricane, Jeanne, which was bar-
reling toward the Florida coast. His over-water journey, as he
soared along on the northerlies, was over 600 miles. By the
twenty-second of September, both Jaws and Tasha were on the
shores of Lake Okeechobee, ending up 10 miles from each other
after making journeys of close to 1000 miles in four days. Jaws
too must have arrived tired and famished from the trip, though
perhaps even better suited to fishing in the lake, given all his
practice back on the Connecticut lakes.

The warm weather, the shallow waters, the abundant fish—
all of it must have tempted the birds to stay. In fact, Florida is
home to one of the few residential osprey populations in the
United States, birds that have decided, over the eons, to say *To
hell with all this migration business.* But neither Tasha nor Jaws
was built that way, and after a day or two something inside them,
some internal prod, was telling them that they weren't quite
done. It was still the season of movement, and soon enough they
would be on the move again, this time heading south to Cuba.

Since I'd returned home, Rob Bierregaard had become increasingly forthcoming, both on the phone and in e-mail, to the point
where I now felt I had a mole inside the BBC camp. The narra-

tive he told me of their journey so far was one of ineptitude and
near misses. For instance, my fears of a BBC helicopter trailing
Tasha across the Albemarle Sound while I watched helplessly
from John's boat had been unfounded. On the day that I had
been out drinking beer and chasing Tasha, the TV crew had still
been up near Cape Charles on the Chesapeake, the same spot
where I'd taken my sunset swim the night before. At that point
Jaws, his transmitter malfunctioning, was to their northwest,
near Washington, and Tasha and I were down on the Albemarle,
where we both spent the night. The BBC decided to chase Tasha
and caught up with her by midnight of the next day, roosting in
a tree near Lake Mattamuskeet. They still hadn't managed to
film any of the satellite birds. But although they had the technology to film at night, they decided, according to Rob, that
they were "too knackered" to film and waited for the morning. Of course, when they returned soon after dawn the next day,
Tasha had taken off.

But over the next stage of migration the BBC crew would
have some distinct advantages over me. For one thing, their government didn't have a decades-old embargo on Cuba and had
not just tightened restrictions on travel to the island. For another, it was now the BBC's turn to be showered with good luck.
On September 23, showing no fear of night or long water crossings, Tasha pushed off from Florida in the afternoon and reached
Cuba around nightfall, followed soon after by Jaws. Over the
phone Rob explained that Tasha had now flown 1693 miles from
her nest, averaging about 123 miles per day. He also explained
that the BBC had made reservations months in advance, and
now, by good luck, they had landed in Cuba on the very same day
as Tasha. On his website Rob posted a note saying that the two
female BBC producers must have been "reporting back to a
coven in Bristol."

The next day I learned that their luck, if anything, was getting better. The day after arriving in Cuba, Tasha flew down the island's green spine, putting in 190 miles before spending the afternoon fishing in a shallow reservoir. It was perfect osprey habitat, not only shallow water but filled with dead snags for perching, just southwest of the town of Camagüey. By sheer coincidence, the BBC arrived in Camagüey only a few hours before Tasha. There they had only to lie in wait for the bird, cameras at the ready.

This was more than a little frustrating for me, trapped as I was on the sidelines. I still had no clue how I was going to get to Cuba, and the migratory season was nearing its end. The fact that I could in no way afford the trip was only a small part of the problem. As the 2004 election approached, the United States was making travel to Cuba next to impossible. For years Cuban travel had been a casual affair in which you headed down through a third country and the Cuban government, wanting the tourism, held off on stamping your passport so you could come dancing back into the States with an easy lie at customs. But those days were over, at least until after the election. The accepted wisdom was that this was Bush's way of repaying the older Cuban population in Florida, who hated Castro and backed the embargo, for their support in the 2000 election, as well as shoring up support for the coming election. Whatever the reason, no matter how I tried, I couldn't dredge up the information, let alone the tickets, I needed. Meanwhile, communication with Freddy Santana had been difficult, thanks in part to the series of hurricanes. Our last e-mail had been particularly stinging: in it he told me he would be leading the BBC crew up onto La Gran Piedra. *Y tu, Freddy?*

At that point I knew I'd all but blown my chance of seeing any of the telemetry birds in Cuba, even if I got there. The two youngsters were already streaming through, and Elsie had

launched herself on a trip to eastern Haiti, a crossing known as
the Windward Passage. My last chance was Bluebeard, who,
loyal as ever, was still sticking it out with his remedial kid back
on the Vineyard. Though I had little chance of timing my trip to
coincide with his, I did make one decision as I sat stranded in
North Carolina. I liked Rob Bierregaard, I really did, and he had
become increasingly generous. But who had decided that his
putting backpacks on them meant that he got to name all the
birds? He liked to make jokes on his website, like the thing about
the coven, and these tended to be jokes with a capital *J*. He was
what once would have been called a card, and this was reflected
in the birds' names, from Bunga to Elsie to Jaws. They were decent names, but I wanted my own. Or at least *one* of my own.
Since Bluebeard was the single osprey I might actually have a
chance of encountering if I ever made it to Cuba, I decided that
he would be the one. So in my journal I began referring to Bluebeard by a new name: Fidel.

Like Tasha in the windstorm, I was suffering through some days
of depression. I no longer felt the excitement of travel, the pleasure of having all my resources and energies focused on one thing,
and I no longer felt the surety that I would see things wherever
I looked. Apparently I'd used up all my osprey mojo back on the
road through Westport, Long Island, Hawk Mountain, and
Cape May.

But it turned out my luck cup was just being refilled. Late the
next morning, the first good omen came. Hadley and I were
walking on the beach, she up on my shoulders, when we saw an
osprey dive. I'd seen plenty of ospreys that fall, of course, and
even a few since I'd been back home, but it had been awhile since
I'd seen this. Dives are what osprey watchers live for, and this one
was something, a brilliant ballet move. Backlit by the sun, its
feathers ruffled and wet from an earlier dive, the bird looked

enormous. It hovered in front of us, readying, the wings beating fast, 50 feet above the surf. Then the plunge down: wings pulled in and held out slightly as the bird adjusted, making the line connecting sky and sea a squiggly one, gaining speed and then kicking its legs back right before striking the water, popping a wheelie, hitting hard, splashing the surface. It came up empty once, twice, shaking itself like a dog. But on the third try it rose clutching a fish in its talons, spraying down a silver-lit waterfall.

It was a heartening sign. My faith was further bolstered at our mailbox that afternoon. There was an envelope with a return address of Nags Head, North Carolina, and when I ripped it open I found a check for three thousand dollars. The only other thing inside was a piece of lined paper with a single word on it, all in capitals: *SOAR!*

I cashed Jon's check at my bank and on the way back home stopped by the school where I teach. For an hour I worked on making reservations for the Cuba trip, a trip I could now at least afford. I typed in queries about how to get there and worked to make sense of the government regulations. By coincidence, a former student of mine was an editor at an adventure travel magazine and had just written an article on travel to Cuba. The article ended with a quote from a former organizer of educational tours, who had said, "Under no circumstances would I recommend going illegally to Cuba now." But when I phoned my former student, he said that I might be able to fight the fines that would be imposed, since I was both a writer and an educator, and he suggested a few websites where I might be able to find out how to get there.

The websites proved fruitless, however, and after banging on the keyboard a couple of times I was ready to give up. No matter how I tried, I couldn't dredge up the information I needed.

In the end it was Google—what else?—that saved me. Exasperated, I typed in something like "How the hell do I get to

Cuba? Foreign travel agents." Two seconds later my electronic genie appeared. The very first entry was the name of a French Canadian firm that was geared toward doing exactly what I needed done. Within five minutes I was on the phone with Jean, a gracious and polite man with a thick French accent, who would be happy to do everything I needed if I was willing to part with a large chunk of Jon's check. "Yes, David," he said. "We can do that all quite easily. I'll work on it this afternoon and get you your itinerary tomorrow."

It was simple, really. U.S. citizens weren't allowed by our own government to spend money in Cuba, and so we paid the Canadians and they paid the Cubans. Of course, I still couldn't fly directly from the United States to Cuba, a flight, as Tasha had just proved, of only a couple of hours. It was still necessary to go through a third country, and so Jean went to work, determining which country that would be.

Things were suddenly falling into place, and the next day I was ready to make reservations for September 30, less than a week away. But before I let Jean run my credit card, there was still the problem of what I was going to do when I got to Cuba and how I was going to find my way. The most recent communication I had had with Freddy was an excited e-mail telling me that he had taken the BBC up to the top of La Gran Piedra and that they had seen over a hundred birds. He'd also expressed misgivings about ferrying me around while the BBC was still there, since he'd made a prior commitment to them. So the next morning I got up early and called him. I'd tried to get through several times since Hawk Mountain but had never reached him. (I'd assumed this was related to the hurricanes, but it was in fact a question of national blackouts.) But this time the phone rang and a woman's voice answered. It was his wife, Ileana, and she handed the phone to Freddy.

From the second I heard his voice I felt better.

"Yes, of course, David, please come. We'll take care of you. We'll show you the birds." His voice was warm and lilting. "Take care," he said as we hung up. "I will be here."

Take care! He would be there!

And now, armed with Freddy's words and Jon's check and Jean's itinerary, not to mention renewed hope, I would be there too. Six days later, on September 30—thirteen days after my Cape Cod–to–Carolina stint ended—I got up at dawn and flew from Wilmington to Charlotte and then from Charlotte to Cancun, Mexico, where I had a layover of several hours. I didn't feel like loitering in the airport, in good part because of something my former student had written in his article on Cuban travel: "Treasury Department officials say that specially trained agents will now be on location even in previously less-watched jumping-off points like Cancun." I was nervous and certainly not in the mood for an encounter with a specially trained agent. And so I went outside and paid for a bus ticket and took the fifty-minute ride to the beach. It was my first time in the Caribbean, and though the Playa de Carmen was touristy, the water was that green-blue I'd seen in pictures and the sand fine-grained, so I took my shoes off, plopped my backpack next to me, and ordered a beer and some salsa. I soaked up the sun and watched the sky but didn't see much other than wobbly turkey vultures. By the second beer I decided the water looked too good, and so hid my wallet under my clothes and dove in wearing my boxer shorts. I returned to the Cancun airport wet, sand-stained, and slightly less nervous, and tried not to look American.

By seven that night I was on the plane to Havana.

CHAPTER SEVEN

FREDDY'S FINEST HOUR

My first sight of Havana, from the air, was a thin strand of glittering jewels near the water. The surprise wasn't the light but how little light shone out from such a large city. Later I learned of the enforced blackouts that traveled the island like manmade weather patterns. As we descended, I remembered a strange fact that I had uncovered in my reading: Cuba itself had migrated. As odd as it sounded, my geology books claimed it was true: the island had been born in the Pacific and had gradually migrated east to its home off the tip of Florida (which itself had moved, of course). This fact seemed to underscore my sense of a migrating world: all was moving; all was change; nothing could be pinned down.

The airport was a sea of drab colors and green military uniforms. After a long wait, I headed into a booth for customs, where, as Jean had promised me, my passport was not stamped. It was too late for a flight to Santiago, so I'd be spending the night in Havana. My cab rides both to and back from the hotel occurred in the dark, but my impression of Havana was not a romantic one. The air smelled of exhaust, and the smell and the feel of the place reminded me of a trip I took to East Germany right after the Berlin Wall fell. Pictures of Fidel and Che were pasted everywhere, and we kept passing buildings that looked like inner-city projects. My cabdriver, Marcos, spoke only Spanish, and soon, for the first of many times, I was silently thanking

Señor Shepherd, my jolly high school Spanish teacher, who had danced and played guitar and sung "Guanatanamera" and done everything else he could to teach me the few Spanish words I knew, despite my almost complete lack of interest. The only English I now heard came from the car's tape player, which blasted the lyrics "Every time you go away, you take a piece of me with you." The car, the make of which I couldn't recognize, wasn't much more than a bulked-up go-cart, and Marcos certainly drove it that way, darting around buses and beeping when he passed a slow-moving motorcycle with a sidecar.

My wife had been jealous that I was going to Havana. She'd always had a thing for it, she said, with its kind of dilapidated former glory and ghosts of Hemingway and martyrs and revolution. But to me both the city and the hotel looked like a rundown junior high school where the student body president had plastered posters of himself everywhere. I was relieved when Marcos picked me up, as we had arranged, the next morning at 5:30. And happy, after two espresso shots and a burger bun smeared with butter, to get on the plane to Santiago. The plane itself, an older model from Aerocaribe, didn't seem to gain enough speed as we rumbled down the runway, but we made it into the air. There was murmuring and then a mild panic when what looked like smoke began pouring into the cabin, but it was only condensation from the ancient air-conditioning system.

Despite the broken-down checkered seats, like those in a low-rent nursing home, I had an enjoyable trip. We flew over orange tin roofs and green farmland and the blue fires used to clear brush, and gradually the land began to rise. Mountains, not craggy and jagged like the Rockies but still wooded, rose as the cloud cover became thick. I tried to imagine ospreys flying this route along the country's spine, navigating through the bulky white landscape of clouds that rose and fell like hills. These clouds were the opposite of wispy, almost corporeal, and looked as if you could climb their sides with an ice ax.

Keith Bildstein had mentioned that clouds like this formed almost every day in the mountains. "I watched ospreys being swept up into the clouds," he'd said. "And then they would fall below, disappearing and reappearing again. When they moved up into those clouds, and I'm talking about groups of ospreys— and this was something I would not have believed had I not heard it myself—they actually called to one another in the same kind of way and for the same purpose that nocturnally migrating birds call to one another: to remain in contact. Since they're no longer in visual contact, they're remaining in auditory contact until they get out of the cloud. That suggests that they're working to be together. Calling out to each other to stay in touch. Their massing is not just a passive aggregation; it's actually something that is being driven by the birds themselves."

This newly observed behavior directly contradicted the stereotype of the ospreys as migratory soloists. Keith had suggested that one of the reasons for their loner image is that ospreys make up such a small percentage—no more than 2 percent—of the overall flight at North American watch sites. But this is partly explained by their relatively small North American population—"probably between 100,000 and 200,000"—compared to, say, 2 million broadwings. What Keith and Mark Martell had discovered in Cuba was something quite different. Suddenly they were watching flights of raptors that were almost pure osprey, upwards of 95 percent. One reason for this was that the water crossing and the flyways coming together caused a bottleneck in Cuba. But it was more than that. Ospreys, despite their reputation, were clearly making an effort to concentrate themselves, to manufacture flocks.

"They were doing this for the very same reason that other

hawks do," Keith had said. "Partly to identify the updrafts and thermals. But partly for safety. Here you are in Cuba, at the end of the land line, and now they're going to make a three-hundred-mile journey across the Caribbean. These are storm-infested waters, and for juveniles, traveling in the company of potentially experienced birds makes a lot of sense."

Santiago proved a revelation after the drabness of Havana. My cabdriver was a tall black man named Edgar, and though he didn't speak a word of English, I managed to get across the purpose of my trip through a mime show supplemented by the words *pájaro* (bird) and *pesca* (fishing). We drove into a green world split by a line of mountains directly ahead, to our north. But it was the road itself, not the farmlands and hills around it, that let me know I had entered a different world: we wove around other exhaust-spewing cars that looked held together with rubber bands and then around carts pulled by donkeys and men on bicycles and antique American cars from the fifties and Russian motorcycles with sidecars and then around a woman who seemed to be herding a single black pig. Turkey vultures hovered above the road.

My hotel, modest but fine, was patrolled by guards who frequently whispered into walkie-talkies. To my delight, I discovered that the hotel was on San Juan Hill, where Teddy Roosevelt had made his famous charge to glory. (I've always been a Roosevelt buff and so knew that despite the popular belief, he'd actually charged up Kettle Hill before joining others racing up San Juan Hill.) Because of the rotating blackouts, the hotel had no power when I arrived. As I unpacked in the dark, I felt two conflicting emotions slosh up against each other inside me. There was exhilaration at having made it to Santiago, after weeks of worry and two days of travel. But there was also a growing sense of "OK, I'm here. Now what the hell do I do?"

That question was answered almost immediately. Though the power was off, the phones were working, and I hadn't been there ten minutes when the front desk rang to tell me I had a visitor. In the lobby Freddy Santana transformed himself from a voice on the phone into a thirty-three-year-old man with a Spanish movie star's good looks and an easy smile. He was thin, had jet-black hair, and stood over six feet tall. After we said hello I invited him back to my room to talk, forgetting that it was without electricity. But when we tried to walk down toward the rooms, the guards stopped us and said that only guests were allowed in that area, not Cubans.

We passed an hour in the lobby talking ospreys, and as we did I became more and more certain that I'd made the right choice in coming. Freddy kept apologizing for his English, but he was much easier to understand in person than over the phone or e-mail, and we communicated with little problem. He explained that because I did not have an official work visa, he would not be able to use his work car to drive me up to La Gran Piedra to watch the birds, so I would have to take cabs to get there.

When he started talking about the watch site atop the rock, his words spilled out. From his wallet he pulled a picture and a crumpled piece of paper. Scribbled on the paper was a misquote from Shelley that an English tourist had given him: "I love all vast and solitary places where what we see is boundless/As we wish our souls could be."

"That is like Gran Piedra," he said, pointing at the paper. "It is my favorite place on earth."

Then he handed me the picture, which was better than the quote: it showed Freddy holding his binoculars in one hand and a dark-haired toddler in the other. "That was the day I saw six hundred and seven ospreys flying overhead. No one had ever recorded over three hundred in the Caribbean before. It was a very happy day for me and happy to have Fredito there. To have my record and my boy at once."

We talked for a while longer and I offered to buy him dinner, but he needed to get home. As we shook hands goodbye, he said he would be happy to accompany me to La Gran Piedra the next morning. But after he left, I couldn't wait. There was still plenty of daylight and, excited by Freddy's descriptions, I didn't want to put it off another day. After all, that was what I had come to see. There were a couple of cabs in front of the hotel, and I asked how much for a round trip to the mountains and back. It turned out it would cost me thirteen bucks to ascend to the top of the world.

There may be better places to watch birds, but there are none more spectacular. The ride was a harrowing series of twists and turns up a mountain road so steep that at times it seemed we were going to start rolling backward. The vistas seemed to alternate, so that in one direction I could have imagined I was in the arid mountains of Colorado, in the other the rainforest. Ferns and palms and red flowers burst from the sides of the road. Much of the land consisted of abandoned coffee plantations, and on the way up we almost hit a guy on horseback with bags of coffee clumped behind him. Then on the next turn we nearly hit another man, this one a shriveled old-timer who was hiking down, carrying a bundle of long-stalked gladiolas over his shoulder like a hobo's stick.

Leonardo, the driver, stopped several times to pick up locals who were hiking up the mountainside. One of them was a young girl, probably nine or ten, who, after we had driven for a while, yelled *"Abre aquí!"* when we came upon a tall truck by the side of the road. The truck held a dozen men in its bed, and more were piling on as it prepared to leave. As it began to rumble off, the

girl yelled *"Abre aquí!"* more desperately. Then *"Papá! Papá!"* as
she climbed out of the cab and ran after the truck. One of the
men in the truck bed called something to the driver, and the
truck slowed, and another of the men casually reached down a
long arm and scooped up the girl before the truck finally made
its way down the mountainside.

Once we were at the top, Leonardo agreed to wait while I
hiked up the big rock, saying I should take as much time as I
liked. La Gran Piedra was the name of both the rock and the village, which consisted of a few buildings along the streets as well
as the modest homes of local farmers and *artesanos* down winding paths that ran off the road. To get to the stairs and the path
that led up to the rock I had to slip through the bar of the town's
one hotel and pay the bartender a dollar, but once I started
climbing, the rainforest closed in, water dripping from plants
and bugs buzzing. Farther up the steps I passed a black pig rooting in the ferns right off the trail. The red mud was slippery and
puddles covered the steps, and my heart pounded from both the
climb and the excitement.

Four hundred and fifty-two steps later I reached the side of
La Gran Piedra itself, a huge hunk of volcanic rock—in fact the
third largest freestanding rock in the world. I emerged from a
kind of tunnel through the rainforest to find a ladder bolted into
its side. The ladder led straight up, and when I reached the top,
I felt dizzy and exhilarated. I'd stood on the top of plenty of
mountains in my life, but the rock had a kind of booster effect,
as if it were a small mountain on top of another mountain. I'd
thought that Freddy's Shelley quote was a little corny, but now I
saw why he kept it. The view *was* boundless.

La Gran Piedra jutted like a great ship out of the rainforest,
and the rock ship sat on a sea of mountains running from west
to east. Another range, or series of ranges, ran parallel to the

north. Off to my left, the south, shone the Caribbean, and straight ahead, to the west, less than 20 miles off below the clouds, was the town of Santiago. The area where I stood was like a small aircraft carrier, and the carrier's landing platform had roughly the surface area of a tennis court. The rock was exposed and treeless; tattered gray clouds blew fast below where I stood. A waist-high fence ran around the top of the rock, which was a couple of hundred feet long and 30 feet wide.

I walked to the west end of the rock and looked toward Santiago, which was capped by a halo of clouds. The town and the ocean spread out below as if on a map, but the main impression, the main sight, was the great mountain range itself, the Sierra Maestra, on which I was perched. Now that I saw the ridge, it wasn't hard to imagine the route that the ospreys would fly, from west above Santiago, to take advantage of the updrafts. Of course it was late in the day, so I didn't expect to see much. But I stayed up on the rock for an hour or more anyway, hoping to get my first sighting. Mostly I saw turkey vultures, and it wasn't until I'd almost given up that I had any luck.

I was walking toward the east end of the rock, where the view was of more mountains and, I soon learned, Guantánamo Bay, when I saw what I first assumed was another turkey vulture. But something about the way its wings hitched said osprey. True, it was so far away that there was a chance I might have been Kathleening it, especially given my desperate desire to see a bird. But if it wasn't the kind of thing I'd confidently report to Hones, I was still pretty sure it wasn't a vulture. It hovered over the second closest ridge, and the more I saw it, the surer I grew. While I can't pretend it was an ecstatic moment—I didn't have any telepathic communication or become a conduit for the Great Osprey—it was quietly satisfying. Here was a bird—not 607 birds, but a bird nonetheless—who had followed the same path that so many of his ancestors had followed. And here was I in the place where almost all the birds I had watched on Cape Cod had flown. No, euphoria wasn't required, at least not yet. It was enough to be standing on top of the mountain watching a single osprey as it traveled along its ancient highway.

The next morning I ascended La Gran Piedra again, this time with Freddy.

Before he arrived I drank two shots of espresso at the hotel bar. Little acrid pools of black in tiny white cups that Keith Bildstein had warned me had an effect "like rocket fuel." I've never been one for sugar in my coffee, but I needed two packs to get the stuff down. By the time Freddy came by the hotel at eight, I was tapping my pen on my notebook pages like a soloing heavy metal drummer.

Freddy wore a tan birding vest and a cap that read *Hawk Mountain* and had a pair of binoculars hanging from his neck. He had an old-fashioned matinee-idol chin that made him look like an actor playing a birder. "Are you ready to see some birds?" he asked. I nodded with caffeinated vigor.

During our cab ride up to La Gran Piedra I told him about my trip the day before, and he promised me we would see more than one osprey today. But when we reached the town, we found the big rock socked in with fog and morning clouds. It wasn't worth going up top until the fog burned off, so Freddy gave me a short tour of the village or, more accurately, the village's flora and fauna. A single street ran along a steep wooded hillside, and as we walked lizards skittered off in front of us. There were over three hundred species of ferns in the area, the most anywhere in the world, and the red-and-yellow bursts of flowers I'd noticed the day before grew from trees called flamboyas.

All that plant life was a magnet for birds, and in a short 100-

yard walk I saw as many new bird species as I'd ever seen in my life. Freddy described the birds we saw in the same calm, lilting voice that had been so reassuring over the phone. Whenever he saw a bird, he motioned for me to be quiet and then pointed it out, often whistling an exact imitation of the bird's song. In short order he pointed out a bee hummingbird (the world's smallest) and a striped tanager with an orange-yellow collar and a flashing black-and-white tail, and then, best of all, a Cuban trogon, with orange encircling its eyes like eyeliner and a blue-green back and long tail. As if on cue, it puffed out its bright orange belly. "It is the national bird," Freddy explained. "It is said to symbolize Cuban freedom. People say it will die if you catch it and put it in a cage. It's also the national bird because it has all the colors of the flag."

He also pointed out the national flower, the mariposa, which was used during the war of independence, when wives took the flowers to their imprisoned husbands, sliding secret messages inside the little tube that juts out from the petals. "There is a word in English for what we call this part of the flower," he said. "Because of how it looks..."

We played a little game of charades as he tried to remember the word before I hazarded a guess. "The clitoris?"

"Yes! Yes!" he yelled. "The clitoris!"

Our walk ended at a small tin-roofed cabin painted pale green, about 100 feet off the road below the meteorological station. Guava trees grew around the cabin, as did some red Dr. Seuss plant I couldn't identify, and as we approached a red-legged thrush flashed in front of the door. Freddy explained that this was where he had stayed with his family during the month that culminated with his big day, when he saw the 607 ospreys. The cabin was owned by the natural history museum that he worked for in Santiago, and his family had been allowed to stay there for a month while Freddy studied migration. It was the only vacation he and Ileana had taken together in years, and they had invited Freddy's brother and sister to take turns visiting during the month. I mentioned that the place really didn't look like it could hold more than one family.

"Yes, it was crowded," he conceded. "But it was wonderful to be up here out of the city. To wake up to the smell of the pine trees. But I'm afraid that for my wife, for Ileana, it wasn't much of a vacation. There were too many migrating ospreys, so each day I was pulled up to the rock."

On the way back up the road Freddy looked at the mountaintop and decided that the weather had broken enough for us to give it a try. I felt anxiety building—after I had traveled all this way, would the weather be so bad that I couldn't see any birds?— but realized it might just be the caffeine that was making me worry. Despite this realization, I stopped in at the hotel bar and had one more shot of rocket fuel before ascending the 452 stairs. Even with that jolt of energy I could barely keep up with Freddy, who took the steps three at a time, practically skipping up the mountainside like a goat. He was a couple of inches taller than me, ten years younger, and thirty pounds lighter, and when I stopped to catch my breath he described guiding the BBC crew. He'd kept talking to them as he guided them up the steps, lecturing on osprey migration, and then he had looked back to find they were no longer behind him.

We climbed up into the clouds. The image of a ship struck me again, though today the sea the ship rode was colored both the green of ponderosa pines and ferns and the gray-white of the clouds. Despite the poor weather, we weren't alone up on the rock. The local *artesanos* were already unpacking their sculptures and carvings and beads, and Freddy said that was a good sign. "It means the clouds will clear. They know the weather better than anyone. They are up here three hundred and sixty-five days a year."

Freddy introduced me to the *artesanos,* three men and a pretty woman in her early twenties named Daimaris. They were all brown of varying shades, just like almost everyone else I'd met around Santiago except for Freddy. Octavio Paz wrote famously of Latin Americans having *dos abuelos,* two grandfathers, one Spanish and one African, but near Santiago the African predominated. Freddy explained that many of the local people's ancestors had come over from Haiti in the eighteenth century or were descended from Africans brought directly to work on the sugarcane and coffee plantations.

For the past year Freddy had been working closely with the *artesanos,* training them as birdwatchers so he could rely on them during the osprey counts. He hoped to outfit them with binoculars and birding books someday. During his big day they had helped point out different groups of ospreys as the birds swooped over too fast for Freddy to count by himself.

We stood on the rock as shreds of cloud and fog flew by. Even when the clouds began to open up, Freddy said that the winds weren't great for migration. He spread his arms out. "The main thing to remember about migrating ospreys is that they do not like flapping. Today requires a lot of flapping," he explained.

He cut a fairly dashing figure up there on the rock, but he was not without a certain scientific geekiness. He took measurements on his handheld barometer and announced that it was 18 degrees Celsius and that the wind was averaging 24 kilometers per hour, with gusts of 37. The humidity, he added, was 100 percent. "This means we have truly become a cloud," he said.

Meanwhile my stomach began to roil from the espresso. If the rock was a ship, then I felt seasick. But I perked up when

Freddy picked out the day's first two migrating birds, small but distinguishably ospreys, flying far off near the coast, where the wind wasn't as bad. At least I now knew I wouldn't be shut out and could say that I had officially seen a bird in Cuba. Then, while we were focused on the coast, one of the *artesanos*, David, saw an osprey to the north. This bird was flapping hard into the wind, obviously not having the best day of migrating.

"On their good days they fly like a mirror of the ridge itself," Freddy said. With his flattened hand, he demonstrated how the birds would rise up and glide down, just the way the silhouette of the Sierra Maestra lifted and fell.

The *artesanos* spoke no English, and Freddy told them that I had come to Cuba to see ospreys. I noticed that when David had seen the bird he had yelled out *"Águila!"* which was short for *águila pescadora,* "eagle fisherman." Freddy explained that in the past the *artesanos* and most locals had called ospreys *guinchos,* which was a much less impressive term. But part of Freddy's attempt to spread the osprey gospel had been to insist that everyone refer to the birds by their longer and nobler name. "They are beautiful birds, and they deserve a beautiful name," he said. "And everyone wants to see an eagle."

It was good to see the birds, but my stomach was now gurgling like a witch's caldron. I knew that puking over the side of the rock wouldn't make a great impression, but at one point I actually had to give in and lie down. The heat of the rock felt comforting, and I curled myself up into a ball as the *artesanos* laughed.

"Estoy muy enfermo," I said.

I would have toughed it out if there were more birds to see, but Freddy insisted it was no use with the winds like this. We retreated a little after one o'clock. Not a great day, or a great start. But at least I'd seen a couple of birds.

I slept away the afternoon. As we'd hiked down the mountain-side earlier, Freddy had stopped at a spot below the clouds to point out a view of the heavily wooded mountains.

"The hills to the southwest have an important history for us," he said. "It was after climbing La Gran Piedra that Castro was first captured. And it was in the Sierra Maestra that he hid when he returned from Mexico to fight. These mountains were the heart of the revolution."

He told me a story that is as much a part of Cuba's national myth as Washington cutting down the cherry tree is in the United States. How Castro, after most of his forces had been slaughtered, looked around to see that he had only a small band of twelve survivors, a group that included his brother Raul and Che Guevara, with just seven rifles between them. Fidel, according to myth more than a little self-created, had then smiled and said, "Good. Now we have won the war."

Over the next few days I noticed that when Freddy talked about Castro, he did so with admiration, and with none of the ingrained cynicism with which most U.S. citizens talk about our leaders, even leaders we support. At one point he mentioned how much better life was for most people "after the triumph of the revolution." Since he was so sophisticated on other subjects, I tried not to dismiss this with my reflexive political skepticism, but it was hard not to. As a relative naïf in Cuban politics, I had no idea whether that admiration was real, or how deep it ran, or whether it might be the result of the fear of being overheard. (Later it occurred to me that it was just common sense on his part: I was a writer, after all.)

Before my trip, in an attempt to learn more about Castro, I'd begun reading Tad Szulc's biography *Fidel*. But I hadn't yet gotten to the part about hiding out in the mountains. So when I woke from my nap, I pulled out *Fidel* and skipped ahead to those chapters. As afternoon began to turn to evening I read about the mountain war in the same hills I'd just hiked through, learning how in November 1956 Castro and eighty-five other revolutionaries boarded the overburdened yacht *Granma* and sailed from Mexico to eastern Cuba, with the goal—unrealistic by almost any objective standard—of overthrowing the dictator Batista. This goal became even less realistic when, after landing in Cuba, almost all of the revolutionaries were killed. Only sixteen—not the apostolic twelve Freddy mentioned—survived, and that group, including Castro and Che, retreated to the Sierra Maestra.

According to Szulc, the story of how Fidel and that tiny band managed to "recover from that terrible initial defeat, start winning against Batista units, and form an ultimately victorious Rebel Army is the story of the extraordinary support he received from Sierra Maestra peasants." The peasants took in Fidel's men, fed them, helped smuggle in arms, and began to swell the rebels' ranks with volunteers. Despite the fact that Batista was strafing the mountains with aircraft fire and constantly sending troops after the rebel camps, the Fidelistas survived by staying in movement for almost a year. Gradually, as the tiny army grew stronger, they began raiding garrisons near Santiago, and these made up their first modest victories. "It was not easy, but I think we identified with the forest as much as the wild animals that live there," said Castro. This time in the Sierra Maestra wilderness became one of the central myths of both Castro and the revolution. And it was a myth that Castro played upon, since he had an innate gift for self-promotion. (Even when he was living like a "wild animal," for instance, he was savvy enough to smuggle in Herbert Matthews of the *New York Times,* as well as a camera

crew from CBS, to help paint the portrait of himself as a romantic bandit.)

Still groggy, I tossed the book aside and headed out for a
walk. The creepy Cuban security guards were whispering into
their static-y walkie-talkies, and they nodded sternly as I walked
off the hotel grounds. Because a large fence encircled the hotel,
I had to leave through the front gate and then cut around back to
the road, but even then it was just a five-minute walk to the com-
memorative park on San Juan Hill. Soon I was standing amid
the monuments, statues, and royal palm trees that marked the
hill. The monuments told their stories in a strange mix of English and Spanish and, depending on the language, referred to the
same war variously as the Spanish American War and the War
of Cuban Independence. A European beech tree that was carved
up with kids' initials stood next to two marble monuments,
one for troops from Massachusetts and another specifically for
troops from my home town of Worcester. Just a few steps beyond
was a Cuban monument that called the capture of San Juan Hill
a "Brilliant Exploit, in which the blood of the brave and true
Cuban insurgents and that of the generous and noble American
soldiers sealed a covenant of liberty and fraternity between the
nations. July 1898–September 1927." *A covenant of liberty and
fraternity!*

I was disappointed not to find any statues of Teddy Roosevelt. I understood that Teddy had his flaws, and that when it
came to killing animals, for instance, he made Audubon look
like a slacker. And there was this question: how much of Teddy
was myth, how much truth? Just as Castro would later invite re-
porters into the mountains, Roosevelt took along a handpicked
scribe during his charge up San Juan Hill. Still, I admired Roosevelt for the reasons so many people did: not only the fact that
he might well have been single-handedly responsible for con-

serving more wild land than anyone else in the history of the world, but the sheer wild gusto of the man, the sense that life was play and that all of it was fun and could be tackled if you threw enough raw energy at it. I also liked him because his life told a story whose moral was that it was okay to brag and even smash and crash sometimes, and occasionally to speak in sentences that ended in exclamation points. Here was a way to be in the world —enthused, outgoing, adventurous—quite different from the way of the earnest nature writer who had offered up the beaver chippings.

Now I stood on the ground, or at least near the ground, that for Roosevelt had been the high point in a life full of high points. He had had to beg to get his commission to fight, and he and his Rough Riders had endured a rocky boat ride from Miami to land at Daiquiri, ten miles to my east. The march from there to here had involved more drudgery than exhilaration, and the charge up San Juan had actually been a brief, crazed burst—"my crowded hour," Roosevelt called it. He began his charge on horseback, right out in the open, exhorting others to follow as Mazur bullets literally whizzed by. Of course accident and chance, as always, played their roles. An equally cocky soldier, Bucky O'Neil, strolled up and down in the line of fire, smoking a cigarette, boasting that "the Spanish bullet isn't made that can kill me" right before he was shot in the head. Roosevelt was luckier. He was swept up in the ferocious moment. "It was as if some primeval force drove him," wrote Edmund Morris. From all accounts his confident state bordered on mania, and his face shone like a gleeful lunatic's. (There is definitely something maniacal—and troubling—about saying to a dying comrade, "Well, old man, isn't this splendid?")

Certainly the glory that came afterward and the medals and the fame were a large part of why Roosevelt looked back on that hour as his life's most satisfying. But there was another factor. While it must have been terrifying to have bullets flying by, it also must have been terribly *engrossing*. For once Roosevelt's always restless energies were concentrated fully. Samuel Johnson said famously, "When a man knows he is to be hanged in a fortnight, it concentrates his mind wonderfully." So too charging into gunfire. Would Roosevelt's mind ever again be so wonderfully concentrated? Would he ever be so absorbed? There was nothing *everyday* about the experience. For a man who relished intensity, here was intensity distilled. Even if you are not the sort to glorify the martial, it is possible to see the beautiful simplification of that hour. Existence was reduced to a single goal, a simple quest. What could be simpler? *Get up to the top.* A life-or-death game of king of the hill.

There in the gloaming, my mind still groggy from my nap, I began to make strange connections. I hiked up a muddy slope toward the deep trenches where the Spanish had made their last stand, the trenches staring like eyes from the sides of the dark hill. A skinny black dog with three working legs ran away from me, as if expecting a kick. It occurred to me that Roosevelt was not the only one whose life's high point had occurred at a literal high point. Just as Teddy had had his crowded hour, Fidel Castro had had a crowded year, living in the mountains. Both had had the good fortune of having their peak moments recorded by journalists who were more than willing to portray them as dashing heroes, and both had then milked their personal myths while scaling the metaphoric heights of their countries' leadership. But the deceptions, and in Castro's case the later atrocities, still didn't take away from the earlier bravery. In the Sierra Maestra, the Fidelistas grew their beards long, rarely showered, ate little, trained hard, and got to know the mountains.

I remembered a quote from the biography attributed to Cecilia Sanchez, the woman closest to Castro while in the hills. "Those were the best times," she said. "We'll never be so happy again. Never."

My reading and thinking were beginning to suggest that elevated states had something to do with literal elevation—that is, that peak moments often occur on actual peaks. If this was so, then I wanted in. Freddy was busy the next morning, so I took a cab to La Gran Piedra. But instead of being driven up to the village, I had the cabdriver let me out at the base of the mountain so that I could make the 10-kilometer climb on my own.

I was stunned by how much I could see on foot rather than by car. As I started the climb the sun slanted down through the royal palms, and the rocket fuel espresso—I hadn't yet learned my lesson—made my blood jiggle and jitter. Occasional thatched-roof homes hid within the overgrown coffee plantations, and red flamboyas lit up the green hillside. A beautiful, tawny brown horse with a ginger mane nibbled grass on the side of the road, and a red-legged thrush, with white patches on its butt and bright orange legs, sang on a branch above me. As I neared the top of the mountain the trees spread out and the view to the north looked like the Colorado foothills. A great lizard cuckoo sat on top of a copse of reeds and clucked, fanning its black-and-white tail and jabbering through its yellow bill, *clik-clik-clik*. When I walked past, it let out a wild jungle cry as if to say, "How dare you ignore me?" A quieter, nobler sight was a small kestrel, no bigger than a blue jay, with a buff chest and owl eyes, sitting on a branch that foregrounded the mountain view to the north. These were birds I had never seen before. I was in high spirits by the time I reached the village of Gran Piedra.

Daimaris was up on the rock, threading beads and trying to sell her wares. But it was a slow day, so she helped me look for birds. When she saw the first osprey before I did, she began to tease me, and then, after I saw one, we began to keep score in Spanish. Seven birds passed by fairly quickly, within ten minutes of my arrival, but it was the eighth that made my day. It came in low and so close to the ridge that I could have jumped on its back if I had been so inspired. Until then the sightings had been distant shapes, but now I saw an osprey as close up as I ever had. It was a large mature male with a wide bandit mask and a full white chest. In shooting past us, it pulled in its wings in the classic *M* shape, and it moved almost as fast as a diving bird. I let out a victory hoot as it zipped down the ridge, and Daimaris smiled but reminded me that she had seen it first. Before I headed back down the mountain, she said something to me that I didn't understand at first. It turned out she was giving the day's final score, which was Daimaris 5, me 3. As a consolation prize, she presented me with a tiny bracelet of red beads to give to my daughter.

As well as seeing a few birds, I had spent my first three days in Cuba thinking about Freddy's record day up on the rock. For me, his big day epitomized and distilled something I had found in other bird people: an enviable ability to become absorbed in and excited by the physical world. An outward thrust leading to inward delight. As I pieced together that day, I liked to imagine it as the peak of Freddy's life. For all I knew, Freddy considered the day Fredito was born or his wedding day or some other day as his life's high point. But in my mind, and in my story, that point came on August 27, 2003.

Of course, the notion that there is a moment—one moment —that defines a person's life is outdated. For post-post-modernists, or whatever we've become, it is hopelessly old-fashioned to think of human lives not just as narratives but as narratives with a climax. We are taught not to accept these fairy-tale notions, and for good reason. What could be more archaic than stamping a narrative on the random moments of existence?

But at the same time we crave narrative. We are instinctively attracted to Roosevelt charging up his hill, his moment of glory finally come, and can see how Americans initially fell for the journalistic portraits of Castro ascending into his rebel mountains. And to that list of glorious days I now wanted to add the day that Freddy saw his 607 ospreys. True, no one had been shooting at him and he hadn't achieved the rank of president-for-life after his day at the top. But for me, Freddy's day was equally, if not more, compelling.

He didn't charge up La Gran Piedra that day, but climbed the ladder in the side of the rock soon after dawn. And while he didn't know it was going to be a special day, it had already been a special month: living in the mountains in a cabin with Ileana and Fredito, waking each morning to the sound of birdsong and the smell of pine. Not only that, but he had seen plenty of ospreys migrating through, enough to confirm the picture that he and Keith Bildstein and Mark Martell had sketched of osprey migration. But his first surprise on that August day was how early the birds began to come. That morning the winds were perfect, a light breeze from the northeast, and by eight o'clock those winds had carried 20 birds out of the clouds above Santiago and past La Gran Piedra. A good day in the mountains at that time of year was 100 birds, and his record, which he had counted with Keith and Mark, was 279. On that particular afternoon Mark had worn a blissed-out expression, at one point laughing and yelling as he pointed at a group of birds, "Look at that big *flock* of ospreys!" He might have been the first ornithologist to use the words *flock* and *osprey* in the same sentence.

That day had exceeded all expectations and had left the three men practically giddy, but by ten in the morning on August 27, Freddy began to suspect that he had something even bigger on his hands. The birds kept coming and coming, not just swooping by his perch but soaring along the coast, where the strong sun had created a perfect day for thermals. Freddy had promised Ileana he would be back down for morning coffee, but how could he leave? When the *artesanos* arrived, Freddy asked them to help, and when they agreed he posted them at different spots on the rock and asked them to call out numbers, which he would then confirm. Between ten and twelve he was getting over 100 birds an hour, and by noon he had already broken the old record.

Then things really picked up. Soon it seemed the rock was under osprey assault. Everywhere patterns of vivid black-and-white against blue sky. They flew by in all the ways that ospreys fly, soaring high above, pulsing along the coast, some charging right at the *artesanos* as if ready to run them through. Ospreys shot past; they glided below; they hovered above. By early afternoon the watchers had doubled the old record, and Freddy had begun to jump around with excitement. He wasn't the only one. If the *artesanos* had always been a little skeptical of his obsession with *guinchos,* it was on that August day that they finally got the old-time osprey religion. They were caught up in the fever of it, hollering out numbers and pointing to the birds and laughing, with cries of *"Águila!"* filling the air. By noon Freddy had positioned them so that each watched a different quadrant of the sky, making sure they didn't miss anything. They may or may not have known it, but they, and the few tourists who happened up onto the rock that day, were seeing something few human beings had ever seen.

At some point in the midst of it all, Ileana and Fredito arrived. Freddy's brother, who was staying in the cabin with them, had gone up to the rock to see where Freddy was and then reported back to Ileana (though it hadn't been too hard for her to guess). She might not even have bothered to hike up to join him if not for Fredito. What brought her up to the top of La Gran Piedra was the fact that Fredito had thrown a rare tantrum and insisted he must see Daddy. "Where is Daddy?" he yelled again and again. "Where is Daddy?" There was no consoling him, so Ileana asked Freddy's brother to carry the boy up the 452 steps to the base of the rock. Then she called up to Freddy, who carried his son up the ladder. Fredito, it turned out, was not content with merely saying hello to his father and then watching the birds with his mother. He wanted a front-row seat, and wasn't happy until Freddy lifted him up in his arms. And so Freddy held Fredito in one arm while clicking the small metal counter with his thumb, somehow managing to get his binoculars to his eyes with the other hand. It would be natural for a one-year-old to become quickly bored by that sort of thing, but with all the birds around, and all the excitement, Fredito was as wrapped up as everyone else. For the next hour Freddy just held him tight and clicked away.

Although he had asked the *artesanos* to call out birds he might not see otherwise, Freddy didn't trust anyone else to do the actual counting. Though he was still jumping around, as his wife later put it, like "a boy with a new toy," he was also concentrating hard. There is a drunkenness to these big moments, but what is required is a reasonable drunkenness. The last thing he wanted to do was overestimate, and he needed to maintain his scientific sobriety despite the day's intoxication. But it was hard as the birds continued to come and he continued to click. At one moment small dark outlines would be soaring over the blue-green Caribbean—a group of 10, or was it 11? *Click, click, click.* Then, riding the north ridge, 6 more, and a dozen way overhead, and now 40 or so flying right by the rock. *Click, click, click.* A single bird would jet by, its wings pulled in a double-jointed style, and then a half-dozen would lift on the mountain updrafts as if riding a roller coaster. *Click, click, click.* For Freddy, one of the true pleasures of that day was the speed with which everything happened. Science, like so many professions, often consists of years of drudgery, of putting in hour after hour, day after day. But as with other professions, things can sometimes, unexpectedly, come fast and furious, and in those moments they lift us out of the quotidian. What has taken years now suddenly takes minutes or even seconds. As Freddy clicked away and his thumb grew raw from the clicking, so many things came together in the rush.

As I imagine that day, that must have been one of its most satisfying aspects: how it wove together all the threads of Freddy's life. First there was the simple visceral experience of seeing all those birds. Anyone who has witnessed the rush of birds migrating knows that the sight connects to something in us, something below or maybe above thought, something that mimics the fast pace and lifting movement of the birds. And of course it wasn't just any bird Freddy was watching, but one that had become his personal totem, one whose black-and-white pattern had long been imprinted on his mind. As he watched them stream around the big rock, he must have felt as if he were standing in the current of a great osprey river.

So there was the physical pleasure of seeing this magnificent sight and counting these wild numbers at his favorite place on earth. But this just formed the base, the root, of his emotions, and may well have been dwarfed by the sheer scientific pleasure. Because here, flying right at him, was confirmation of what he had been working toward since he had first found that dead banded osprey seven years before and reported it to Keith Bildstein. That accidental discovery and simple action had led him on an unexpected journey, which had included a season in the United States during his internship at Hawk Mountain and then years of fieldwork exploring his own country and poring over maps in hopes of discovering just this sort of osprey river. What he saw now was a validation of something he first suspected during a 1998 field trip to the Sagua Baracoa range, where he had seen 43 ospreys fly by in less than 17 minutes, and a validation of the theory that he had then developed with Keith Bildstein and Mark Martell. His earlier trips to La Gran Piedra with Keith and Mark had already begun to confirm this theory, but this was different: not just a confirmation, but a celebration. *Jesus Christ,* he must have thought as he watched the streaming birds, *we were right!* It would be hard to imagine a more physical sense of both discovery and confirmation. It was as if Louis Pasteur had seen pasteurized milk flying toward him or light bulbs had rained on Edison. Bird after bird after bird.

And there was another feeling he must have experienced, a swelling of something that might be called "career joy." Freddy is a sweet-natured man, true, but he is also an ambitious one. Suddenly he was a player in the raptor world, a force to be reckoned with, a name in the ornithological game. He had dreams of writing a field guide of his own, the first great national field guide, and of lifting Cuba out of the ornithological dark ages. And now he could see this happening—yes, this too was really happening. Possibilities were becoming real as quickly as the birds rushed at him.

And finally, how perfect to cradle Fredito in his arms. During and after college, Freddy had studied the biology of both dolphins and birds, but he had never quite *felt* biology the way he had since Fredito had been born. That moment in the delivery room something had cracked and opened in him, and he had begun to feel an even deeper connection with the animal world. At this moment, with his flesh and blood in his arms and the birds filling the sky, that connection was stronger than ever. This would be the first of many birding trips Freddy took with Fredito, and after this day Fredito would forever say goodbye to his father in the morning by yelling, "You do good work today, Daddy!" Unlike so many kids, he would know just what kind of work Daddy did.

It wasn't until midafternoon that the migration tapered off. Freddy had a word for these big days. He called them a "push," a day when all the meteorological conditions and timing and other unknown circumstances were right and the ospreys clearly decided, at least at some level, that it was time to move. By the time this push ended, a blister had bubbled up on Freddy's thumb from using the metal counter. By late afternoon the birds slowed to a trickle. The number had already passed 600, but Freddy stayed up top until dark to make sure he was there to count the last, the 607th osprey. By sunset he was exhausted and had spent every daylight hour on the rock, so that even the backs of his ears were sunburned. He hiked back down the path to the village in the dark.

The *artesanos* stuck with him almost to the very end, and as the day wound down there was an air of celebration up on the rock. Before they packed up and left, Freddy saluted them. He held up his binoculars as if in a toast and said, "Without you, we wouldn't have counted our six hundred." As I mulled over Freddy's big day, I found myself wondering if there had been any real toasts later with his family, with Ileana and his brother, down in the pale green cabin below the weather station. A bottle or two of champagne might have been the logical conclusion to Freddy's finest hour, but I understood by now that my new friend really wasn't much of a drinker. Of course it didn't matter. It wasn't as if he needed alcohol to change his state. He had already spent the day drunk on ospreys.

CHAPTER EIGHT

SOARING WITH CASTRO

Ospreys share with us the inability to stay still. It is hunger that drives them on, hunger that keeps them moving. In the past I'd defined the birds by the place where they nested and spent their summers, but the limits of this definition were becoming more and more apparent during my time in Cuba. Different places required different behaviors, like massing and calling out to each other through the clouds, to name two. And even as the juvenile birds changed place, they were changing in another way, beginning to lose their black-and-white checkering and orange eyes, turning into something else. My definitions needed to change along with the birds.

Reg Saner, a good friend and great writer, has said that our *where* affects our *who*. This was true not just of the juvenile birds but of Freddy Santana. If he had lived in the United States, he would have been celebrated for his achievements and would probably be working in the Cornell Lab next to Alan Poole. But ornithology is in its infancy in Cuba, and his own country has been slow to recognize his work.

When I went over for dinner on my third night, another difference became obvious. Freddy and Ileana were quite proud of the home that they owned, since owning was a rarity. But by American standards there was little to be proud of. Their apartment building looked like a housing project in a bad part of the Bronx. The apartment itself, one of a hundred other apartments, was a cramped, two-room concrete bunker that a single college kid might consider living in, not a place you'd expect an up-and-coming young scientist and his working wife and toddler son to inhabit. But they had made the place a home, putting up gauzy curtains over the gash in the wall and flowers on the tiny kitchen table.

It was in the minuscule kitchen, with its ancient cyborg re-frigerator (made up of some of its original Soviet components as well as spare parts from Germany and the U.S.), that Freddy had spent the better part of the afternoon. Ileana was pregnant and couldn't stand strong smells, so Freddy did most of the cooking. For his guest he had prepared a feast of thinly sliced pork, rice and beans, and plantain chips.

While Freddy cooked, I played with Fredito and talked with Ileana. Fredito had turned two in September. He was only eight months older than my daughter, but he could already name most of the birds in Freddy's field guides in both Spanish and English. The boy got his gift for language, and his dark looks, from his mother, who worked as a translator and relished the chance to have a long conversation in English. Between bouts of stirring things in the kitchen, Freddy would run out and point to a king-bird or crow or warbler or parrot in the field guides, and Fredito would sing out its name in both languages, and we would all smile. At one point Freddy pointed to the bespectacled author of his American field guide and Fredito said, quite clearly, "Sibley."

As well as birds, Fredito loved Pooh and Tigger, though he knew the latter only from the half-section of Tigger's body that adorned his pajamas. I asked Ileana if I could send books from the States, and she said that though the customs agents usually stopped and scanned everything, books would make it through. I had been thinking mostly about sending the dozens of extra children's books we had lying around the house and making sure

Fredito got to know Tigger's other half, but Ileana said that she'd love it if I could also send any adult books in English.

Before we ate, Ileana found a shoebox filled with pictures. In earlier photos Freddy had hair down below his shoulders, so he looked like American television's clichéd idea of a Colombian drug lord, and when he next popped out of the kitchen I asked him about it.

"There is much fear of homosexuals in Cuba," he said. "I wore my hair long to bother the traditional people who think you must be a homosexual if you wear it long."

Just as we were about to sit down to eat, we were interrupted by the bread truck, an old van rattling on the street below. Along with all the neighbors, we headed out to the small balcony and lowered a bucket, into which the bread man placed the daily free loaf.

Dinner was delicious. Rice and beans were the usual fare, and it was only on special occasions like this one that meat made an appearance. Freddy had even bought some beer, a rarity in the house. We finished the meal with fruits and cake, and then I hugged Ileana goodbye and high-fived Fredito. I could easily have called it a night, but Freddy insisted that we take a walk downtown for the Saturday night festival, Noche Santiago.

At first I regretted the decision. Freddy walked into town with the same long-legged stride with which he climbed mountains, and I, exhausted from all the travel and the big dinner, had a hard time keeping up. He seemed eager to show off the town, but I couldn't help but wonder what there was to show off. Buses retched clouds of exhaust, and trucks that served as informal buses drove by, holding as many as thirty men in their beds. A blackout was in effect, and people sat out on the sidewalks in lawn chairs in front of dirty storefronts and rundown apartments.

The walk was long, but by the time we reached downtown I understood why Freddy had brought me. On Saturday night, downtown Santiago spills over with people, a New-Year's-Eve-in-Times-Square kind of crowd, though not quite as thick. Old men sold pork sandwiches for twenty cents and kids rode in circles on tethered ponies. We headed down a narrow street where a band was playing African Cuban music, three men and a beautiful woman banging on drums between wild dances, the crowd throbbing into the street from the sidewalks, many joining the dance. The next block brought the famous Casa de la Tabja, where an old black couple played behind jail-like bars, the man strumming his guitar while the woman sang, their song a slow-paced counterpoint to the riotous street music. The road continued downhill, emptying us into Céspedes Square, with its statues of martyrs and a famous hotel called La Casa Granda. "Céspedes was a rich man who freed his slaves," Freddy said. "Like Abraham Lincoln."

Next to the hotel stood an old cathedral with an angel on top, and next to it, incongruously, an ugly Soviet-style bank. We headed into the hotel and took an elevator to the rooftop bar, where I bought a Cuban beer, a Bucanero Fuerte. We sat outside on the balcony that overlooked the square and the harbor beyond as music drifted up to us from three directions, the song of the old couple, the dance music of the African Cubans, and what sounded like a marching band. Above the stench of pollution, a sea breeze blew in cool.

"You could watch ospreys from up here," I said.

Freddy told me that he had once had lunch here with Keith Bildstein and Mark Martell. Dessert was almost over when Mark looked up and pointed with his fork toward the harbor. From the top of the hotel they were almost at eye level with a large female osprey flapping right toward them. Mark looked at it through his binoculars and laughed. "It's one of ours," he said, handing the binocs to the others. The bird wore a small back-pack, and a wire arced down from its back.

To my delight, this story led Freddy into a session of un-prompted ragging on the BBC crew. "When I first studied the ospreys," he said, "I learned that they usually came into our country at a spot called Santa Clara, north and east of Havana. I would see sixty on a dam and forty circling above the dam. When the BBC came to Cuba, I told them that they should go to Santa Clara, because that is where their birds would enter. But they went to Havana instead, because they thought Havana had good stories of people and was good to film." He shook his head. "Havana might be good for people. But it is not a big deal for ospreys."

Then he laughed and told me about the filming on top of La Gran Piedra. The crew had pointed the camera at him and asked why ospreys migrated through the mountains. "They kept mak-ing me answer, six or seven times, from different angles," he said. "But I am not an actor."

For once I could sympathize with the BBC. Of course they would want to get footage of Freddy, who was about as close as they were going to get to a sex symbol in the osprey world.

Then Freddy told me the position of the BBC ospreys, which he had checked on the Internet at work earlier in the day. As of the day before, Elsie, the first bird to pass through Cuba, was still hanging out in the Dominican Republic. She had spent enough time there to make Rob Bierregaard wonder if she might even winter in the Caribbean, since a small percentage of the telemetry-tracked birds had stopped short of South America. Tasha had joined her in the Dominican Republic and seemed ready to make the jump to South America. But the bird I was most concerned about was the osprey formerly known as Blue-

beard. On September 26, four days before I made my own trip to
Cuba, Bluebeard/Fidel had finally left Martha's Vineyard. Right
up to the end he had been feeding his offspring, but then the kid
disappeared, having either taken off south on his own or, in Rob's
word, "perished." From the Vineyard, Fidel flew over Westport
and toward New Haven and then headed straight toward Keith
Bildstein, and Rob's early reports were that the last of the robobirds would probably be "joining thousands of other raptors
riding the updrafts along Kittatinny Ridge as a south-bound es-
calator." But at the last minute Fidel had a change of heart, cutting down toward Washington, and he had now made it through
Virginia into North Carolina, averaging 112 miles per day.

I told Freddy that I'd renamed the bird Fidel and that I fan-
tasized about rendezvousing with him at La Gran Piedra.

He laughed but then thought about it for a second. "It could
happen," he said seriously. "You may still have your meeting. But
it will take much luck. And much tailwinds."

As we sat there enjoying the sea breeze, I thought about how
ospreys had opened up the world for Freddy, leading him to
Hawk Mountain, for instance, which made him one of the few
Cuban professionals to travel to and be trained in the United
States, but also introduced him to a larger community, a community beyond borders, a community that I was now part of,
too. How nice to be able to forge a friendship in a country where
I wasn't technically allowed to be. While flight has been over-
used as a symbol of freedom, it is worth noting the obvious: that
the ospreys were flying in and out of the United States and Cuba
(and Haiti and the Dominican Republic, for that matter) without passports. There are strong reasons that flight has always
been so closely associated with freedom, that an *águila* is our national symbol. Movement is our first freedom. On the most basic
evolutionary level, flight allows for freer movement than other

modes of getting around. (When Castro was being tossed about on the seas on the *Granma*, he said, "I wish I could fly.") Freedom, at its essence, is the ability to move without restriction.

I thought of the ways that Castro had restricted the freedom of his citizens and then of the way that we had tried to restrict Castro. I asked Freddy how he felt about the longtime embargo that the United States had kept on Cuba. He seemed equally fond of the United States and proud of how far his country had come, particularly when it came to education. He admitted there were still problems in Cuba. "I am not angry at the United States," he said. "But it is obvious who the blockade hurts." He pointed down into the square. "The people," he said.

We headed back down to the street. If freedom is the ability to move freely, then by this definition our walk home through Céspedes Square was not particularly free. We pushed through the jostling crowd, fighting upstream. The mood was still festive, but there were pockets of less joyful chaos. On the way home we passed a young man shouting at his girlfriend in the street. He grabbed her by the arm and hollered in an over-the-top way, as if he were in a street opera.

After we passed, Freddy shook his head. "Cuban pheromones," he said. He nodded his head back toward the man. "That is why Cuban men aren't allowed in the room when their children are born. Doctors are afraid the men will start yelling once they see what they are doing to their women."

Freddy explained that he was an exception to this rule and had been able to be present when Fredito was born—but only after calmly explaining to the doctors that he was a scientist, a biologist, and that he would not, in his words, "freak out."

Over the next couple of days I developed a routine. Each morning I would catch a cab up to La Gran Piedra and each night take another back down, picking up locals who were on their way either home or to work (in both directions, down to Santiago or up to the hotel/bar). One woman, María, even made my cabs into her regular commuter transport, going so far as to ask me to be at the bottom of the hill at a certain time every morning. Having so many people jammed in a small cab made it tough to drive up the steep sections, but it gave a festive air to the trips. By then I had become almost entirely unselfconscious about jabbering freely in my bad Spanish. I was learning that I was bilingually garrulous, and I would now spew about anything: the weather, what life was like in the U.S, and, of course, as always, *águilas pescadoras*. I felt a little like my daughter must have felt back home, trying out new words, and just as Hadley made her first full sentences there, I was doing the same here. It made clear to me just how obviously encoded, how physically ingrained in our brains, is this desire to communicate, to verbalize our experiences. Like Hadley, I took pure physical pleasure in the new words pouring out of my mouth.

Up top I would say goodbye to the gang from the taxi and head through the bar to the steps up to the big rock. I no longer had to pay a dollar to climb the steps, since I'd been blessed by Freddy, and it was known that I was the American bird guy who was obsessed with *águilas*. Reynaldo, the bartender, said hello and served up my regular morning shot of rocket fuel (I now kept it to one or two shots, at most), and then, properly fueled, I would make the climb up into the rainforest, through spiderwebs spanning palm fronds and occasional sunbeams shafting down through the mist. Although I liked driving up with the car full of villagers and liked buying my coffee and chatting with Reynaldo in the bar and also liked the ritual of the climb, what I really liked was getting to the top to the rock. From the moment I arrived and said hello to the *artesanos,* the teasing osprey competition would begin with Daimaris. There was also my more serious relationship with David. He was a good guy, about thirty, with a thin mustache and an air of sophistication despite having spent his whole life in that one small town. He also had the best eyes for birds among the *artesanos*.

When I would get overexcited about a speck that appeared above the mountains near Santiago, thinking I had an osprey, David would laugh and reach for the binoculars. *"L'aura,"* he'd say after a second. Then Daimaris would laugh, too.

L'aura, or *la aura*, was slang for "loser," though they weren't calling me that. The word was also the Cuban nickname for turkey vultures, which, just as at Hawk Mountain, were treated with disdain for being so common. Though I had gotten better at picking them out, they could still fool me once in a while from a great distance.

David often spent the morning flipping through my Sibley guide and occasionally asking questions. By the fifth day I'd decided to leave the guide with him when I flew home, and I wished I'd thought to bring more gifts. Daimaris had given me a small carved wooden eagle necklace and liked my suggestion that she start carving osprey statuettes.

When tourists began trickling up to the rock, the *artesanos* spread out their various statues and jewelry. None of them were pushy salespeople, and they hung back and chatted casually with the tourists, never pressing their wares. Their job was a little like fishing, hanging around all day to see if they could get a few bites. It wasn't a bad job, really—they all professed to like it, and all it took was a sale or two a day for them to make more than they would at a regular job. They chatted up customers, and at its best the mood on top on the rock was like that of a good party.

But if it was a party, it was occasionally a slightly bizarre one. One thing I'd noticed about the visitors to La Gran Piedra,

from my very first visit on, was that there were a disproportionate number of couples made up of old men and extremely
young women. This was bad enough, but even worse, these mis-
matched couples seemed to regard the rock as a kind of makeout point. Particularly repellent was one shriveled, overtanned
Frenchman in his fifties who wore a white muscle shirt, white
clogs, and a kind of Crocodile Dundee hat with a large feather
in it. He stood with his arm around a woman whom I first assumed was his daughter but whom David said was Cuban. Their
common language, other than love, was bad English. They
spoke in loud stage whispers, as if no one could hear them (which
would have been for the best).

Not 10 feet from me, the shriveled fop leaned over, fed his girl
a grape, and asked "Hungry?"

"Mmmmmm" was her answer. "Only for you."

Before I could turn away, they were necking like teenagers.

After they had gone, I leafed through my Spanish-English
dictionary and found the words *ridiculous* and *disgusting*. I read
them out loud to David, and he nodded vigorously.

The *artesanos* weren't the only ones whose job was like fishing. I too sat there gazing out at the clouds over Santiago, hoping
for a nibble. Of course osprey-watching was fun when they were
really biting, but often what was required was simply sitting still.
And so I sat. My days were quiet, and it often took a while before
I had my first bite. When a spot appeared on the horizon, I
would watch it carefully for a few seconds before I made the call,
making sure it wasn't another *l'aura*. When I finally did yell out
my first *"Águila!"* there would be a round of applause from the
artesanos.

It wasn't until my fifth day that I saw a textbook demonstration
of why the birds used these mountains as their highway. A single

bird rode the updrafts off the mountains just as Keith Bildstein had described, as if it were flying off a ski jump, and then continued to spiral up like the birds I'd seen back at Hawk Mountain and Westport. It circled, circled, gaining more and more altitude. Then, when it had lifted almost out of sight, it decided, for whatever osprey reason, that it was high enough. It pulled in its wings and started the roller-coaster ride down. The beauty of this sighting was that rather than heading off over a distant mountain, the bird came right toward us. As it closed in on the rock, I lowered my binoculars. It was not quite as large as an eagle but looked large enough eye-to-eye. Soon I could see the yellow gleam of its irises behind the dark-brown bandit mask.

The afternoon turned out to be decent, with a dozen more ospreys and a couple of peregrine falcons. It was blisteringly hot, however, and around two I told David I was heading down for a siesta. The difference between this day and my other days on the rock was that I'd decided to rent a cabin up in the mountains, and so, rather than taking a cab down to Santiago, I would be spending the night in the town of La Gran Piedra. I had to leave in just two days and needed to watch at least one sunset on the big rock. Freddy had had his transcendent month in the mountains; I would have my single night.

When I climbed down the ladder, I discovered that Daimaris and two other women were eating lunch in the shade of a rock. They asked me to bring sodas when I came back up, and instead of telling them that I was leaving for a nap, I decided to hike down and get their drinks. When I returned, sweat was pouring off me and my heart was pounding as if trying to escape my chest. They held out coins for the sodas, but I said, *"No pagar"* and then said that in the United States people actually paid for the opportunity to do what I'd just done. Then I tried to explain the concept of Stairmaster in Spanish.

Since I was already at the base of the ladder, I decided to climb up for one more look. I stayed for another half-hour and didn't see any birds, but I was glad I'd gone back. It was just David and me up there in the heat of the afternoon, all of the other *artesanos* and makeout couples having decided to find some shade. We passed the time looking up birds in the Sibley guide and chatting.

I tried to explain the situation of the bird called Fidel/Bluebeard, which took some doing. Harder than describing satellite telemetry, it turned out, was getting across the name that Rob Bierregaard had originally given the bird. After a fairly elaborate mime show of piracy, during which I danced about and swung my imaginary bottle of rum and talked to my imaginary parrot, David finally yelled *"Sí!"* But then we had to work our way to the name of the specific pirate, which we eventually did after I pointed back and forth between my beard and the sky several dozen times.

"Sí! Barba Azul!"

Yes, *Barba Azul.* Bluebeard.

Then, before I left again, David asked me a question. Though I hadn't known it, it was a question I'd been waiting for the whole trip.

"Te gusta rum?"

I smiled. *"Sí, me gusta mucho."*

A plan was hatched. We would meet later that evening; I would bring the colas and David would bring limes and rum. Then we would proceed to get *borrachos.*

My mountain cabin was cool and dark, overlooking a steep hillside of ferns and hummingbirds and palms. It was like a cave, perfect for sleeping, and I dozed for over an hour. I woke abruptly to a noise that I first misidentified as a car alarm and then, placing myself, realized was the loudest donkey I'd ever heard in my life. Once the animal finally stopped braying across the valley, I passed the rest of the afternoon in my cool shaded room reading some books on migration, as well as dipping into the stolen Whitman, which I'd brought along. Around four-thirty, I loaded up my backpack and headed up to the rock again.

One thing I already knew, as I hiked back into town, was that the nature of my adventure was changing. Perhaps this was just a case of reading too much Whitman, but for whatever reason, I had begun to conceive of my journey as a quest not just for ospreys, but for moments. Maybe this was partly rationalizing, too. Recently the BBC had been beating me like a rug: in one hour they'd seen more ospreys from La Gran Piedra than I'd seen over the past five days. What's more, without regular access to a computer, I couldn't be sure where either the BBC or the robobirds were.

Still, my trip *felt* successful. Since arriving in Cuba I had become almost wholly absorbed in this new life, despite pangs of longing for my wife and daughter. Ospreys added an organizing principle to the journey, transforming it into something beyond mere vacation. I was relearning what I'd first learned on the way from Cape Cod to Carolina: that there was joy in reducing life to one thing, and that—here was the sneaky part—it really didn't reduce anything. As John Muir had promised, you could pick up one thing and find the rest of the world hitched to it. I liked the feeling that all the usual worries, the everyday anxieties, the quotidian burdens were subsumed by the quest to see and learn about the birds. Having a quest seemed, among other things, a way of both organizing and intensifying the unruly mess of life. Better, it gave life a plot line. There is an undeniable pleasure in a certain amount of monomania, if there can be such a thing. The people I admired most, like Freddy during his big day, were like good-natured Ahabs, their pursuits filling and focusing their lives without pushing them over the edge.

After my nap, I headed over to the bar to see if Reynaldo had any cigars. *"Lo siento,"* he said—he was all out. But just then I saw Evangelino, another of the *artesanos* whom I'd be meeting later for rum, and I called out and asked if any cigars were available in the village. There might not have been any Internet access in La Gran Piedra, but the communication network was effective, and soon Evangelino had run off to tell a group of men hanging out near the meteorological station, who then spread the word to others passing by. I was confident that I would soon have my cigar.

The reason I needed the cigar—preferably a big fat perfect mythic Cuban cigar—was as a kind of prop for a fantasy that had been slowly building in my head. I had gone through a brief cigar infatuation in my twenties, and back then I liked to smoke two in a row, right down to the nub, which provided me with the nearly hallucinogenic buzz I was after. One day, after I had pushed it and inhaled three whole cigars, my girlfriend found me vomiting into our toilet. I stayed there for almost an hour, and at one point she came in to see me lying on the tile in just my boxer shorts. "Why do you do that to yourself?" she asked. Barely able to speak, I lifted my head a little off the cool tile and, wiping flecks of vomit and spittle from the edge of my mouth with the back of my hand, found myself thinking not of my pained, pathetic state but of the great earlier high from smoking three in a row. "If I had the choice," I croaked, "I'd do it again."

That was the me of my twenties in a nutshell, craving highs and exaltation at any cost. And that thrill-seeking adolescent still slumbered, sometimes quite lightly, inside the middle-aged man I'd become. Now, greedy for narrative, I imagined taking my big fat cigar and climbing to the top of the rock as the sun blazed down into the Santiago harbor.

That was just the beginning of the story, however, and to fill it out I needed another character. As I stood there on the prow of my rock ship, staring out nobly at the endless mountains and sea, a small shape would appear out of the orange blaze above the city. There it would be, flapping slowly and strongly as it rose— a single osprey, heading right toward the rock. It would be visible only with binoculars at first, but then it would grow larger and larger, this magnificent loner, and finally it would glide right toward me as if it wanted to impale me on its hooked black bill. But I, desiring contact but maybe not quite that much, would step aside like a matador and watch it pass by, listening to the hushing swish of its wings. Then, for one moment, one glorious and—why not?—Whitmanesque moment, I would be the bird and not myself. And in this exalted natural state I would notice something not so natural. From the primary feathers of this beautiful bird a small wire arced up, and looking closer, I would see the straps of a small brown backpack crossing its chest.

So there I would be—there I *was*—standing on top of the world, or at least the top of Cuba (if not the highest point, then, at 1257 meters, one of the highest), and I would put my arms out at my sides and feel the lift of wind below, and then, still sucking on my fat cigar, I would soar with the bird that I had rechristened Fidel. And as he flew by I would follow him with my eyes—and my spirit, of course—as he flapped—no, not flapped, *soared*— past the rock, to the east, growing smaller but still looking like the perfect symbol of freedom (were it not for the fact that he was now headed toward freedom's opposite). But not even Guantánamo Bay, out there beyond those four or five peaks like a Chinese landscape painting—not even Guantánamo could pull Fidel down tonight. Though on second thought it might pull him down, since it was late and he would have to fuel up and rest rather than attempt the crossing to Haiti at night. But in the morning he would rise again—and I would climb the rock at dawn to try to see him—and he would climb the air on mountain updrafts, up and up and up, knowing that he needed to gain great height for what was to come, and then, when he was as high as he could go, he would pull in his wings and begin the downward glide across the Windward Passage to poor hurricane-devastated Haiti. Then, perhaps even later that same day, he would cross another international border, into the Dominican Republic, before he fueled up again for a final crossing, all the way to South America.

Or that was how I imagined it. The fact was that Evangelino's search of the town proved fruitless and he soon returned, shrugging in failure. So I ended up standing on top of the rock with a pack of cheap cigarettes—a Cuban brand called Vegas— that Reynaldo sold me, instead of my mythic cigar. Also there were no ospreys in sight, and for good reason. Night was coming on fast, without the melodramatic blaze I'd hoped for, and clouds were sweeping in from the north, accompanied by the loud rumbling of thunder. The rumbling grew louder as the clouds closed in, and every sane impulse told me to get down off the rock. But I ignored those impulses and lit my unfiltered Vegas and took a slug from the beer I'd smuggled up, a Bucanero Fuerte. I had smoked only about twenty cigarettes in my life, but this one tasted good and seemed to bring with it the promise that my earlier fantasy might play out. Soon I was enjoying myself, sucking in that cheap tobacco smoke and drinking the beer in those clouds, surrounded by dramatic weather, trying to summon up Fidel.

The odds, of course, were less than slim. To have made it down here from his previous location in North Carolina, he would have had to fly at a record-setting clip, or would have had to repeat the tailwind luck of Tasha and Jaws. Either way, he wouldn't be flying through weather like this at nightfall.

Right before I finished the cigarette, a loud crack echoed off

the rock. Over the past few days I had spent a lot of time thinking about hilltops and mountaintops as places of great exhilaration and triumph and had neglected considering the fact that
they were also places of danger. At least one acquaintance of
mine had been killed by lightning: she was a beautiful young Ultimate Frisbee player, not much older than twenty, who had been
hiking in the mountains in Utah. Then I remembered a similar
death, that of Dennis Puleston's son, Dennis, who had been
struck by lightning on top of a mountain in Mexico. As a new
father myself, I couldn't imagine losing a child, or, more to the
point, I could and often did imagine it. For all the joy of father-
hood, it had also brought pricks of fear and horror that I had
never felt before. Now I really had something to lose.

Which should have made me run right down off that rock
but instead made me think again of Fidel, or Bluebeard, or
Barba Azul, or whatever the hell he thought of himself as (some
osprey variant of *me*). If ever an osprey had been a dedicated
father, it was Fidel. *My god,* he must have thought, *I keep feeding
this kid and feeding it more, and still it isn't learning anything.* Had
he finally just given up? Or—the happy ending—had the young
bird finally gotten it and speared enough flounders to give Dad
faith that it might, just might, be able to make the trip south?
Whichever it was, the reason that there was even a tiny chance
that I might see Fidel flying overhead, tomorrow if not tonight,
was that Fidel's fledgling had taken so long to figure out the osprey game. I could see it: as the fall weather came to the Vineyard and the eelgrass reddened and the cranberry bogs were
harvested and the leaves began to fall, some instinct would push
at Fidel to leave, leave, leave, while another instinct—something biological, something ancient—would be making him
stay, making sure that this kid—*his* kid—had at least a chance
at survival.

I knew I was anthropomorphizing and that any scientist

would rightly find my putting osprey thoughts in osprey heads laughable. But I also knew that feelings toward one's young are not just human feelings, or osprey ones, but feelings that unite all of us, all people and all animals, in ways that can open us up to the world—a world not of borders and restrictions and boxes and graphs and constraints, but of flesh and scales and blood and feathers, a world where there is a basic unity between different peoples and different creatures and where all operate from a basic and sensible humility. And a world where—as hokey as it sounds —there are at least fleeting moments when we understand that we are all one.

These were my thoughts as the thunder rumbled. Which might make you suspect that I had swallowed a tab of acid and not merely puffed on a cheap Cuban cigarette. But then again, they were not just stoned thoughts but sober ones, and the result not just of a cigarette and a beer but of time spent observing the animal world, the physical world. They were thoughts that I still stand by as I type them now, in a much less exalted state. And as I finished my beer, I felt good about coming to La Gran Piedra and good about my quest, even though it was unlikely I would ever see Fidel, or Tasha or Elsie or Jaws, for that matter.

And that should have been enough—*enough! enough!*—since the rumbling was louder and the dark shredded clouds were whipping by the prow of my rock ship, and I should have climbed right down the ladder, but instead I pulled out another Vegas and lit it and stayed up top. I could hear my wife from a thousand miles away calling out to me, yelling, "Why are you risking your life standing up on top of that stupid mountain in a thunderstorm when you have a baby at home whom you love more than anything? And, by the way, why are you smoking a cigarette?" And all I could say back across that void was that I just felt like pushing it and staying and seeing what might happen up here in these wild winds.

And then, as if on cue, I got a little taste of what I'd been asking for: instead of being struck by lightning, I saw the clouds move by like mist, and for a brief moment a hole opened up in the cloud wall to the west and the orange sun blazed out. It was not a sunset, exactly, but dramatic—a sun portal, an intense blaze of orange about the size of a coin on the horizon. Then, almost as fast as it had opened, the hole closed, and soon I was again inside the clouds and the thunder was again rumbling. It took another loud crack for me to finally get it that not only was I on top of a mountain, but I was on top of a rock on top of a mountain, a rock that, not incidentally, had a large metal pole jammed into it like a conqueror's flag to mark its peak. And so I finally beat a retreat across the big rock and down the ladder. My brief shining moment was over. It was time to get the fuck out of there.

Back at the bar Reynaldo served me a mojito and a pork steak. I ate outside in the dark below the steps that led up the mountain while a tiny tree frog serenaded me with a high-pitched chiming song. Then, demanding my full attention, it leaped right up onto my table. Its song chimed crisp, bell-like, and perfect, and another frog responded with love from across the hill. The frog was no bigger than my thumbnail, but its eyes took up a disproportionate amount of its body. I stared into those black eyes.

After dinner I walked over to the closed hotel down the street where Evangelino was working as the caretaker for the night. I took three cans of Ciego Montero soda, which tastes like ginger ale, and a few Cokes. Four of us—David, Evangelino, Ugando, and me—sat in the empty dining area of the empty hotel and worked our way through two bottles of Ron Mulata white rum. David sliced up limes the size of oranges—*limones*— and plopped them in our plastic cups. We toasted Freddy and his big day and *águilas pescadoras* and my trip.

Evangelino apologized for not finding me a cigar, but I told
him that the cigarette had worked just as well. I tried to say
"Close but no cigar" in Spanish *("Próximo pero no cigaro")* and
then spent ten minutes attempting to explain what that expression meant. I finally gave up and said that while I was a professor
in the United States, here I spoke like a caveman. But the word
caveman proved another tough one to get across, despite my attempt to pantomime clubbing someone and walking with my
arms low like an ape. Finally Evangelino dredged up an ancient
Spanish-English dictionary from 1957, the year after Castro
sailed from Mexico, and I put together the phrase *"un hombre de
la caverna,"* and they all nodded.

Despite the language barrier, we had a jolly time of it. David
admitted it was fun to have someone new around for a while.
They had all lived in the village their whole lives and had known
each other since birth.

"Everyone in these mountains knows each other," said
Ugando. "It is nice to drink with someone new."

I asked him if there was much drinking in the mountains and
he nodded, but then added, *"Pero no drogas"* and made a motion
like slapping handcuffs on his wrist.

After a couple of hours, we all swayed home along the main
road. The moon had been sliced cleanly in half and what was left
shone with an orange aureole. That light was the only one in the
village, and I asked if this was the result of a blackout. But it
turned out, he explained, that the inhabitants mostly kept their
lights off at night. Whatever the cause, the sky was black-black
and the clouds from earlier had been blown off to the south and
fierce stars pierced the blackness. David said the stars promised
that the next day would be a good osprey day.

And it was, dear reader, it was.

I know that it will strain credibility if I say that I saw a "push" on my last day on the rock. But at the risk of being considered an unreliable narrator and, worse, of Kathleening, I must tell you that I did, I did. On that last hike up those 452 steps, I sweated Ron Mulata from every pore. On top the morning was quiet, except for Daimaris teasing us all for being hung over. But then the real action started. At 11:55, the day was clear enough to see a far-off blur that Daimaris said was Jamaica, and the feeling of being on the deck of a ship had never been stronger, with the winds blowing into our faces. In fact, I wanted to yell "Thar she blows!" when the first osprey came gliding along the north ridge. While I was still following that bird, David shouted out *"Águilas!"* and I ran over to the south side, where two beautiful young birds were soaring overhead, about halfway between our rock and the Caribbean. Then they really started coming: some shooting by, a few hovering above, some gliding below our ridge. A large adult osprey flew by with its double-jointed wings shaped like an *M,* but the larger impression was of black-and-white patterns against a blue sky, black-and-white so distinct that I wondered if it made a sort of direct neurological impression on the human brain. And then I remembered what the pattern reminded me of: the black-and-white mobiles we'd hung over my daughter's crib during her first months.

I now got a sense of how the ridge led, even ushered, the birds to our rock and beyond. And as the birds flew by on either side, I also saw how La Gran Piedra could act just like a great boulder in a river, the stream of water splitting to either side. For almost an hour the ospreys came: ten, fifteen, twenty, twenty-five, twenty-nine. I knew from watching with Freddy that we had missed at least as many as we'd seen and that our total was closer to twice that. I didn't know if this actually qualified as a push—maybe a mini-push—but it gave me a sense of what a push felt like. For one hour my senses were heightened. I ran from side to side on the rock as Daimaris and David called out birds. I loved watching them glide right toward us, and I'd barely follow one by with my glasses when another would show up, hovering over Santiago. A couple of redtails and a merlin flew by, but there was little doubt that we were smack in the middle of what Keith had called "a single-species corridor." What had it been like when five times as many birds were passing by the rock in a single hour?

Almost on the hour the osprey charge ended, as abruptly as it had begun. Though the weather remained perfect—the best I'd had all week—there were no more birds. Had that been a particular group that had been flying together and begun the day in central Cuba, perhaps near Camagüey, where Tasha had paused for the night? Had they all sensed the weather and felt the winds that morning and decided it was a good day to travel? Had they left at the same early hour and made their push? I didn't know.

"That was a flurry," I said to David in English when they were gone.

He asked what a flurry was, and I told him as best I could in my weak Spanish.

"A flurry," he repeated.

I watched for a while longer, but it was clear the push was over. The birds had headed toward Guantánamo, where they would probably rest, just as my fantasy bird had rested the night before. Then in the morning they would rise high in the air before they tackled the Windward Passage.

Before I left, I gave David my field guide. I shook his hand, hugged Daimaris, and then descended the steps for the last time. I took a cab back down to the hotel, where, soon after, Freddy showed up to say goodbye. In our few short days we were approaching something like friendship, and I was already looking forward to getting home and mailing back piles of my daughter's Pooh books for Fredito.

When I asked Freddy to have a beer with me in the bar, he agreed and laughed. "For you, David," he said.

I told him about my big day, and he said that it was likely there had been three or four times as many birds as I had seen. They came through high up, he said, and often even the *artesanos* missed them. After we finished our beer, I handed my camera to the bartender and asked her to snap a picture of us with our arms around each other. It was the last shot in the roll, and so I popped out the film and gave the camera to Freddy. "It's worth a lot more down here," I said.

He thanked me and then told me something he'd never mentioned before. "When I first went to Hawk Mountain, I had some ancient binoculars. They were only a little better than seeing with the bare eye. Very bad. One day Keith Bildstein saw me trying to look through them and he walked up and took them away. 'You need better binoculars. So take these.' He gave me his binoculars." Freddy shook his head and smiled. "That was a new beginning for me," he said. "I *loved* those things."

Though Freddy and I would soon be separated by borders, I liked to think that a more vibrant line would continue to connect us. He would keep watching ospreys on his end of migration, I on mine. United we stood.

Of course it wasn't that simple. We live in restrictive times which are getting ever more restrictive, and the odds were pretty good that we'd never see each other again. What's more, it would turn out that I was naive to think that my flight to Cuba could easily mimic that of the birds.

I thought I'd seen the last of Freddy, but he showed up again right before I checked out early the next morning. We hugged goodbye, and I was about to carry my bags to the cab when the manager came out of his office and walked up to me with a piece of paper. It was a ticket, a summons from the immigration office in Santiago. My plane left in two hours, and I had been told to be there early. I felt a mild panic rising.

"It is not uncommon to get this kind of ticket," Freddy said calmly. "And the office is just a kilometer away."

He volunteered to accompany me, but the directions sounded easy enough. Rather than taking a cab, I headed down the street on foot, carrying my backpack and suitcase. The streets were crowded, and I watched as a commuting business-man with a briefcase climbed into the back of an old truck with two dozen other men. When I got to the address on the ticket, there was just a series of rundown houses, nothing that looked even vaguely like an office. I stopped a woman holding hands with a young boy and asked where the immigration office was, and she said the office had moved and pointed down the street, making a leftward sweeping motion with her hand. I went down the street and turned left, lugging my bags, and found nothing except another crowd of people. The next two strangers I ques-tioned offered up completely different answers to my query, and by then I was covered in sweat and tamping down a deep panic. My trip was over; I'd seen my birds; I wanted to go home. But instead I was walking through the crowded maze of Santiago, lugging my luggage, sweating through my clothes, and getting different directions from every person I met.

Finally I found myself standing at the door of a yellow-trimmed Victorian home—no doubt the home of a wealthy in-dividual before "the triumph of the revolution." Though there was nothing to identify it as the immigration office, a man out front assured me it was. Inside a grim-faced woman told me to wait in the hall and then returned to her wooden seat behind a small desk. She was typing out a form on an ancient typewriter, filling in answers given by a woman sitting across from her. An old, unsettled feeling came over me there in the dark hallway, one I barely remembered despite the impact it had had on me at the time—that of being called to the principal's office as a kid. My hair and Hawaiian shirt were drenched in sweat from the walk, and I couldn't imagine that the principal was going to be very impressed. I pictured my plane leaving and me being stuck in Cuba with my money running out.

Twenty minutes later I was in another room, sitting on a hard-backed chair across from two women and a scary-looking man in a suit and tie. The scary guy asked for my passport and I handed it to him. One of the women wrote down everything I said, and the other explained that she was there as a translator. The translator looked friendly enough, but her English was not much better than my Spanish, and so the interrogation took place half in Spanish, half in English. The questions started: What do you think of Cuba? *Me gusta mucho!* Have you talked to people about the government while you were here? *No, no!* Did you take only official taxis? *Sí, sí.*

As the questions continued, the scene grew creepier and more Orwellian. But at the same time it partly felt like a game, like when I was in college and was pulled over by the college cops, not the real cops, after tearing down a street sign as a prank. These people had stern looks on their faces, but that had to be perfunctory, right? I had a feeling that it would all end well.

And then that feeling passed.

Why did you go into the mountains?

Here is where I thought I could really win them over. *"Porque me gustan mucho las águilas pescadoras. Yo escriben una libro de las águilas. Para mí las águilas es muy importante..."* And so on and so forth in my mutilated Spanish, trying to explain my love affair with ospreys and the books I had written, and would write, about them. What could be more winning? Who wouldn't love the story of a simple guy who loved birds—innocent little *birds*? Caught up in the momentum of my story, I painted a picture of a future when people from all over the world would flock to La Gran Piedra to see the great river of ospreys.

But strangely, instead of smiles and nods, the three brows across from me began to furrow and the three heads nodded sternly. I had meant my spiel to sound enthusiastic, but now I worried that perhaps it had carried a whiff of fanaticism. Finally the man in the suit spoke to me in English, a language that I hadn't realized he understood.

"In our country, this is not allowed," he said. "You can come for tourism in our country, but not for work on birds."

A cartoon light bulb went off over my head. Instantly I became a sixties sitcom husband who, caught in a lie to his wife, furiously backpedals. "But birds are my tourism," I said, deciding to stick mostly to English now. "It was all just for fun. *Turista!*"

The man scribbled something else down. "Did you meet any people up in the mountains?" he asked.

"I met people. But it wasn't deep. Just hello."

With that he got up and walked out of the room, carrying my passport. A second later the stern woman stood and followed him. The translator just sat looking at me. She shook her head slowly and sadly. She said, "To work here you need a visa."

We sat there for ten, fifteen minutes in silence. Visions of Hadley and Nina and home swirled in my head. I wished that I could beam myself back to the United States or, like Castro on the *Granma,* that I could fly. I looked down at my watch and mentioned the time of my flight to the translator. She stood up and left the room, and I sat alone for another fifteen minutes.

This was long enough for me to dissolve in a puddle of sweat, sweat that now came from panic. I wondered how I would stand up to torture and decided the answer was not too well.

But suddenly the translator was walking back in, wearing a smile and waving my passport. She sat down and then leaned toward me and patted my leg. "It will be all right," she said. "They are just calling the airport to hold your plane."

She asked me if I had any children, and I pulled a picture of Hadley from my wallet, and by the time the other two returned we were having a great time talking about our kids. In a spasm of relief I went on about how Hadley was learning to talk while I was away, and then the translator started to describe her two girls, one older and one younger than Hadley. Then she interrupted herself. "We must stop now for you to catch your plane," she said. "You had better hurry."

A direct flight from Santiago to North Carolina is, as the osprey flies, about 800 miles. Tasha, with the right tailwinds, could do it in two days.

It took me longer than that to get home. First it was back to Havana for a night and then to Cancun for most of the next day. In Havana I spent the night in the same crappy hotel and wondered again how that city had achieved its romantic reputation. Maybe I was just in the wrong part of town, but in my mind the city paled next to La Gran Piedra. The bed was uncomfortable, the room hot, and after I finally fell asleep in a pool of sweat, I was awakened by a great roar coming from the street. The next day I realized that this was due not to some midnight rally for the glory of the revolution but because the Yankees—the dreaded Yankees, dire enemies of my Red Sox—had won a playoff game in extra innings. Thanks to their Cuban players, especially El Duque, the Yankees were a local favorite.

I spent the next day flying from Havana to Cancún, where I passed an unpleasant six hours in the airport listening over and over to a recording of a woman's voice, apparently the same one used everywhere in the world, repeating, "Unattended vehicles will be ticketed and towed" in Spanish and English. My nerves were shot from the interrogation and travel, and I was both longing to see my family and dreading dealing with American customs. Though I didn't have a stamp in my passport, I had two stamps for going in and out of Mexico through Cancún, and that would take some explaining. I had decided not to lie about where I'd been. For one thing, I knew I was going to write about it later, and therefore I felt that it was better to take whatever penalties were being doled out than to perjure myself.

Even though I was nervous, a part of me, the writer part, sort of hoped that the interrogation in the United States would mirror the one in Cuba, just for the poetry and symmetry of the thing. But the truth was that even in the age of Bush, I never felt quite as worried when I was questioned in Charlotte, in part because I was in my own country and in part because it all took place in English.

Once I admitted I'd been in Cuba, I was shunted toward a desk where a chubby black woman in a uniform stood. She took my passport and asked me if I knew that it was illegal to travel to Cuba.

I said I was a journalist and a researcher and that I believed I qualified under the general permit.

"There is no longer any general permit," she said sharply.

She asked a dozen more questions and had me fill out some forms, but she grew friendlier as we talked, and I never felt the real fear that I'd briefly experienced in Santiago. The only bad moment was at the end, after she had handed back my passport.

I said goodbye and she said the same. But then, as I was walking away, she spoke a line I thought people said only in movies. She was not a particularly impressive woman, but she delivered her line impressively.

"*They'll* be in touch," she said.

CHAPTER NINE

WINTERING GROUNDS

"They" were indeed in touch, though not for a couple of months. In the meantime I settled back down on our new home island of Wrightsville Beach, catching up on my schoolwork and spending time with my wife and daughter. Hadley seemed to have changed dramatically in the week I was away. She had entered that stage which child development specialists call "fast mapping," when words have to be repeated only once to stick to the mind like flypaper. Suddenly her vocabulary was burgeoning, bursting: *moon, cheetah, Go to beach, good dog,* and, of course, *bird.*

It was a pleasure to be home, to be staying still, but while I rested, the ospreys raced onward. As expected, my vision of communion with Fidel/Bluebeard on top of La Gran Piedra proved mere fantasy. We really didn't miss our rendezvous by that much, since, as Rob Bierregaard put it, "Bluebeard made his move through Dixie in a hurry." Along the way he took in many southern hotspots, flying from Charleston to Savannah before pushing hard through Florida to the Everglades. If he had kept riding that momentum, we might have met at the big rock, but instead he paused in southern Florida.

It wasn't until October 8, the day after I left Cuba, that Fidel finally crossed the water, settling down near Santa Clara in northwestern Cuba. Though the length of Cuba can be crossed in three days by an osprey with a nice tailwind, the birds usually take longer, using the island as a pit stop for refueling. In the scientific paper that Freddy had written with Keith Bildstein and Mark Martell, they had concluded that ospreys sometimes even took twice as long. But Fidel apparently liked Cuba so much that he hung out for a full nine days before leaving the Santa Clara area. This adult male osprey was again proving just how individual an adventure migration tends to be. The fishing was good near the Santa Clara dam, and he was in no hurry, thank you very much. Though finally migrating, he was at heart a settler. He had taken his own good time leaving the nest back on Martha's Vineyard and he would take his own good time leaving Santa Clara.

When he finally did get going, he really went: he flew directly down the spine of the island and through the Sierra Maestra to La Gran Piedra before making the Windward Passage to Haiti, pausing only briefly there before bee-lining straight south across the Caribbean to Colombia. This was more than a 300-mile trip across open water and made up approximately a ninth of his total mileage of 2647 since leaving his nest.

And he wasn't done. He barely rested upon landing on the Guajira Peninsula in Colombia before he took off again, speeding southward, crossing the equator on the twenty-seventh and flying deep into the Amazonian watershed, nearly into Brazil. Then he stopped on a small river, a tributary of the Rio Negro, a jungle world of vines and crocodiles quite different from his Martha's Vineyard summer home. If he was like most adult ospreys, he would stay within just a dozen miles of this spot until late winter, when he would begin the trip home.

Winter is the least understood part of an osprey's life, and I wanted to know more. Over the next couple of months I tried to cobble together the puzzle of the year, reading what I could about osprey wintering grounds. One thing I learned was that for ospreys, winter is fraught with its own dangers. In the paper Freddy had put together with Martell and Bildstein, he wrote that "the shooting of raptors is common in Cuba" and that "the talons of ospreys are sometimes used as spurs on the roosters used in cock-fights on the island." Alan Poole also e-mailed me a paper about how birds were shot at aquaculture facilities in Colombia.

The climate in Colombia is ideal for aquaculture, and over the past twenty years fish-farming plants have sprung up all over the country. The problem, from an osprey's or osprey lover's point of view, is that one of the main species raised on these farms is tilapia, a surface-dwelling fish that is perfectly snack-sized for an osprey. They are raised in large areas of shallow, impounded water that must look every bit as inviting as the goldfish back in the pond on Long Island. "The day I visited one of the farms the owner said he had just shot twelve ospreys the week before," wrote the report's coauthor, Marc Bechard, in an e-mail. "Every time they dive into the pond they come up with a fish and sometimes two. That makes the owners go nuts." Understandably frustrated by watching their crops being dive-bombed, the farmers had begun shooting the birds. At one facility alone, 270 ospreys had been shot.

The literature on wintering grounds was scanty, so after Christmas I decided it was time to make another short migration, driving the five hours to Charlotte to talk with Rob Bierregaard. Rob was just as I'd expected from his online and phone persona, maybe a little corny with the jokes but open and affable, and he invited me into his home for an hour or so of osprey talk. We sat in his living room and I got right to my questions.

"It's true we don't know much about what they do in South America," he said. "With one of the first birds we tagged, HX, he did kind of the same thing as Bluebeard. He landed on the Guajira Peninsula in Colombia, rested for a while, then took straight off south. You could tell he knew exactly where he was going, flying straight and fast, and you could almost hear the brakes go on when he got there. Then he spent the winter there before heading north. And the next year, when he flew south again, he ended up three miles away and headed back to the same tree."

Rob slipped into another room and returned with a picture. It was of an osprey diving for a fish. "That's Jaws in Colombia," he said.

Jaws and Fidel/Bluebeard were the only birds Rob was still monitoring. True to form, nature's cruel triage had winnowed the five birds down to two. While Bunga had succumbed back in Connecticut, her mother, Elsie, had migrated all the way east through Hispaniola to Puerto Rico, one of the few birds to do so, and for a while it looked as if she might overwinter there. But then, after a couple of weeks in Puerto Rico, she suddenly flew south across the Caribbean to Venezuela. It was there that her signal had gone dead.

As for Tasha, the young bird whose journey had mirrored my own, after flying across Cuba and Haiti, she had suddenly stopped moving in the Dominican Republic. Her last signals came from just north of Cabo Beata, which was a regular jumping-off point for the trip south across the Caribbean. Since her transmitter hadn't been functioning well for days, there was still a chance that it was her radio, not her, that was dead. But Rob assumed that she had expired, either before or during her final water crossing.

"Jaws is the real success story," Rob said as I studied the picture. "He's the only young bird to make it, and thanks to him we're getting to see what a young bird does in South America."

He explained that Jaws had first landed not far from where Bluebeard later landed on the Guajira Peninsula. "That was an exciting moment for me," he said. "We had so little data on young birds in winter. Jaws had the whole continent in front of him and no special place to go. But it turned out he ended up not going anywhere. Right after landing he lucked out and found osprey heaven. It's a vast shallow bay called Bahía Hondita. There must be a couple hundred square miles with three to six feet of water. Jaws is living the good life. Lots of fish and no one else around but some flamingos and ospreys. He roosts with six or seven other ospreys in a stand of mangroves and horses around with the gang a bit each morning before heading out to fish."

I was glad that Jaws, who had always acted like the most type A of the young birds, was doing some horsing around. Back in August, the time pressure of migration was great, but now life had loosened. And play is an important aspect of learning in young animals, a way to discover new possibilities, new techniques. Not to mention the obvious: play is *fun*.

I asked Rob why Fidel—for Rob's sake, I called him Bluebeard—hadn't taken advantage of the same good life that Jaws had found in Bahía Hondita when he arrived there two weeks later. Why not just fatten up at the same *hondita* where the living was easy instead of launching off for another thousand miles of migration?

"It all comes back to that first time the young bird makes the trip. Maybe the first time Bluebeard flew down he didn't land as close to the Hondita. That place is a dry landscape, and maybe Bluebeard's idea of a wintering ground is a jungle river. Why do birds fly so far into South America? My feeling is that the migratory urge is turned on for about a month. Some kind of hormonal switch is thrown, and you just go until the switch is turned back off. Some years, if the weather's good, that might carry you down to Brazil. Some years, like this one, you might have hurricanes to contend with and might not make it that far. A lot of it is chance. You play the winds as they hit you. And if you're blown off-course and end up wintering in a strange place, then you imprint that strange place. And from then on you keep going back to it. Again and again and again."

Before I left, I needed to ask one last question. My funds were completely depleted and my traveling days were over, at least for a while. Not so the BBC. They had just flown the whole crew down to the Guajira Peninsula in search of Jaws and the elusive closeup. But while they had money, I also knew that during the entire trip from Cape Cod to Cuba they hadn't yet gotten a single good shot of any of their birds. When I asked Rob if they had gotten a good shot in Colombia, he shook his head slowly and described Jaws as "camera-shy." "They did get one brief shot of him from a distance," he said. "But they really didn't have great luck."

"That's too bad," I said, shaking his hand goodbye. Schaden-freude is an unpleasant emotion, I understand that—something people don't really want to see. So I tried to hide my smile.

As a fan of complexity and diversity, I have never been a great believer in Thoreau's exhortation "Simplify!" But over the holidays my own life simplified nicely. In the mornings I got up early and drank coffee and typed up my story of chasing birds from the Cape to Cuba. In the afternoons I took Hadley to the beach and watched as she did some bird chasing of her own. She would toddle-sprint after gulls and wave her arms while bellowing her war cry, "Fly, birds, fly!" As an ornithologist she was still no match for Fredito, but she wasn't bad. Before she turned two she would learn the names of purple martins and great blue herons and brown pelicans, and she could already do a fair impersonation of an osprey's warning cry.

Around this time I reviewed a book by the historian Jon T. Coleman that contained these lines: "Some naturalists argue that the categorization of living beings forms the basis of human cognition. Human brains learned to think by wrestling with the differences and similarities between animals." It was easy enough to see this sort of development repeat itself in my daughter. I was struck by how much of a child's imaginative world is made up of animals. Words and beasts are constantly tangled, from Baloo singing "Bare Necessities" to the Pooh books to the stuffed elephant Hadley dragged everywhere.

We saw real animals too. From the shore we watched dolphins sea-serpent in and out of the waves, and for almost a week we were visited by a rare right whale, one of only about three hundred in the world. Then, on a wonderful January afternoon, Hadley and I witnessed a particularly wild congregation of birds. In the foreground, close to the beach, more than five hundred gulls swarmed after bait fish. Through this mass of gulls, brown pelicans crossed every which way, plunge-diving as they followed their great bills into the froth. Once they had speared their meals, they sat in roundup circles, digesting and draining their pouches, bobbing together on the water. Behind the pelicans, farther offshore, was an even more arresting sight: a thousand gannets diving for fish. Gannets are large snow-white birds that spend their summers off Nova Scotia and points north, and I had always thought of them as a cold-weather bird, but here they were in my southern home, and my bird book confirmed that they wintered all the way down to Florida and beyond. Their dives were spearlike and different from ospreys', as they entered the water headfirst and then tunneled after fish below the water. They hit the water like feathery missiles, and when they found a particularly good spot, thirty or forty birds could hit the water each second. At those moments they looked like they were all being sucked into a great vortex, or like filings pulled to a magnet. They sliced into the water, one after another after another, as the world filled with their jangling energy.

I thought about different strategies of survival. A large part of the survival game is the conservation of energy, or rather, how to expend energy effectively. Ospreys are not energy misers, animals that do little or consume little (which is certainly another common winter survival option for many mammals and reptiles). But neither do they have the wildly excessive habits of these gannets, plunging again and again, having figured out, through some species-wide calculus, that they can balance this expenditure by gobbling many fish. An osprey, by contrast, particularly a wintering osprey, will be looking to eat a couple of fish a day, and to a certain extent will pick its spots. As I watched the gannets' spectacle of gluttony, I wondered just how many fish they had to eat each day to sustain this level of intensity.

The next afternoon was one of those crazy North Carolina days that defies the calendar and has everyone wearing shorts in January. The gannets moved in close to the beach, muscling out the gulls. I was standing alone on the shore, thinking, *I've never stood so close to diving birds before,* when it occurred to me that I could be much closer. On impulse I stripped down to my boxer shorts and swam out into the thick of the action. My legs were numb, but it was worth it. From below it was a little like being one of those carnival assistants who acts as a knife-thrower's target; I could see just how bladelike the gannets became right before they hit the water. Then a couple of pelicans started diving close by, and I felt like ducking my head. The birds ignored me and sometimes splashed down within 20 feet of where I treaded water. For the first time I had a fish's view of diving birds.

A less romantic moment also occurred in January. "They," as promised, were in touch. The Bureau of Foreign Assets, a branch of the Treasury Department, contacted me and sent along a questionnaire about my trip to Cuba. My brother-in-law's law firm agreed to handle my case pro bono, and I began to work with a lawyer who specialized in just this sort of thing and who gave me a history of the Cuban embargo. The United States had now maintained its embargo against Cuba for more than forty years, though during different times the intensity of the restrictions varied. During the second Clinton administration, U.S. travel to Cuba became fairly commonplace, but Bush had returned things to the cold war days, and my lawyer warned me that a fine of up to $11,000 was possible. Since this was about $11,000 more than we had in our bank account, I was a little troubled. Furthermore, the lawyer was initially pessimistic about my case and thought the best we could do was lower the fine by showing that the trip had been a misunderstanding on my part. But the more we worked together and the more information I sent him about my osprey research, the more optimistic he became. At one point he paused during one of our long phone calls. "They're quite something, these birds, aren't they?" he said.

One of the many questions I asked him was whether my pending case would impede my ability to travel outside the country. The answer was no, which was good, because by late January I was again feeling the itch to follow the birds. As usual, there were obstacles, both financial and otherwise. For one thing, I had classes to teach, which I would have to find someone to sub for. For another, Nina didn't exactly love the idea of my taking off again, particularly considering the places where I was thinking of traveling. Cuba had been one thing, but following Fidel into the jungles of Colombia was another. I looked into Venezuela as a safer option, and at one point it seemed that a scientist friend of Rob Bierregaard's would be willing to take me by boat up the Orinoco delta to watch ospreys. But then, abruptly, the woman stopped returning my e-mails.

Without a clue of how to proceed, I e-mailed the ever-dependable Keith Bildstein, asking if he had any contacts in

Colombia and Venezuela. He sent back the name of Adrián Naveda-Rodríguez in Venezuela, whom I promptly e-mailed. Adrián explained that he was the head ornithologist at a natural history museum in Henri Pittier National Park, which contained 50 percent of the bird species in his country. He also said that he would be happy to put me in places to see ospreys. "I do not have a problem to attend you," he wrote. "Please I apology for my bad English." The note was vague but had a whiff of Freddy Santana's generosity to it. I wrote back, and Adrián's response was even more informative, more gracious, more thorough. He had obviously been in touch with birders around his country, and he sketched out several places where I might see the birds. I wrote a third time with more questions, and this time he said he would be willing to take a week off and travel around Venezuela with me if I rented a car. It was beginning to look like I had my next osprey man.

There were still impediments, however. Money was first on the list. It was time to apply for another loan from the bank of Jon, and so I swallowed my pride and contacted him, sticking out my tin cup. Over the past few months I had hinted at a winter trip by e-mail and had half hoped that a spontaneous sequel to his wonderful *SOAR!* check would arrive in the mail. Now I sent him an exploratory note as to the feasibility of another loan. His reply was only slightly longer than the note that had accompanied his first check: *Go to Venezuela, goddammit!* By then it was February, and many of the birds were already flying back north. Would there be any ospreys left to see? But with the support of my benefactor, I began to call travel agents.

As soon as I definitely decided to go, a rash of articles appeared in the sports pages about various kidnappings and murders in Venezuela. My father-in-law sent me one of the articles with a note that read: "The main point is to be cautious if you visit this country." The articles were in the sports pages because many of the victims of these crimes were professional baseball players, and since I doubted I would be mistaken for a baseball player, pro or otherwise, I thought I might be okay. But other friends came out of the woodwork with horror stories about Venezuela, with a particularly gruesome emphasis on carjackings and kidnappings. One well-traveled friend of my wife's described how President Chavez's goal was to be the "next Castro" and how many people in his oil-rich country had a not-so-unreasonable fear of the United States. "I have heard that crime is pretty brutal down there," the friend e-mailed Nina. "And I guess that Chavez is getting a little paranoid about all things American, so maybe Dave will end up in a Venezuelan jail or something. I know you're not actually paranoid if they're really out to get you, but Chavez is a little off the deep end lately about preparing for 'American invasion this' and 'American invasion that.' Please tell Dave to get good photographs of any violent street fights he wanders into." Other than managing to scare me, this message wasn't very helpful, but it did hold one piece of concrete advice. It was best not to travel alone.

I had already taken care of that by inviting along Mark Honerkamp, who had played the role of my trusty sidekick in previous adventures in the Belizean jungle and Utah desert, among other places. I'd learned that many of the pro baseball players who lived in Venezuela during the off-season had bodyguards for themselves and their families, so I would have one too. The truth was that Hones had a wide passive streak and wouldn't have really passed muster as a bodyguard, but at six foot four, 240 pounds, he could at least act as a kind of large, hairy scarecrow.

Hones and I had met more than twenty years before as teammates on an Ultimate Frisbee team in Boston called the Hostages. To support our ultimate obsession, many of my teammates worked briefly in a local warehouse for a ski company. For Hones the stint at the warehouse hadn't been quite so brief, and now, twenty-two years later, he still worked there. His was a kind of deal with the devil. He lived fairly cheaply and alone and each weekday worked from seven to three in the warehouse. But he took some of the most exotic vacations of anyone I'd known, from Bolivia to Costa Rica to Belize, and sustained himself emotionally between these trips by going fishing almost every minute when he wasn't either asleep or at the warehouse. We liked traveling together, for the most part, and did it pretty well. As well as a love of the natural world, we shared passions for large amounts of beer and food.

We had our differences, however. Mine was a more spontaneous approach, and I had been known to change my mind fairly quickly. Hones, in contrast, liked to plan things out and was understandably unnerved when I started wavering before confirming the tickets ten days before we were to leave for Venezuela.

"I'm going to do it, I think," I said to him over the phone.

"'I think'?"

"I think."

The next day I called him back and said the same thing more definitively.

Less than two weeks later we were on a plane to Caracas.

We spent the first night in a cheap hotel on the coast. There had been a fairly heavy military presence at the Caracas airport, and it was late by the time we took a cab to the hotel. Along the way we passed a roadblock where a driver had been pulled over and was being frisked, and I, just like a typical American, was reminded not of real life but of a movie: *The Year of Living Dangerously*. The next morning the world felt a little safer, and we stared out at pelicans and magnificent frigatebirds from a rock wall above a point where a beach had once been. Flooding and mudslides had wiped out the beach, as well as many of the homes on the mountainside behind us. I'd forgotten about Hones's surprisingly sharp eye for birds. As we walked back to the hotel he pointed out a great kiskadee with a black eye band and a yellow breast.

I'd also forgotten his tendency to provide a running commentary about whatever was occurring at the moment with his bowels, and after his first cup of strong Venezuelan coffee he started musing. "Sometimes traveling all day binds me," he said. "But I think this will loosen me up."

He lit a cigarette, and I realized that this adventure would have a different flavor from my solo trips during the fall. I headed back to the room to pack while Hones stayed out by the water, smoking. When he got back to the room, he was sweating profusely. "It's a Bob Stanley out there," he said.

We had traveled together so often that we were like a married couple, right down to the private language. Sadly, I knew just what he meant.

"A steamer," I said, nodding. Stanley had been a notorious relief pitcher for the Red Sox, and "Steamer" was his nickname.

We took a cab back to the airport to rent a car. We hadn't wanted to rent one late the night before, because of the potential danger, and the plan was to meet Adrián at the rental car counter. We knew him only through e-mail exchanges and had no idea what he looked like or how old he was, and he surprised us with his youth. He was a slightly plump twenty-five-year-old, the weight the result of both remnant baby fat and fact that, we soon enough discovered, he was a trencherman on a par with Hones. Right away we could tell that he was a good kid, quietly engaging, and his smile took up most of his face.

The rental car people screwed us out of about two hundred

dollars more than they'd estimated when we made reservations from the States. They did this because they could: we were there and we needed a car and what the hell else were we going to do but plop the money down? The car itself was a slightly cramped Toyota Echo. We drove off through the mountains and hillside slums of Caracas, with me at the wheel and Adrián navigating in the passenger seat as Hones leaned forward over the console (a seating arrangement we would keep for the better part of the next six days). The plan was to drive the two and half hours west to Adrián's home in Maracay, the city that would serve as our base of operations. Adrián's English wasn't quite on the level of Freddy Santana's and we conversed in a mix of his passable English and my bad Spanish. (Hones's Spanish was even worse than mine, which was quite an achievement.)

"We will see birds tomorrow, yes?" Adrián said.

Yes, I said, I hoped we would.

"No, no, we *will* see them," he said. "But it is a question whether to try to see them at the lake near my home, or to go into the north to the seashore, or to head to the south to Los Llanos."

As he laid out the various options I felt a stab or two of anxiety. In Cuba it had simply been a question of ascending a big rock that stood in the middle of the ospreys' flyway and waiting for them to show up. Venezuela, on the other hand, had no known watch sites and no reliable center of migratory information. No less an authority than Alan Poole had warned me that it might be smarter to head to the Everglades to watch the ospreys returning from South America—better that than trying to chase migrating birds around a country that was roughly twice the size of California. "It may be like looking for a needle in a haystack" had been his less-than-encouraging words.

But Adrián had done his homework, and it quickly became clear that despite his youth, he knew both his birds and his bird

people. At fifteen he'd begun working as a volunteer in the
Maracay Zoo, and he had eventually become what he called "the
reptile keeper" at the zoo. In college he'd studied to be a natural
resources technician, but his interest was really sparked when he
became involved in a study of the harpy eagle. And it was when
he was doing research on the harpy that he visited the Museum
of Natural Resources in Maracay and the director offered him
his present position as head of ornithology.

For our trip he had called various parks and ornithologists,
and he used his cell phone to confirm our plans with them as
we drove. He didn't do this by talking, however, but by writing
text messages, which he whipped off with his thumb. Though
Adrián was never without his trusty cell phone, I saw him actually talk on it only once or twice. All of the rest of the time it
was thumb-pushing, which at times was fairly nonstop. One
of the messages he received while we drove was from a birder
friend confirming the fact that he had witnessed at least thirty
ospreys on Lago de Valencia, right near Adrián's home in Maracay. We decided that we would rent a boat the next day and get
out on the lake.

When we reached Maracay we drove to Adrián's parents'
home, half of a gated two-story stucco house with caged parrots
in the front yard. Adrián had a room in the house, as did two of
his sisters. We sat in the kitchen in the blazing heat, sweat dripping off Hones's nose, and Adrián's mother offered us espresso
and cake, which we happily accepted. We were in the middle
of polishing off the cake when Adrián's brother-in-law walked
in with a case of Polar Ice (pronounced *EE*-say), the country's
most popular beer. It came in tiny bottles (about .22 liter) so it
wouldn't get warm in the tropical climate. I don't usually like to
pile depressants on top of stimulants, but when Hones and I
were offered two cold bottles, we felt it only polite to accept, fol-

lowing our espressos with beer chasers. Since the beers were so little we also said *sí* when another round was offered.

We checked into a hotel around the corner and then headed up into the mountains with Adrián. The mountains were due north of the town, and if you continued north over them, you reached the Caribbean. Adrián's museum stood at the base of the mountains, but the gates to it were closed, so we wound our way toward the clouds for about half an hour and then pulled into the Rancho Grande Biological Station.

The huge question-mark-shaped building looked like something out of a Werner Herzog film, as if it had been long abandoned in the jungle, which in fact it had. My guidebook told me that the building had originally been commissioned as a "posh country hotel" by the dictator Juan Vicente Gómez but that it "was only half completed by the time Gómez died and it was deserted by the workers when they heard news of the dictator's death." Deserted it remained until the park's founder, the scientist Henri Pittier, converted it into a biological research station. But the conversion had apparently not included any substantial improvements to the dilapidated building: trees and vines grew in and out of broken or glassless windows, the rainforest crowding in around the old hulk. We climbed to the vine-covered top of the station, and from there we could see the town of Maracay laid out below. I pointed toward the huge lake next to the city.

"Yes," Adrián said. "That is where we will go tomorrow. That is the lake where my friend saw his thirty ospreys."

I felt a small pang of disappointment that we hadn't headed directly to the lake. We had been in the country almost twenty-four hours without seeing an osprey, which by my recent standards was unacceptable. For the moment I had to make do with watching songbirds from the upper deck of the station. Hones pointed to a honeycreeper that shone with the malachite green of a Van Gogh self-portrait, and Adrián explained that the female honeycreeper would build a nest in the fork of a tree, attaching it to the branches with spiderwebs it collected. We also saw lesser swallow-tailed swifts carving the sky overhead and a blue-gray tanager—full of clean gentle whites and delicate blues—landing on a tree at eye level. From the top of the station we could also see eye-to-eye with a groove-billed toucanet in a fig tree and stare down at the nests of oropendolas hanging like scrotal sacs from branches. As the day lengthened, the oropendolas let out their wild jungle cries, a crazy upward gurgling that mixed with the din of howler monkeys from the rainforest.

By the time night fell, Hones and I were both exhausted from traveling, and I drove back down the mountainside bleary-eyed. If we had both been surprised that Adrián was just a kid with chubby cheeks, we were quickly learning that he knew his birds and that he had a quiet, unflappable style (granted, we hadn't yet given him much of a chance to flap). But what did Adrián think of us? He had perhaps expected reputable international ornithologists rather than two large, hairy men with a taste for beer and scatological humor. Hones, for instance, had already discovered that his favorite Spanish word was *flatulencia,* and he found a surprising number of opportunities to use it in conversation. But he had been in his element up at Rancho Grande. While he could be juvenile, even imbecilic, when detailing his bowel movements, he knew his fish and mammals cold and had a keen eye for birds. He hadn't finished college, but his mind was sticky for facts. I'd often thought he'd make a great park ranger. Before we left the mountain we had taken a short walk into the jungle at dusk, and Adrián had said he smelled a peccary, a wild pig. It had been fun to watch Hones come alive with expectation.

We decided to take Adrián out for dinner and get our first

taste of Venezuelan cuisine. Meat, and meat alone, dominated the menu. Unlike Cuba, where mixing even chicken with your beans was a rarity, this richer country featured a menu spilling over with *carne*. Hones took full advantage, and soon the table was covered with tiny beer bottles and plates full of steak, sausage, chicken, and pork. Adrián and I had similar eating styles, wolfing down our food, but Hones had a more consistent, even dainty approach, carefully slicing up his meat into little triangular wedges and then drowning each wedge in hot sauce. He was still eating long after Adrián and I had finished.

I pointed my Polar Ice bottle at him. "You are amazed by my friend, yes?" I said to Adrián. "That he can eat so much and still live."

Adrián nodded vigorously. "Yes," he said. "He likes meat, so he will like my country very much."

I slept poorly, my stomach gurgling with *carne* and my mind anxious about ospreys. In the middle of the night the TV suddenly came on on its own, blaring—a bad omen. I was even more anxious by the time Adrián arrived at our hotel at eight. My main worry was the huge investment we had made in the trip, but a smaller worry was that Hones would think I had been Kathleening my way through my fall journeys. Sure, I had magically seen ospreys at every turn while traveling alone, but what would happen now that I had a witness?

We stopped to get gas and water before heading to Lago Valencia, "the lake of thirty ospreys." A liter of water was cheap, only 1000 bolivars, or about fifty cents, but a liter of gas was less than a tenth of that, 97 bolivars. We filled up the tank for less than two bucks. "No wonder they think we'll invade them," Hones said as he topped us off.

I was antsy on the drive out to the lake, and maybe a little unjustifiably irritated with Adrián. This was because at first our plan didn't really seem like much of a plan: we were to drive out to a little lakeside village and try to find the house of some guy who owned a boat, which we would rent. Since we didn't have the address, our strategy was to stop people we saw along the road and describe the guy and in that way hope we could find the house. The village of Punta Palmita had no center but was rather a long series of tin shacks built along the curving lakeside road, as if the road itself were a river mirroring the coastline. With no sidewalk between the shacks and the street, people sat at the edge of the dirt road, using it as their stoop. Kids played baseball with rocks and naked toddlers stumbled about and listless dogs barely moved when I beeped. We pulled up to one apparent storefront, where an old man stood behind a window in a wall and Polar Ice banners flew from the awning. We were about to get out and ask directions when Hones spoke up in the back seat.

"I think I see one," he said.

No sooner was I out of the car than I heard the *kew, kew, kew.* And not just from one direction. We stood on the side of the road where we had a view of the lake and the mountains behind us, and before long we were seeing ospreys everywhere.

That would be the last of my worries about Kathleening for the trip. The last of my worries about anything, really: the next few hours were Ospreypalooza.

Above us, toward the mountains, at least thirty birds spiraled upward: a kettle of turkey vultures, black vultures, and a half-dozen ospreys. Some were very light—*"Blancos,"* Adrián said —which meant they were Caribbean ospreys. But some were darker, and as they kettled, becoming specks in the sky, I suspected they were migrating through.

While I studied the kettle, Hones spotted several more ospreys out over the lake. One bird flew right over us with a small black fish in its talons. The talons of an osprey are unique among diurnal raptors, in that one of the toes can be reversed, which allows the birds to carry their fish like a torpedo in a torpedo bay, straight forward and aerodynamic. As the fish-carrying osprey sailed by, its long dark-brown primary feathers pointed like human fingers.

"Holy shit," Hones said, gesturing at the sky. Two more ospreys flew right toward us with similar black fish in their torpedo bays.

Adrián smiled at our smiles, perhaps understanding his immediate boost in status. As more and more birds flew past he was being instantly transformed, in my mind at least, from a kid who liked birds into an accomplished international ornithological guide.

"It's fucking osprey heaven," Hones said.

He was right. The small bay near where we had parked was the perfect habitat for the wintering birds. Surrounded by sugarcane fields and semideciduous forests, it was shallow and clearly burgeoning with those black fish. And this was just one small finger of a lake that extended almost 30 miles from Maracay to Valencia. By the time we climbed back in the car we had seen well over twenty birds.

Next came an unexpected lesson in just what the ospreys were having for breakfast. One of the villagers gave us directions to the house of the fisherman who would rent us the boat. We pulled in at a lopsided shack and parked in a yard full of broken-down boats and boat parts and trash where, improbably, banners for Polar Ice hung between two trees like Christmas lights. We haggled a little with the old fisherman about the price of the boat and got the rental down from fifty to forty dollars for the day, which was still a great price for him (one that could buy 200 gallons of gas). We asked if Hones could fish but were told that we could fish only with nets on this lake. Then the fisherman said that he would not be our guide. When we asked where we would find our guide, he pointed to a small path through the briars of his backyard.

We followed the path through the trees past an aboriginal burial sight and down to the water. There we found a small clearing where two women stood by a wooden table covered with small black fish. A boat, not much bigger than a rowboat but powered by an outboard Yamaha motor, floated just offshore, tied to a tree. It was filled with the same kind of fish. Two boys worked at unloading the boat with baskets, while a man at the long table filleted the fish, dropping the scraps down to a dog and two black cats that had stationed themselves below. Another boy, maybe fifteen years old, wandered in aimless circles, waving an ancient blunderbuss in the air. He was a scrawny kid with brown-stained teeth, and he occasionally pointed the gun and pretended to shoot. He kept up a kind of high-speed monologue as he waved the gun, and though I didn't understand much of what he said, I couldn't help but notice that every third word or so was *americano.*

Hones and I looked at the table piled with fish and then at each other. "Bingo," Hones said. This was what the ospreys had been carrying; this was what all these ospreys were dining on; this was what they were here for. Adrián told us the fish were tilapia, the same fish raised in the aquaculture farms in Colombia. They were heaped up in a great pile, their black eyes and white-tinged scales smeared with occasional red slashes of blood. Perfect osprey size and osprey weight, and apparently the lake was lousy with them.

The boat's owner had told us that for legal reasons we could not get on the boat here, so we said our goodbyes and walked back to the car to drive to a beach club called Bahía Paraíso, where we could be picked up at an official dock. When the boys were done unloading the fish and cleaning the blood off the boat, one of them would pilot it over and meet us at the dock. We drove the winding dirt road along the coast, staring up at elaborate thornbird nests, like spiny hand muffs, that hung down from trees above the road, sticks jutting every which way. Adrián pointed out a squirrel cuckoo that landed in the muscular bare branches of what he called a "naked Indian tree." We stopped for supplies at a little bodega in a steep hillside town called Gabrielle. The grocery store was quite literally a hole in the wall, though again bedecked with the ubiquitous Polar Ice banners, which draped from its roof across the road to another building. "The national flag," Hones said, which made Adrián laugh.

We bought a tin of tuna, rolls, and some plantain chips as well as a round of Polar Ices to celebrate the morning's triumph. While Hones and Adrián were putting the groceries in the car, I scanned the trees with my binoculars. Sure enough, an osprey was roosting on the steep wooded hillside above us. Before we left, it pushed off the branch and swooped down toward the lake. As it spread its wings its chest feathers gleamed in the morning sun like a blooming white flower.

Since it was Sunday morning, the club Bahía Paraíso was deserted. The only people around were waiters in stiff white shirts, and since they had nothing to do, they wandered down to the water to chat with us while we waited for the boat. One of the waiters was going to visit some family in Michigan in the coming summer and had a long talk with Hones about snow and the local Michigan beers. While we waited, a military boat pulled up, with six soldiers wearing what looked to be riot gear. Even more impressively, most of them had their machine guns pointed at a single prisoner, whose hands were cuffed behind his back. They ushered the prisoner off the boat and down the dock.

Once the prisoner was out of sight, the soldiers got into a long discussion with Adrián, who then came over and translated for us. "He says that because you are Americans, we will need to have a soldier come along on the boat with us," he said.

"To watch us?" I asked.

"No, no," he said. "For *your* safety. Sometimes there are bad people on the water. What you call . . ." He was at a loss for the word.

"Pirates," I suggested.

"Huh?" he said.

Then I remembered one of the words I'd learned in Cuba. *"Como Barba Azul,"* I said.

"Yes, yes, like Barba Azul," Adrián said, smiling.

"What?" Hones asked.

"Like Bluebeard," I said. "They are worried about pirates."

Hones shrugged and smiled, as if this notion were merely funny, not worrisome. But the soldiers apparently felt quite serious about it: they took our passports and wrote down all our information. As they were finishing, the small fishing boat we had rented pulled up at the dock. At the helm was the crazy kid with the brown-stained teeth who had been waving the gun and yelling about *americanos*. As soon as he landed, he launched into an animated discussion with the soldiers, and then Adrián joined in and they all started speaking so fast that I could catch only every tenth word. The upshot of it all was that we wouldn't have an armed escort after all: instead, one of the soldiers gave Adrián their phone number and Adrián agreed to call them on his cell phone if we ran into pirates. (It occurred to me that Adrián, being Adrián, might instead thumb out a text message: "Pirates approaching—come fast.")

The soldiers wished us luck, and a couple of the waiters gathered at the dock as we pushed off. *"Viva Michigan,"* Hones yelled to his new friend, and we puttered out through the algae-green edges of the lake and onto the dark water. The view was spectacular, the lake endless and island-filled and surrounded by mountains. We hadn't gone 50 yards when I pointed to a stand of dead trees in the water. The trees were filled with about a hundred cormorants, but one of the birds was shaped a little differently. This was the first osprey we saw on the lake, but not the last.

The boat took on water, and I noticed that while several of the holes in the bottom were caulked, one was simply jammed with a section of a sandal and a T-shirt, then polyurethaned over. The name of our crazy kid captain was Pelón, and he drove standing up, holding the throttle, wearing a white tank top and smoking a cigarette. He handled the boat expertly, scooting us along the west side of the lake, past marshes and avocado plantations and more naked Indian trees, stark and barkless. Water hyacinths clogged the shoreline, but we coasted in close anyway to inspect trees that at first looked like they were dotted with snow. The snow turned out to be flocks and flocks of egrets, roosting in leafless trees along with cormorants and anhingas. Pelón maneuvered the boat close below another tree that held twenty white egrets and a single brown-and-white osprey. Then we headed to the north end of the lake, where another stand of trees held about a dozen roosting ospreys. It was a textbook illustration of osprey wintering behavior—a bunch of birds amiably hanging out between bouts of easy fishing—and Adrián beamed with our success.

At first I'd been anxious about having the gun-wielding Pelón as our pilot, but he was nothing if not enthusiastic, and soon he got caught up in it too. Sometimes I spoke to him directly, but he just half smiled and stared at me uncomprehendingly. Then Adrián would have to translate my Spanish into real Spanish.

We followed a couple of the birds out to the middle of the lake, where they began fishing. Pelón gunned the engine so it was as if we were flying right along with them, directly below, staring up at their deep, slightly labored wingbeats. Never have I gotten a better sense of how the birds row through the air. From below, the white of their chests was the same gleaming white of the egrets, but it seemed even whiter because of the contrast with their dark feathers. The two birds joined a larger group diving for fish, and it was all happening so close that Hones and I put down our binocs and watched several dives with the naked eye. Before they dove, the birds hovered in the air, flapping their wings hard and looking like some primitive form of animation, the kind where you flip the pages of a book. We watched one young bird dive from 40 feet, catch a tilapia, shake its wings like a wet dog, rise, and then fly back to the north-end snags to eat and rest.

Pelón cut the motor in the middle of the lake, and we drifted while watching a great variety of dives: vertical plunges and stoops and perpendicular skims with talons held out front. The air was full of tension. At one point we saw two successful dives within ten seconds. I thought of the poor fish: while the ospreys bombed down from above, dozens of cormorants simultaneously tunneled below the water after the same quarry.

Watching the various dives, I found it easy to speculate about how Jaws was spending his winter: taking it easy for most of the day and occasionally flying out to spear a fish, using the techniques he had honed back on the Connecticut lakes in August. Wintertime, and the living was easy. Maybe even hooking up with a female, though nothing like the true breeding that would begin the next year. During these months the birds lived as Thoreau had recommended, "with a broad margin."

Pelón got into the spirit of things and, through Adrián, told us about an osprey nest that he claimed was on the hill behind his house. We were dubious, because ospreys were not supposed to nest here, just roost in trees. But then I wondered: Why the hell not? Why not, with the habitat so perfect? Why fly back to cold wet Cape Cod when you have perfect weather and a lake full of tilapia? When I asked this question out loud, Adrián provided at least part of an answer. Rainy season might be the key, he explained. From June to November fishing would not be quite so easy, since the lake's surface would be obscured by rain. And so the ospreys would move for the same reason they always moved—hunger. But that led right to another contradiction: if the fishing was bad, why did the first-year birds stay through the summer?

Clouds were gathering up in the mountains, but the sun blazed down on us, and the tops of my feet were burning around my sandal straps. When we'd finished watching the diving ospreys, we spent an hour or so buzzing around the small, hilly islands that rose in the middle of Lago Valencia. Pelón wasn't exactly what you'd call an environmentalist, and he drove fast and close to shore, startling the birds and sending clouds of herons—great blues and tricoloreds and greens and little blues —and egrets and ospreys flying off before us. Bird-lovers as a rule don't want to scare a roosting bird. Since energy expenditure is so much a part of the game of survival, a person who lets his dog run on a beach, for instance, might be tipping the scales against the plovers that the dog chases, particularly during nesting season. But when Hadley chased the gulls back on Wrightsville Beach I didn't worry, since those gulls were fat and bloated and dined on human scraps and garbage all winter, along with the abundant fish. Likewise, I could now rationalize that these birds were living off the fat of the land: all we were really doing was briefly interrupting their afternoon siesta, and as soon as we passed they flew back to their branches.

Whatever my rationalization, the most obvious thing about what we were doing was that it was fun. Maybe there is an innate pleasure in moving fast and seeing a lot. As Pelón cut closer to the edge of one of the islands, dozens of species flew up in great numbers and variety, and the four of us could have easily yelled out Hadley's war cry: "Fly, birds, fly!"

As it was, Hones called out the ospreys he saw as we flew along: "There's one in the branch and one flying off and another fishing..." We laughed as the day's osprey count passed one hundred. This happened near a small island called El Burro, which had formerly been a prison, and sure enough, our one hundredth osprey stood guard nobly atop an abandoned gun tower. By the time we stopped for lunch in the shade of a giant fig tree on the lee side of La Tortuga, or Turtle Island, we'd counted 116 ospreys, by far the most I'd ever seen in a day.

We tied the boat to the thick fig roots, which bulged like tendons below a canopy of leaves stained white with guano. Adrián cut the tuna tin open with his knife and Hones spread the fish on rolls, while I stuck to the plantain chips. After lunch Pelón and Hones smoked cigarettes and I lay down in the bow and stared up through the branches of the tree. Water lapped against the hull, and shadows and light pulsated on the branches of the fig. No sooner had I thought, *Hey, I might be able to see an osprey just by lying here* than number 117 landed in a tree above us. Then another osprey, 118, flew by, dipping its feet in the water and skimming along, not to fish, apparently, but just to cool off or, as Hones suggested, to clean off its talons. Before we left our lunch spot we'd also seen an oriole blackbird with a wild yellow chest, a caracara with a buff chest, and, best of all, a wattled jacana, or Jesus bird, walking on top of the hyacinths with ridiculously large feet.

On the way back to Bahía Paraíso I noticed another kettle of ospreys rising up toward the clouds. At first we thought they were fishing, like the birds we'd watched earlier, but then they lifted almost out of sight. It occurred to me that they were probably migrating, using Lago Valencia as a stopover point. To these birds, flying north from southern Venezuela or Brazil or points even farther south, this lake must have looked just like it does on the map: a great bull's-eye of fresh water—the largest and most obvious refueling point before they made their ocean journey. What halfway intelligent osprey wouldn't stop here for the night, or at least pick up a lunch to go? Most likely the birds we were seeing were a mix: for some this was their winter home, while others were just passing through.

Using the results of satellite tracking, Rob Bierregaard had guessed that the Guajira Pennisula was one of the main routes into and out of South America, but here, not 500 miles east, was another branch of the osprey highway. Later, when I e-mailed Alan Poole to tease him about his needle-in-the-haystack comment, I estimated—I think conservatively—that there were well over six hundred ospreys on Lago Valencia. We'd covered only a small section of the lake, after all, and by the time we turned toward the Bahía Paraíso we'd seen over 120 birds. On the way back we passed a few more snags and several more fishing birds to get the count to 133.

We tipped Pelón on top of the forty bucks and he apologized to Hones about not being able to fish. Through Adrián, Hones said, "It was like a day of fishing where you catch over a hundred." I thought of John, the boat captain back in Hertford, North Carolina, and his line about how looking for ospreys was like "fishing the sky."

The beach club, which had been asleep that morning, was now wide awake. Venezuelan families swam and played volleyball and danced and crowded the outdoor bars. We retreated to a table below a thatched roof, where our waiter, who turned out to be Hones's Michigan friend, brought us six Polar Ices, two each for starters. Next to us sat a couple of the soldiers from the morning, machine guns resting against the table, and they held up their own beers in greeting. Michigan disappeared and returned with a heaping mountain of barbecued beef and chorizo sausage. You could see Hones lathering at the sight, but before we dug in, Adrián held up his first tiny beer and proposed a toast.

"El día de ciento treinta y tres águilas," he said.

CHAPTER TEN

THE RIVER NORTH

Of course it occurred to me that after that one full day on Lago Valencia, I could have flown home and called the trip a success. The reason for the journey to Venezuela had been to see how ospreys lived in winter, and our ride around the lake had certainly helped me fill in that missing piece of the year. If I had been a scientist, the sensible thing to do would have been to return to Lago Valencia each day we were there, counting birds and studying the population (indeed, that was what Alan Poole urged me to do over e-mail). But I wasn't a scientist and was curious about other kinds of wintering habitats. So we got up early the next day and drove three hours west and north into the province of Falcon and the town of Chichiriviche.

The road followed the north side of the lake, and we had to resist the temptation to stop to watch the birds. But we stuck to the plan and soon found ourselves cutting through the unpleasant industrial city of Valencia and up into the mountains. On the way we got caught behind several huge, lumbering trucks. These trucks had signs on their backs that said CARGA LARGA instead of WIDE LOAD. And that's what I began calling Hones, to Adrián's delight, a nickname that stuck for the rest of the trip. He didn't mind the name, of course, and joyfully fulfilled it by daintily devouring four shark empanadas at a roadside stand on the other side of the mountains.

Near Chichiriviche we pulled into the local ranger station,

which was under the auspices of the Ministry of Environment
and Natural Resources, the same governmental branch that
Adrián worked for. Once again Adrián's connections with the
locals made all the difference. We loitered at the ranger station
for a while, until a few men who were at least loosely affiliated
with the station hooked up a small outboard to a trailer and had
us follow them down to a landing with a broken-down dock. A
man named Alfredo piloted us along a winding river through a
mangrove swamp, which he told us would lead out into the Gulf
of Cuare and eventually, if we kept going, the Caribbean. We'd
put in in open water, but soon we disappeared into a watery path
below mangrove branches that cantilevered above us. The roof of
branches formed such a tight tunnel that only occasional shafts
of sunlight broke through, the beams reflecting upward in the
dark water. We traveled this way for fifteen minutes or so, until
the tunnel opened up into the gulf and the sun returned, dap-
pling the limbs of trees and burning the tops of my legs. It was
great habitat for roosting ibises (which we saw) and American
crocodiles (which we didn't). Dozens of frigatebirds fought high
in the sky, which was a little like watching a series of wrestling
matches between children's kites. We also saw storks and herons,
but the stars were the scarlet ibises soaring overhead, birds that
were so red they looked as if they'd been set afire. For wings they
stuck out diaphanous flames, and we laughed out loud at their
unreal color.

Of course, inevitably, we saw ospreys. Around ten that day,
most of them roosting on mangroves in this saltwater habitat,
quite different from the lake the day before. But what wasn't
different was the relative indolence of the osprey lifestyle and the
ease with which they caught fish. The day had the same basic
bird rhythm: lots of hanging out punctuated by the occasional
dive, which seemed motivated by boredom as much as by hunger.

In fact, as if in confirmation of this thought, many of the dives had a high degree of difficulty. One was particularly flamboyant: a steep spiraling approach with a sudden veer that turned it into a kind of horizontal skim dive, like the one by the bird we'd seen wetting its talons the day before. Hones and I clapped in recognition of this stunning athletic moment. Adrián, as usual, smiled his slightly bemused but proud smile.

The bird wasn't the only one to have a successful fishing day: As soon as we got out on the bay, Alfredo pointed at Hones's rod and said, *"Pesca ahora."* Hones dropped a line over while I watched for ospreys, and so we simultaneously trolled both sky and water. Before long Hones had caught two fish, both jacks with yellow tails. I knew this would keep him happy for the rest of the day. Once he'd caught and released the second one, he put the rod away and we steamed across the bay to the south side, where sheer limestone cliffs shot up hundreds of feet in the air. There we pulled into a small cove that Alfredo told us was called the Cave of Saints. Thousands of crosses and statuettes and lit candles rested on ledges of rock, flames reflecting shadows on limestone and water dripping from white-stained walls, occasionally sizzling in the small fires. The statues were, predictably, of Mary, Joseph, Jesus, and various local saints I didn't know, but also of Charlie Chan and Marilyn Monroe. As well as saints and celebrities, Polar Ice bottles and baseball caps decorated the crevices and ledges. Alfredo beached the boat on a small sandy shore at the back of the cave, below a single enormous mangrove. We climbed out, and while the others explored on foot, I swam out in the clear water below the cliffs and statues and burning candles. When we were done with the saints we explored the next cave over, called the Indian Cave, climbing through a petroglyph-covered tunnel into an amphitheater that reached up 800 feet.

Once we got back to shore, we invited Alfredo to dinner. We ate outside, at a small restaurant in Chichiriviche, and decided to emulate the ospreys and be piscivorous, forgoing *carne* for the night. Hones's meat withdrawal was alleviated by the bottle of Santa Teresa rum that we bought and took back to the hotel to drink. But sadly for Adrián, we all slept in the same small room. During an earlier trip to Belize, Nina had claimed that the volume of Hones's snoring was competitive with mine, which she had previously considered the world's loudest. Poor Adrián got to sleep in the bed between us, our snores blasting in stereo.

The next day was more or less ruined by another one of Adrián's local contacts, a guy named Waldo, who also worked for the Ministry of Environment and Natural Resources. Hones called him "the mayor of Chichiriviche," since he seemed to stop and shake everyone's hand and slap his back when we walked down the main street of town. But I didn't like him from the start. He had a short but extremely wide frame that had just crossed the border into fat, and something of the bullying manner of a junior high school gym teacher. He more or less hijacked us into spending the day on the floodplain, slamming and bottoming out our rental car along rutted nonroads in search of nonexistent ospreys. At one point he asked to look through my binoculars, and that was the last I saw of them for over an hour. When I finally took them back, he turned around and grabbed Adrián's binocs right off his neck. Adrián responded with a shrug and the usual bemused smile. My mood wasn't helped by the fact that it was my anniversary; I knew that Nina wasn't thinking particularly warm thoughts about her AWOL husband. Our grand total for the day was one sickly looking osprey flying over an impounded puddle of a pond.

On the other hand, we saw vermilion flycatchers and pink flamingos that flew like Day-Glo sticks with wings, not to mention a jaguarundi, a wild black cat, slithering across the road. And at one point we witnessed the upside of Waldo's aggressiveness, when he noticed what he thought were flamingo poachers and wouldn't leave the area until he was sure they were not. He told us that local flamingo poachers were ugly sorts and that they would sometimes go so far as to hang fish hooks off kites to snare the flying birds.

But despite some bright moments, the best part of the day was its end. On the way back to our cheap hotel we stopped at a large tourist hotel to pay to use its Internet access. We did this so I could show Adrián Rob Bierregaard's website, but while doing so I remembered something that I had somehow forgotten. I'd been so caught up in my adventures that I had misplaced an important piece of information: it had been in the very state we were now in, Falcon, that Elsie had landed after her trip down from Puerto Rico, and in this very state that she had suddenly disappeared, her radio gone dead. I sent Rob Bierregaard an e-mail marked "Urgent" asking him for Elsie's last known coordinates. To this point we had been following a seat-of-the-pants itinerary in Venezuela, deciding what we would do each morning. But as we drank our evening rum, I knew two things. One, I didn't want to see Waldo again, preferably ever. And two, it was time to track down Elsie.

At dawn we checked out and drove over to the fancy hotel to look for any e-mail. Sure enough, Rob, good guy and double agent that he was, had written back with Elsie's last known coordinates: 69.105 degrees west by 11.356 degrees north. These numbers determined the course of the day as Adrián plotted them out on a map. The spot wasn't too far, about three hours' drive away, though to get there we would have to double back over the previous day's turf, through the floodplain we'd visited with the bullying Waldo. After the plain we headed up into the hills, the road deteriorating as the world grew green. The homes became less shacklike and slummy and the steep hills were covered with palms; though I was a shore person, all in all this seemed a better place to live. A half-hour later Hones announced that he was "getting horny for caffeine." Adrián asked me to translate, but I declined, instead pulling over at a café in the little town of Capadre. Half the town was sitting outside the café, and everyone greeted the exotic, unkempt strangers with elaborate shows of affection. So much for the dangers of Venezuela.

A lush green hilltop rose above the town, an evergreen forest mixed with palms and cotton trees, and when an osprey came soaring over the hilltop I cried out *"Águila!"* to the amusement of the locals. But one man—the butcher, it turned out—came over and started a spirited discussion about the birds. He said that they had ospreys in Capadre year-round, *"siempre todos los años."* I told him that that meant some young birds were spending their first summers there.

As we continued northwest toward the town of Píritu and the coordinates Rob had sent us, I tried to imagine Elsie's last days. Here is what I came up with:

First of all, Elsie was a mature bird, no rookie, and had made this trip before. But the hurricanes, and the remnants of the hurricanes, had messed with her, blowing her west and then east. Perhaps it was all the chaotic weather that had led to her taking refuge on Hispaniola, spending sixteen days there. And perhaps it had crossed her now cross-wired osprey brain to forgo her traditional wintering ground and spend the next months in the perfectly suitable climate of Haiti. Until the urge to get home overpowered her. Until whatever it was triggered, or in this case retriggered, her, and she headed east through Puerto Rico until she ran out of land. When she finally did make the turn south,

she was farther east than any bird yet recorded. She would have
landed well east of Caracas if not for something, some midtrip
correction by her internal GPS, which sent her veering westward
over the last 100 miles of her cross-water flight.

For some unknown reason, many of the ospreys that have
been tracked by satellite have made their last Caribbean crossing
at night, a fact that was originally brought to my attention by
Paul Kerlinger in Cape May. At first I felt this contradicted
much of what I'd learned about the birds and their migration.
How could they avail themselves of solar power in the dark?
Over the winter I had called Keith Bildstein about this mystery,
and he had suggested that the birds were riding "sea thermals."
"I would have told you about them back in the bar," he said. "But
you only gave me five minutes." He described how trade winds
from the northeast blow south over the increasingly warm water
of the Caribbean as they move closer to the equator. This creates
a difference in temperature between the water and the relatively
cool air, just like the temperature difference over parking lots in
the Northeast, and the ospreys can lift on this rising air while
riding the favorable trade winds. And because the sea thermals
are dependent on *stored* solar energy, they are open around the
clock. (Think of how much more quickly a parking lot cools
than the ocean.)

These were the thermals Elsie rode as she flew through the
night and arrived in Venezuela wet, ragged, and ruffled. She
made landfall on the Gulf de Cuare and probably caught her first
good meal just about where Hones had caught his yellow jacks.
She rested there awhile, in that bay of blazing scarlet ibises and
candlelit limestone caves and overreaching mangroves. Then,
once she had gathered enough strength and was ready to continue, her senses—her internal compass and perhaps a magnetic
sense—told her that she was far to the east of where she usually

landed. So rather than heading directly south, she began to fly west over the floodplain we had just crossed. She flew through crowded skies, full of great flocks of flamingos and more scarlet ibises in loose military formations, and she would have dipped down into the many lakes to snack. But she didn't rest long, eager to escape the oppressive heat of the plain, and from the coast she flapped inland, following our morning route up over the moist forest and hills that vaguely resembled those she knew in New England. The peaks above Capadre would provide lift, so she could spiral up toward the sun and then gently glide down over the dry lowlands of cactus and dust. Perhaps she was harassed by the local caracaras, who played a kind of vulture role here, and was serenaded by the local cardinals, wildly pompadoured versions of the birds she knew from Martha's Vineyard.

Flying above this drier landscape, she would have grown hungry, hoping for a lunch to go, but the only water was a winding brown river—though winding might be an overstatement for its lazy meandering. The river was murky, but she kept above it for a while, traveling lower than she would have liked while hoping to catch sight of the brief flash that meant fish. The place was quiet compared to Hispaniola: a few more caracaras, some vultures, thrushlike songbirds, tropical mockingbirds, a heron or two hunting from the banks and the shallows. She might or might not have hazarded a dive into the murk.

And that was it. That was where my fiction ended. As we drove, hot on her trail, I couldn't pretend to solve the mystery of her demise. At exactly the point of her last coordinates, Hones, Adrián, and I were on the outskirts of a small village of the sort you see all over Venezuela—tin roofs, tin walls—though the place felt less impoverished than the coastal towns. It occurred to me that maybe it was her hunger, and the subsequent need to fly low over the murky river, that did her in. Certainly the residents of that town wouldn't feel any qualms about shooting a big, low-flying bird to put in a pot with the rice. Still, meat wasn't exactly scarce, and as we stopped to talk to people along the street, everyone expressed surprise at the idea of shooting an *águila*, not for moral reasons but simply because it didn't seem like a very traditional—or tasty—meal.

I had grown used to getting ridiculously lucky, so as we pulled up to a bunch of mechanics working outside, I imagined the *jefe* replying to my query with *"Sí, como no!"* and, after heading into his shop, emerging holding an osprey upside down by the ankles, the bird complete with backpack and antenna. But instead the boss just snarled and said in gruff Spanish, "I don't look at the sky." We talked to other people and searched the fields, but Elsie's death remained a mystery. I still liked to think that it wasn't a death at all but a malfunction of her radio and that maybe her journey had continued first west and then south —maybe right now she was roosting in the thick canopy of the rainforest in her usual winter haunt in the branches of a strangler fig, occasionally dipping down to snare a *pavón*, or peacock bass.

But that was the happy ending. The sad endings included shooting, which, even if disdained by the locals, was still a common cause of death for ospreys in South America, or being hit by a car or truck (no doubt a *carga larga*).

Hones, for one, didn't buy the last notion. "How often do you see them flying low over a road in the States?" he said. "Not often. And down here there are hardly any cars on the road to hit her, even if she did fly low."

On our drive back from Píritu, he pointed south toward a more likely culprit, huge electric pylons strung with power lines. I nodded: I knew for a fact that back in Massachusetts, sometimes up to a dozen ospreys a year are lost to electrocution when they hit or land on power lines during rains. The birds act as gi-

ant feathery conductors, and I had seen gruesome pictures of
fried ospreys hanging from the wires. Of the choices for Elsie's
end, if it was her end, this seemed to me the most probable. Flying low to fish and landing on or colliding with a wire, a shock
followed by a gradual dying descent to the other side, the north
side of the road, where her last signal came from and where she
came to her final rest in this unfamiliar land.

It was a day of marathon driving.

The night before, over another bottle of Santa Teresa rum
and lime, Adrián had suggested that we either head northwest to
follow Elsie's trail or make the long drive south into the plains,
Los Llanos, to see another habitat at the El Pao dam. Now, after
our morning hunt for Elsie, I said I wanted it all: we would attempt the trip to Los Llanos before sunset. It was a preposter-
ously long drive, but if I expected a mutiny, I didn't get one.
Adrián said "*Sí,* is fine." (As Hones would later say, Adrián was
so accommodating that he would have said, "*Sí,* is fine" if I had
suggested driving off a cliff.) As for Hones, he just nodded. Then
he pointed out hopefully that this meant we would pass the
roadside stand where he had bought the four shark empanadas.

By the time we reached the empanada shack at the foot of the
mountains, I had already driven for more than four hours that
day. After eating, we puttered up the mountain, trapped behind
carga largas, and then down the other side, cutting back through
the city of Valencia before heading south to the plains. I liked
Valencia even less this time, and for an hour we were caught in
standstill traffic. As we sat there, Hones read from the Lonely
Planet guide about the city we were trapped in:

> It had not yet reached its seventh anniversary when Lope de
> Aguirre, the infamous adventurer obsessed with finding El
> Dorado, sacked the town and burned it to the ground. Twenty

years later the not-yet-fully-recovered town was razed by Carib Indians. Then in 1667 the town was seized and destroyed again, this time by French pirates. The town's proximity to Lago Valencia doesn't help either. The disease-breeding marshes brought about smallpox epidemics that decimated the population and scared away many survivors. Then in 1812, a devastating earthquake shook the Andean shell, leaving Valencia in ruins yet again.

Hones read on for another paragraph or two of slaughter, disease, and disaster, bringing the town's history almost up to the modern day, but then the traffic eased and we began to escape the poor doomed city. I'd spent a decade driving in Boston, but even that couldn't prepare me for the Venezuelan highway. The drivers were every bit as chaotic as they were aggressive, and *carga largas* would suddenly switch lanes with no indication while pedestrians ran suddenly across the road. People drove at two speeds, unbearably slow or terrifyingly fast. Hones again read from the guide: "Officially, traffic coming from the right has priority. In practice, however, it seems that right-of-way depends on the size of the vehicle rather than regulations."

As we left behind the blighted environs of Valencia, I felt the joy of release. Gradually the land dropped away and we wound down into Los Llanos, the hot region of savannas and rivers that makes up over a third of the country's enormous land area. I imagined that these grasslands were something like the spot where Jaws was spending the winter, with water amid an almost desert dryness. The humps of the hills browned, and along the roadsides *artesanos* sold beautiful earthen pots. Around mid-afternoon we pulled over for cheap gas and a round of Polar Ices, and then we made the interminable trek east through a military zone to the El Pao dam.

Throughout the trip we had been stopped frequently at roadblocks called *puntas de control,* where armed guards peered into the car before—so far at least—waving us on. As we drove through the military zone the *puntas* came more frequently, and, my nerves frayed from driving, I was growing tired of men in fatigues pointing machine guns at me. I'd had it by the time we finally reached the town of El Pao, at around four, and, ten minutes later, the El Pao dam. My spirits lifted a little when we pulled up to the small park on top of the dam, stepped out of the car into the blazing heat, and Hones spotted an osprey flying toward us, then another. But despite this initial lift, our overall reaction to El Pao was disappointment. The gates to the park were locked, and it took Adrián fifteen minutes to convince the *jefe* to let us inside. Even then, the prospects were less than spectacular. Though it was a beautiful place, a peninsula jutting out into a huge lake, the sun blazed so hot that standing still meant becoming soaked in sweat. When we scanned the opposite shore of the reservoir, we identified three ospreys roosting in trees—a large population by New England standards but scant compared to our high standards. We were spoiled, and I now wished we had just headed back to osprey-filled Lake Valencia.

Over the next twenty minutes, I halfheartedly looked for birds, Hones scoured the shore and dreamed of fishing, and Adrián chatted up the *jefe* before returning to the shade to punch out a message or two on his phone. The ospreys were every bit as listless as we were. Soon Hones and I met and agreed the place was kind of a bust. We decided to give it another ten minutes before making the long drive back to Maracay.

But then, for whatever reason—maybe because we would have felt foolish driving for eight hours to spend just half an hour there—we stayed. The park served as a kayaking camp for kids, and there were large stands for the spectators of kayak races, where we all met to sit in the shade. Hones smoked a cigarette and I watched as an osprey lazily dipped into the water to cool off and then circled back to its roost. We were all, birds and men, lazy, hot, not eager to move. Hones mentioned that he sure wished he could drop a line in the water, so Adrián wandered over to the *jefe* and then wandered back and told Hones it was fine to fish. As Hones and Adrián headed to the car to get the rods and some Polar Ices, I walked down the peninsula. While Lago Valencia was much more dramatic and osprey-dense, El Pao also gave a pretty good sense of what wintertime is like for an osprey: a lot of sitting around, a few siestas, some dipping in the water, an occasional spasm of fishing. The dog days of winter.

Things picked up when the sun dropped. On his first cast Hones caught a strange yellow fish, a type of *pavón*. Not long after, the osprey I'd been watching left its branch and began a slow descent toward the water, then a kind of horizontal skimming flight that turned into a sudden dive, from which it came up with a fish of its own. The skies reddened the trees and the lake held their bloody reflections. The *jefe* had said to Adrián that fishermen usually came to this lake before the sun came up and right after dark, and dusk seemed to energize the ospreys too. Before long there were three crisscrossing out on the lake. Meanwhile, teenagers, future shortstops by the look of it, slung a baseball around artfully in the near dark, and iguanas climbed the trees.

I headed back to Hones to bum a couple of cigarettes and smoked the first while walking out to the peninsula's farthest point. One of the birds soon flapped out to where I stood, its wingbeats deep, the wings crooked at the wrist. On the ride to the dam Adrián had said that when he studied the harpy eagle he became very fond of its qualities, especially its reliability and sheer power. I smoked the second cigarette and thought of the osprey qualities I loved: the clarity of vision, the near monomania for fish, the obviousness and transparency, the need to be close to water. Not to mention the sheer commitment. I thought again of the many stories, only some apocryphal, about ospreys being dragged down after sinking their talons in fish too large to handle, being pulled under like feathery Ahabs.

I felt lucky to have stumbled on this particular bird as my obsession. I had always been calmed by watching ospreys; for me, the birds worked better than Prozac. It is easy enough to let the world crush down on you; anyone can see that we live in dire times, with a ravaged environment and a political world that gives little reason not to be depressed. Earlier, as I had driven through the numerous *puntos de control,* I had indulged in a dark fantasy where such things would come soon to the United States. Maybe, maybe not, but it was no longer as inconceivable as it had been only a few years ago. *Control* was the issue. Always the issue. Keeping people from moving freely. *Tracking* them.

In contrast, the ospreys were all about movement, even the poor sad telemetry ospreys. And when I was with the birds, I felt briefly connected to something deeper than the political, something beyond or below the *puntas de control.* Something animal and physical. I had ospreys to thank for that.

I stared at the three adult birds flying over the reservoir and realized that these were late birds. Soon they would have to stir and leave this place of easy living and begin their journey north. If ospreys had a bumper sticker, it would be *We move for food.* It was all about hunger, after all—or was it? Maybe, as Keith Bildstein suggested, it wasn't quite that simple. *We move because we were built to move. Hey, look at these wings—wouldn't you move too? We move because we* can.

As I finished my second cigarette it occurred to me that maybe I should take up smoking, which, combined with birdwatching, seemed reliably to provide these moments of lift for me. But I was already feeling a tobacco hangover by the time I got back to Hones and Adrián. The dragonflies were out and Hones was in heaven, having caught two more fish: a strange-looking creature called a horseface and a guabina. He excitedly explained that this was a *little* guabina, and that the big ones could grow up to forty pounds and sometimes ate ducks and lizards. It was dark now, and after he threw the last fish back, we trudged to the car, anticipating the long drive to Maracay.

The hills out of Los Llanos were alive with *carga largas*. We puttered behind them as they lumbered uphill, blocking the road ahead. I made occasional life-threatening dashes in attempts to pass them, but all in all it was a slow and ugly trip. At one point we pulled over and ate huge steaks—it seemed we hadn't seen a vegetable in a week, and I wondered aloud whether Venezuelans got scurvy. Hones, for one, wasn't worried. He smothered his steak in a green sauce called guasacaca he'd become addicted to and then belched with delight. After the meal we were even more tired, but there was no choice but to drive on. We arrived bleary-eyed back in Maracay well after midnight.

As with eating, so with life: I was more of a sprinter, Hones an endurance man. While I sagged, dragging myself out of bed the next morning, he was ready for more, a shaggy, eager, middle-aged puppy. He had been patient with all my osprey-watching but had been itching to get up to the cloud forest. I was tired and had seen enough birds and so I gave in, agreeing to spend the day in the mountains. But on the way there we checked in at our old site on Lago Valencia, the site of our first-day glory. Attempting to recreate the moment, we pulled over by the road at the same place where Hones had spotted the first osprey. Mist enshrouded the lake, but soon enough an osprey, a large female, cut through the mist with a fish—a tilapia, no doubt—and alighted on a

branch just 100 feet up the bank above the road. She was a striking bird, with a freckled necklace on her chest and white epaulets
on her shoulders. She sat there on the limb, in no hurry to eat,
her tail feathers crossed like the scabbards of swords. When she
finally began to tear apart the fish, the inside of her mouth shone
bright red, and it occurred to me, not for the first time, that this
would all be a different, gruesome story from the fish's point of
view. It was a terrible way to die, to be almost fully asphyxiated
before the stabbing began. Then, if you lived long enough, you
got to experience being pulled apart.

The osprey took its time with the killing, casually picking at
the fish, in no particular rush on this hot morning. Through the
scope my view was made rubbery by a garbage fire burning by the
side of the road. After a while a young teacher came along with
several of his students, barely teenagers, and they all took turns
looking through the scope. Before the teacher left I teased him
about his Yankees cap, gloating a little as a Red Sox fan. He said
something in Spanish that I only half understood, so I asked
Adrián to translate. "He says, 'Boston will never win again.'"
Hones and I nodded, the two of us New Englanders, one born,
one adopted, but both fatalists, sure that he was right.

After the teacher and kids left, I watched for over half an
hour as the female osprey went about methodically devouring its
breakfast, paused to look around for a while, and then spent another twenty minutes finishing up.

"It eats more like Hones than you or me," I said to Adrián.
"No comida rapida."

Adrián laughed at this, just as he laughed whenever I referred
to Hones's eating habits. *"Sí,"* he said. *"Muy despacio."*

These would be the last slow days for a while for this adult
bird. Very soon her life would speed up. Something would prod
her from inside, or, perhaps better put, something in the world

—sunlight, weather—would prompt something in her, and it would be time to move. As a rule, females return to their nests a few days later than males, who are usually there waiting for them on their return. Ospreys, like eagles, are said to mate for life, but they don't migrate or winter together, taking separate vacations before hooking up again each spring. Perhaps, however, as we learn more we will find a few exceptions to this rule, couples who do spend the whole year together. It wouldn't entirely shock me, given how individual some of the other migration behaviors were proving to be.

When the female had finished her languorous meal, we climbed into the car and headed into the mountains. After we passed Rancho Grande the hills turned steep and narrow, which didn't keep *carga largas* from bombing up and down. I was exhausted from driving the day before, and my mood quickly soured. On the way down the other side of the mountain, heading out of the cloud forest toward the shore, we stopped at a roadside restaurant for empanadas. I took one bite and pushed the food away from me like a petulant child.

"I need to take a fucking nap," I said.

Adrián looked puzzled, in his bemused, smiley way. Hones, however, knew me almost as well as my wife did.

"If he doesn't rest, he will kill someone," he said. "Probably me."

We wound down out of the foothills to the beach. Though the vista was spectacular, it wasn't particularly private, and there was no place to get away from the crowds. But Hones had a brainstorm. He ran over to a local merchant and rented a kind of one-person cabana, a beach awning that Adrián called a *toldo.* When he came back from talking to the man, he pointed at the awning. "It's all yours, Your Highness," he said. "On me."

I staggered over to the *toldo,* lay down on the sand, and slept hard in the shade. While I snoozed, Hones and Adrián walked the beach, watching frigatebirds and boobies and hoping to see some ospreys heading north. Forty minutes later I woke re-freshed, reinvigorated, a new man, and went for a swim below the diving birds. Soon we were driving back up a mountain and down the other side to Rancho Grande.

We were there so that Hones could bird-watch in the jungle, but the cloud cover made it hard to see. We stood on top of the great abandoned hotel turned biological station as mist blew be-low and bats zipped through the glassless windows.

The week had exhausted me. We were leaving the next day, but in my mind the trip was already over. I thought I had nothing more to learn, that my Herzogian jungle adventure was over, but I was wrong. In fact, what happened next seemed to spring more from the imagination of a George Lucas or Steven Spielberg than a Werner Herzog.

Hones and I had come to watch birds, but instead we stood there fascinated by bats: dozens of them, zipping in and out of the broken windows, moving so fast that they looked as if they were being sucked into a vacuum. While we watched, Adrián talked to an older man near the quarters for the resident scien-tists, and when we strolled over he introduced the man as the caretaker, Juan. Juan was speaking rapidly and gesturing to Adrián, waving a self-rolled cigarette like a conductor's wand in front of his chest. I didn't like the looks of him at first, maybe just because I was still a little cranky, but then Adrián told me that Juan had been caretaker of the place for more than thirty years, and Juan pressed a picture into my hands. The picture showed a woman holding an immature osprey that had been caught in a mist net, a thin, gauzy net that scientists use to catch birds so they can weigh and band and release them. I asked Juan where the bird had been caught, and he began speaking rapidly again while pointing to the west with his cigarette.

Adrián translated: "He says it was caught in the notch in the mountains where all the birds fly through. Over there, just a few hundred yards away. In October every year he watches the ospreys fly through this gap and then float down to the lake." Adrián pointed toward Lago Valencia, laid out as always like a map far below us.

It was almost dark and it was time to go, to end our trip. But this was too good. We thanked Juan and headed directly to the gap. We walked down the hill from Rancho Grande, out the main entrance, and up the mountain road to a small sign that marked the opening of the trail to the gap. The grasses were long and wet, the trail untrampled and muddy. Despite sinking to our shins, we made our way up to the notch just before darkness settled. From the notch you could look south to Lago Valencia or north to the Caribbean beach where I'd swum earlier.

"This is by far the lowest point in these mountains," Adrián said.

At just that moment, something shot by our heads. And then something else, another of whatever it was, darting and moving fast—fast like the bats we had watched, but sturdier and wedge-shaped.

"Nighthawks," Adrián said. "Nacunda nighthawks."

Of course. All birds would use this notch in the mountains to travel from one side to the other. A low point, particularly a low point dramatically lower than the surrounding peaks, would act as a funnel for birds. Which meant that this would be part of the osprey highway, in fact would be a kind of natural tollbooth on that highway.

Adrián, Hones, and I all realized this at about the same time. I wanted to laugh out loud. Life had taken on all the subtlety of a *Scooby-Doo* episode. Here we were on our last night in Maracay and a gnarled old caretaker had shown us a sepia-toned picture—well, not really sepia-toned, but old and close enough—

and pointed toward a gap that turned out to be part of the osprey river. We said nothing to one another, but in that moment we could all see it. The exhausted birds, having just flown across the Caribbean, would arrive on the beach in late September and October, and after resting and feeding at the seashore, they would fly up through this notch in the mountains and then glide down to their winter home on Lago Valencia, where hundreds of other ospreys waited. And now, in spring, they would fly back up to this notch and back to the sea, the first leg of their trip northward.

As Venezuela goes, so go the birds.

That sounds nice, but what does it mean? It means that with a phenomenon like migration, we can't just conserve a place, we need to conserve a process. The flyways that migrating birds follow cross state and national lines, and the birds depend on many stops along the way. And so as Venezuela goes, as Cuba goes, as Cape Cod goes, as Carolina goes, so go the birds. If Fidel Castro or Jeb Bush, say, declared osprey hunting legal, or even encouraged it, in their respective provinces, then not just the Cuban and Floridian birds would be wiped out, but the Venezuelan and New England birds too.

Which makes us all responsible, all linked by the chain of migration. Another example is DDT. Although the banning of DDT was a great environmental victory in the United States, ospreys still gather the deadly chemical in their lymphatic systems each year. This is because similar victories did not occur in Latin America, and the chemical, like the birds, does not respect international borders. Though we often seem loath to admit it, the fact that our country is part of a larger world is undeniable.

Migration is the real worldwide web, the closest thing that nature has to connecting the entire planet. "Bird migration is the one truly unifying phenomenon in the world," writes Scott Weidensaul in *Living on the Wind*, "stitching the continents together in a way that even the great weather systems, which roar out from the poles but fizzle at the equator, fail to do." But if the stitches are ripped in one place, the whole is easily torn.

The next day we fought our way back through the god-awful rush hour of Caracas, just making the plane. From Caracas we flew north along the classic osprey route, over the 300-mile open-water leg and then over the western tip of Haiti and the eastern end of Cuba, almost directly over Freddy and La Gran Piedra. From there it was up over Florida to Atlanta, where Hones and I said goodbye, and then, for me, on to North Carolina.

Back at home, I had the usual catching up to do. That was the by-now-established rhythm of the year: intense bursts of travel followed by almost equally intense bursts of making up for what I'd missed. This included family time: Nina, Hadley, and I spent the whole weekend together. On Sunday we went to a park near our house called Airlie Gardens with some other professors and their families. I was walking ahead of the group down one of the garden paths with Hadley on my shoulders when I heard the familiar high-pitched cry. She knew the sound too, and when I pointed she yelled out, "Osprey!" We looked up at a beautiful natural nest in the crook of a tree. The pair had obviously just returned from their winter away and were setting about spring's first business: repairing and bolstering last year's nest. The male flew off and returned with an oversized stick while the female padded the nest's bowl with Spanish moss. When Nina and the others caught up to us, I turned ornithological lecturer, going on about the birds until my listeners began to look uneasy.

A week later, on my birthday, Hadley and I drove north to the town of Hampstead and the house of a local birder, Jack Steiner. Jack wasn't at home but had left instructions to roam his property freely. From the dock behind his house we watched an extremely white-headed osprey try to drive a pelican away from the water below its nest, but while the osprey dove again and again, the pelican just floated serenely, a feathered Buddha, calm and unruffled. We also saw a berry tree fill up with cedar waxwings, their crowns golden yellow in the sun. But the sight of the day was two fledgling great horned owls sitting on a branch near their nest. They looked like twins, leaning in close and glued to each other, though one kept its eyes open and the other closed. From the waist down their feathers were great fluffy boas, and when I carried Hadley close, the open-eyed one let out sharp clicks of warning. The whole way home Hadley clicked and hooted in imitation.

For the ospreys at Airlie Gardens and Hampstead it was a family time of year, a time of both reunion and preparation for the coming of young later in the spring. For me it was also a family time. Two days after visiting Hampstead I was in flight again, but this time I wasn't going it alone. On March 17, Nina, Hadley, and I flew to Sanibel Island, off the coast of Florida. When my earlier book on ospreys had come out, the first talk I had given was in Sanibel, at the annual meeting of the International Osprey Foundation. At that time we had stayed at the home of the foundation's ever-generous president, Tim Gardner, and this time he did us one better: he let us use the home of a friend of his who was away, a house on the water with a bald eagle nest out back and ospreys all around. We were in paradise, and when Hadley discovered the pool in the backyard, we couldn't keep her out of it. "Water," she yelled over and over, "Water," until we were worried that she would sneak out and drown while we were sleeping.

On our first night we went out to eat at a locally famous restaurant called the Bubble House and sat next to a couple named Len and Sam Foster. When Hadley melted down during dinner, we apologized, and they lied nicely: "Oh, she's fine." Then Sam asked us what we were doing on Sanibel. When I replied, they smiled at each other. Their boat, it turned out, had been built in our island town in North Carolina and had been christened *Pandion*, as in *Pandion haliaetus*, the scientific name for the osprey. They had just been to the Players Golf Championship, where ospreys had a nest on the thirteenth green. They described seeing Tiger Woods concentrating over a putt but then breaking out of his stance and scowling at the loud *kew, kew, kew.*

On the first day in Sanibel I pushed off from our house and kayaked down the tidal river in the backyard. Light pulsed on the trees, the fish were jumping high, and the male bald eagle soared above me, its head that unmistakable, vibrant white. One of the reasons I had come to Sanibel was that Florida was a kind of missing link in my osprey year, but another was to survey the damage from Hurricane Charley. Sanibel had taken a direct hit, with winds up to 140 mph, and friends of Tim Gardner's who had decided to ride it out on the island described sounds like rifle shots as branch after branch cracked. The ospreys, according to Tim, had moved lower and lower in the trees, until they hunkered down near the ground in the brush. But no amount of hunkering could protect them. After the storm, Tim hadn't found any osprey corpses, but all 118 nests on the island had been blown down. The remarkable thing was the birds' resilience: those that had lived through the hurricane had come back to rebuild on the same spots.

Or approximately the same spots. The coast, which had been dense and jungle-lush when I last visited, now looked like a war zone full of injured and dead trees. The few remaining trees jutted up like broken spars above the chaos on the ground. The

Australian pines, which were not really pines at all but shallow-rooted plants, had been pulled right out of the ground, and the slash pines hadn't fared much better. The only thing I could compare it to was Monkey River Town, a Belizean beach village I'd visited where the surrounding rainforest canopy was ripped apart by a hurricane, destroying all the howler monkey habitat. But as I floated down the estuary, the resilience that Tim had spoken of was much in evidence. Only six months later the osprey population was coming back strong: I counted six, seven, eight, nine new osprey nests. It occurred to me that the single spars of the remaining trees might even make *better* places for their homes. After all, ospreys were birds that didn't like to be hemmed in, that preferred a nesting spot with a panoramic vista near the top of a branchless tree. Now almost all of the trees on Sanibel were branchless.

The next morning, after getting Nina her coffee, Hadley and I took a detour and drove into Ding Darling National Wildlife Refuge. Luck was with us and the park's crocodile, the only American crocodile north of Miami, was sunning itself by the edge of one of the many lakes. I held Hadley in my arms and watched from a safe distance with five or six other people. The croc was 12 feet long and exactly my age, forty-three. It had a mouthful of huge white teeth. I knew some of its history from my last visit to the park: it had once been captured and transported 30 miles south to parkland in Naples, but the next year it swam back to its home in Ding Darling.

Like everything else in the world, at least in my world, this crocodile had an osprey connection. From my last trip, I knew that for a long time the crocodile had spent its nights next to the driveway of a renowned local osprey expert named Mark "Bird" Westall, who'd lived within the confines of the park at the time. I had toured Ding Darling with Bird, who, among other attributes, had the most convincing and authentic osprey call of any human being I had ever met. (It even fooled ospreys, who would look over, curious, then confused, and finally impressed.)

"My wife and I got used to having the croc in our driveway," Bird had said. "The neighbors didn't like it swimming in their pool, but it never bothered us." When he toured the country giving bird talks, he never worried about whether his wife was safe from intruders. "Not with a four-hundred-pound croc in the driveway," he said.

Hadley and I finally took Nina her cold coffee, and we all spent the afternoon around and in the pool. For the first time in months I was starting to feel like a halfway responsible family man, but then Tim Gardner called, around three. He told me about a guy named Mike McMillian, who was watching and counting ospreys in central Florida on Lake Istokpoga, where he claimed to have the largest concentration of nesting ospreys in the world, with 214 active nests. Of course I had to see *that*, but I really couldn't take time away from the family, so the next morning I got up at 4 A.M. to make the drive. On the way I took a detour to Lake Okeechobee, where Jaws and Tasha had stopped on their way south, but I couldn't find a way to get to the lake, which was encircled by a cement dike.

Lake Istokpoga, on the other hand, was one of the most perfect and romantic osprey habitats I'd ever visited. Around nine in the morning I pulled into the Cypress Isle fish camp, a small, rundown RV park and marina squeezed into a grove of beautiful cypress trees. Spanish moss swayed in a cool, almost cold, fall-like wind, and the lake wore its fall color of cold blue, a viridian blue painting with white slashes for the occasional whitecaps. There was only one building; on the stoop was a woman in her thirties and, standing hunched in a sulky teenage way, a boy in an army jacket. Both of them scowled at me as I got out of the car and approached.

When I told them why I was there, the boy's face relaxed into something close to a smile. His name was Carl, and he had been helping Mike McMillian with his osprey surveys since he was nine. "I'm fourteen now," he said proudly. As we walked across the camp, ospreys flew every which way through the cypresses, their bellies white and tail feathers a light, almost diaphanous brown. Within the square footage of about a football field were six active nests, nests that put our artificial New England platforms to shame. These sat huge and shaggy, decorated with Spanish moss, in the crooks of great cypresses. The roots of the trees tunneled down into the water, and the thick gnarled branches, mirroring the roots, reached upward to the blue sky. I marveled at how close the nests were to one another.

"This is nothing," said Carl. "Around the lake we got places with two nests in one tree."

Just then Mike McMillian arrived in his truck, towing a Boston Whaler. He wore a flannel shirt and had short gray hair and the kind of open, friendly face that instantly signals "good guy." We immediately launched into an animated osprey discussion. He told me that Mark Martell had put four satellite transmitters on the Lake Istokpoga birds back in 1999, and that to everyone's surprise, the birds had flown to four different countries in South America: Colombia, Brazil, Ecuador, and Venezuela. This was surprising because the accepted wisdom was that birds living south of Gainesville did not migrate but instead simply dispersed around Florida.

As an example, Mike pointed out at the lake. "People used to ask, 'Why don't northern ospreys just stop in Florida for the winter? Why go to South America?' The old answer was 'Because they won't stop when there is a resident population.'" But new studies, he explained, were showing that northeastern birds sometimes *did* winter in Florida. Migration, it turned out, was quirkier than anyone had supposed.

It was clear that I had found another member of my osprey tribe, and we no doubt could have talked for hours. Mike invited me to come out and do the osprey survey with him and Carl, but I told him I had to get home to my family. The truth was that after a year of ospreys, I'd finally had enough. But before I left I mentioned the BBC's documentary, and Mike laughed. It turned out that the BBC was farming out some of the production to American filmmakers. Just the week before a Florida filmmaker had accompanied Mike and Carl on their survey to get footage for the BBC film.

Mike described how at one point they had pulled the boat close to an occupied nest and the filmmaker had said, "Carl, you look kind of Hispanic. Let's get a shot of you up in the bow. Can you say something in Spanish?"

The filmmaker then explained to Mike that this was just in case the BBC didn't have any good footage of Cuba.

When Carl climbed into the bow, the filmmaker pointed the camera at him. "Okay, now we're all in Cuba," he said.

On the drive back to Sanibel, I thought about the similarities between the BBC's project and my own. Not just the obvious ones, but how telling a story about something changes the story itself. I could hardly take umbrage if my competitors occasionally played fast and loose with their material; that wasn't so different from what I did in my so-called creative nonfiction. Even when you are simply telling the truth, there is still the job of choosing which truths to highlight. And if there is something slightly suspicious about this, it isn't so different from what storytellers have always done. The facts are always there, random, formless, and someone has to come along and give them shape. That was the job I would start to face when we got home from Florida.

But if artists are allowed to shape the facts, there are times we take it too far. I was thinking of one particularly appalling example from a movie I had at first loved, *Winged Migration*. *Winged Migration* tells the story of bird migration all over the world and is filled with unbelievable shots that leave the viewer wondering, *How the hell did they film that?* I especially wondered that after the antihunting scene, in which several geese are shot out of the sky. It is a moving scene, particularly so since the film leads its viewers into a personal connection with the birds. I imagined that it made some moviegoers think critically about hunting birds for the first time.

But there was one small problem with the scene. I wondered: did they just happen to be filming when the hunters shot the birds? No, it turned out. The geese were taken to the area in crates by the filmmakers. Then they were released and flew off, within range of the hunters the filmmakers had hired. With the cameras rolling, the hired hunters blew the birds out of the air.

Fidel finally began his trip north while we were in Florida. Leaving behind the Caqueta River in Colombia for another year, he launched himself on the return leg of his 7000-mile annual trip. He left on March 19—late by osprey standards, particularly northeastern ospreys, almost the same day when the ospreys annually returned to the marsh behind Don Mackenzie's violin studio on Cape Cod. Fidel took his time about it, too, and was still in South America when we flew home from Florida on March 21, the vernal equinox. He gradually made his way up past osprey heaven on the Guajira Peninsula, where Jaws would spend the next year, and made it to Cuba a week or so later. Then he passed a day or two fishing near the dam in Santa Clara, where Freddy had seen the birds enter the country, a region Fidel knew well from spending a week there in October. Finally he pushed off for the States, spending the night of March 29 on Lake

Okeechobee before catching a nice southern wind and picking up speed. He flew from Jacksonville to Savannah to Raleigh, and from there more or less followed the bird equivalent of Route 95 up through Washington to the Chesapeake and then to Philly and on to Stamford, Connecticut. He picked up speed near the end of his trip and was back on his nest on Martha's Vineyard above the cliffs of Aquinnah, a.k.a. Gay Head, on April 8, after traveling 3420 miles in twenty-four days.

By then school was winding down and Nina and I were preparing for our own trip north. One of my last responsibilities at the college was being a guest lecturer at an introductory creative writing class of over a hundred students. I was sure most of the students knew nothing about their school mascot, the sea hawk, and so I decided—what the hell—to talk about the nesting and migratory habits of ospreys. After the lecture, one of the students wrote an e-mail to the professor who ran the course. "That guy *really* likes ospreys," it said.

After school ended, we began packing. In the twenty-plus years since I'd graduated from college I had lived in many beautiful places, often right on the water. But the economic realities of living on or near a beach meant that I had to move out almost every summer, when coastal rents skyrocketed. This cycle was continuing in our rental home on the beach in North Carolina, and during the summers we packed all our belongings into a storage locker. Which was unsettling, to say the least, though like any migration it had certain advantages. "Migration allows ospreys to pick the best place to breed as well as a super place to overwinter," Keith Bildstein had said. "They really don't have to compromise, because they're capable of having the best of both worlds." And something like that was true for us too. This summer some old friends from Cape Cod would be traveling and had agreed to let us squat in their home. So we packed up our stuff

and piled ourselves and our belongings into our car. It was time
to pull on my trusty hose sock again, and in late May we began
our drive north, more or less following the route that Fidel had
taken. It occurred to me that it might add something to my osprey year to swing by Hawk Mountain or the Puleston compound in Long Island. But with Hadley in the car, there was no
time for detours. This was a more practical migration.

We had barely settled on Cape Cod when I uprooted us once
again. I decided it was finally time to meet Fidel face-to-face.
Though I had followed the satellite birds through the year in
imagination, I had yet to see an actual satellite-tagged bird. Of
those five birds, three had perished, or at least had had radio mal-
functions, and Jaws would remain on the Guajira Peninsula for
another year. But Fidel was back on the property of the Outermost Inn on Martha's Vineyard, so on Monday, June 13, we
headed out to see him. I have to say, with only a little exaggera-
tion, that traveling from Cape Cod to the western end of the
Vineyard with a two-year-old was more stressful than flying to
Venezuela. But we made it, and before long Jeanne Taylor, the
generous hostess, was greeting us in the living room of her beautiful inn.

No sooner had we walked in than she began ushering us to
the telescope that pointed to the backyard nest. And there was
Fidel in all his glory. No need for nicotine-induced fantasies or
wild imaginings this time: a real bird with a wire jutting out of
its back, sitting on the perch next to his nesting mate. Fidel had
very dark wings with a white scapular patch, a brown cap where
a man's bald spot might be, and wore the kind of crazed raised-
eyebrow expression that ospreys' masks sometimes give the birds.
The band on his leg made him look, to me at least, like an es-
caped convict. A section of blue plastic tarp flapped in the typically unkempt nest. House sparrows lived downstairs, in the

interstices of the sticks that made up the nest, a sociable living arrangement quite common in osprey nests.

Jeanne explained that it had been a cold, rainy spring and that Fidel and his mate had gotten off to a delayed start. At this late date they were still incubating their eggs. "And we've seen some strange behavior," she said. "Yesterday there were two females up on the platform with him. One had a fish and the other was on the nest."

She looked to me for an explanation, but I didn't offer one. I thought back to Gil Fernandez in Westport and his insistence that all ospreys had perfect manners, and remembered the way he'd handily made this notion jibe with bigamy. Maybe Fidel was just this sort of happy, well-mannered bird.

When Nina and Hadley headed up for a nap, I explored the territory. At Jeanne's suggestion, I followed a trail through some fields down to the beach. Like most of us, I like all different kinds of environments—mountains, rivers, woods—but my first love is the ocean, and as I hiked down the path and saw the Atlantic I felt that reliable lift that the sight of the sea always brings me. Jeanne had told me which way to walk, but what she hadn't told me was that I was about to experience some of the most spectacular views I'd seen anywhere during my past year's travels. At first the place was just like a larger version of the bluff habitat I loved back on Cape Cod: eiders bobbing on the surf, terns diving, a white rock covered with black cormorants, a cliff riddled with holes, which I knew were the tunneling homes of bank swallows. But then the cliffs rose twice as high as those I was used to, then three times as high, and then the colors swirled, streaks of red, black, and white clay running down the cliffs and red clay rivulets crossing the beach. By *clay* I mean not just earth but actual clay, like modeling clay. Someone had taken advantage of this by sculpting a small red bunny and a lobster on one of the rocks. Gulls rose over the banks, some kiting into the wind, staying perfectly still.

And then, of course, an osprey. The first one sailed through the mist, looking so ghostly that its black-brown markings appeared gray. Caught up in the sight, I didn't get my binoculars up quickly enough to see whether it had an antenna or not. It joined another osprey, and they both hunted off a sandy point a quarter-mile ahead of me. I watched two dives into the surf and then a third bird joined the other two. I hate to end my story by Kathleening, but on this last bird I was 70 percent sure I saw a jutting antenna.

After a while I cut up from the beach and followed a path through *Rosa rugosa* and scrub brush toward the Gay Head lighthouse. My day so far was, on a small scale, proving the whole point of migration. Basically, it had been a great pain in the ass to get out to the inn. First there was the forty-five-minute drive to Falmouth, the shuttle bus to Woods Hole, the ferry across the sound, the two buses to get to the far western end of Martha's Vineyard. All that with a baby, and for what? To sleep one night in an unfamiliar bed? Sure, I had expected to see Fidel on his nest, but it was the unexpected, my walk below the cliffs, that made it all worth it. Maybe that, as much as hunger, is the impetus for movement. New places, new territory, new knowledge. Not just food.

Though the food wasn't bad. After the girls woke up, we ate grilled lobster rolls—perfect and not mayonnaisey—and fish and chips at a clam shack below the lighthouse and then headed back to the inn. There Nina had a glass of wine and I a glass of rum while we spoke with Larry, the bartender. I'd talked to Larry over the phone and he had expressed interest in my project—for obvious reasons, it turned out. As well as being on good terms with the pair of Outermost ospreys, his life had until recently followed a regular migratory cycle. He'd married a woman from the town of Guantánamo in Cuba, and they had a five-year-old daughter named Dayana. Beginning in 2002, they had spent the winters in Cuba and the summers on Gay Head. But during the second summer, George Bush had decreed that Cubans could return home only once every three years and had stopped Americans from traveling to the island.

"I remember the date exactly," Larry said. "June fourteenth. Bush talks about family values, but he doesn't value my family. So many families have been broken up. And he has redefined family according to American standards. In Cuba, family means aunts and uncles too. Now people can't visit their relatives or even send more than three hundred bucks every few months." He pointed to the nest. "I now spend more time with Bluebeard than I do with my little girl. What kind of law is that? It's not even a law, but an act. Like a royal decree. Thanks to the decree, I don't get to see my wife or see my daughter grow."

Of course he had found a way to get down to Cuba, and had been fined by the same governmental *they* who might soon be fining me. I told him about my own case, still pending, and we toasted civil disobedience.

We were soon joined at the bar by Hugh Taylor, the host of the inn, who also had migratory stories to tell. Thirteen years before he had purchased a catamaran, which he had christened *Arabella*. Rather than store *Arabella* in dry dock during the winters, Hugh had begun sailing it down to the Caribbean, and during one of these trips had discovered that he loved the Bahamas. Now he and Jeanne, in osprey fashion, spent every winter there, from late October to May, returning north with the spring. I didn't mention that I hoped this year was the beginning of my own annual migration—that is, I hoped I could find a way to keep bringing my daughter north to Cape Cod each summer, so that she could see the land that I had imprinted when I was her age.

I looked through the Taylors' scope and mentioned that Fidel, or Bluebeard, seemed to be stabbing at the backpack with his bill. He pecked at the spots where the straps went under his wings and then turned his head around 180 degrees, like an owl, and scratched at his back. Hugh reassured me that he had just started noticing this behavior the day before, and he thought that the bird might just have lice from the nest. But he too admitted some ambivalence about the telemetry packs. (As we talked, I kept thinking that Hugh looked familiar, but it wasn't until later, walking back to my room, that I saw the framed photo of him with his brother, the singer James Taylor.)

We slept well, and the next morning I woke at six to the cries of ospreys. I walked outside and saw that Fidel had returned with a fish. Hugh and Jeanne had given us a seldom-used room, above the kitchen, where I could set up my own scope focused right on the birds, and I watched Fidel rip apart the fish and then dish off the remains to his mate. At seven I went downstairs for coffee and then brought it back up to my crow's nest and watched some more. It had taken over nine months and 3000 miles, but I was finally keeping the rendezvous with Fidel that I'd hoped for on La Gran Piedra. Other than the wire jutting up, he didn't look all that different from the hundreds of ospreys I'd seen over the course of the year. A casual observer would look at this bird and think he had nothing better to do than preen and eat and laze, never guessing that he had just finished a journey of 7023 miles, roundtrip. In fact, that same observer might think that Fidel was an idler, a ne'er-do-well, when the truth was that he was living what Teddy Roosevelt, my old friend from San Juan Hill, would call "the strenuous life."

This late in the year, Fidel's chances for reproductive success were slim, but that didn't stop him from trying. He, after all, had some experience with late starts. As I watched him on the nest, I didn't indulge myself in any mystical ceremonies, though I did take some small pride in the fact that the bird and I had made similar journeys, both going out and coming back. But now my adventure was over, and it was highly unlikely that I would ever make the trip again. For Fidel, in contrast, the year was a continuous circle. He was back where he had begun but already feeling the pressure of the year ahead, the need to mate and incubate so his young could hatch and learn to fly and fish in time to make their own trip south. For me this was an ending, but for Fidel it was just another beginning.

A KIND OF HOMECOMING

If you listen to nature long enough, you will hear the story it tells over and over: a story not just of abundant and varied life but of extravagant loss. "Follow your dreams" is a cliché of our pop culture, as if dream-following were a kind of force field against loss. But in the natural world, or the real world, as it might be rightly called, dreams are no defense. Tasha had followed her dream—her procreative, instinct-propelled dream—with a passion that would have made Rocky wilt. But it had not guaranteed success.

So too with human beings. Success stories and biographies are often told in retrospect, with youthful dreams serving as a first chapter. But sometimes those first chapters are all we have. Not long after my trip ended, so did the life of one of the Cape May interns. Jason Starfire, the most exuberant, the most lively and vital of the interns—the one who would have been voted "Most Likely to Become a Keith Bildstein–type Teacher"—died suddenly, at the age of twenty-four, in August 2005. I had known him less than twenty-four hours. But I remembered him vividly in his early budding, a charismatic young man intoxicated by the notion of becoming that phrase of his own invention: a field ornithologist.

My osprey year ended on the solstice, June 21, when I headed out to the Cape Cod nest where I had seen the birds learning to fly the year before. It's hard to say that one time of year is your favorite, when there are so many different flavors. But if you had to pick one day, you could do worse than solstice, with light shining through and silver tinting and green bursting.

The young birds were on the nest again, a new group but exhibiting the same behaviors as the young of the year before, already rising and floating above the nest, trying to earn their wings. They had no idea what was ahead of them (though if we had spoken the same language, I could have recommended a nice lake down in Venezuela). Or maybe they did have some idea, a map already etched out on a level deeper than memory.

For these soon-to-be fledglings, this green saltwater marsh was their first home, and they would imprint it in their minds and return to it or near it, if they survived, year after year. But it would not be their only home. They would see and come to know other places—the lakes of Florida for one, the mountains of Cuba for another. And perhaps they would pass their winters on a reservoir in Los Llanos or in the jungles of Colombia or on a mangrove river in the province of Falcon or even on a large lake near Maracay. Whatever the specific place, they would imprint it too. In the end it was a human game trying to decide and define what true home was, and the ospreys didn't care one way or another for these distinctions. But I was a human being, and as one of the fledglings lifted off the nest and hovered, treading air for a second or two, before falling back, it occurred to me that perhaps their true home was in flight. Perhaps their home, like all our homes, was a place in between.

ACKNOWLEDGMENTS

The success of migrations often hinges on accident and luck, and my luck was so good as to sometimes border on the preposterous. But my single luckiest break was getting to know Keith Bildstein at Hawk Mountain. Not only did he serve as a character in the book, but he was a fount of both information and contacts in the bird world. To top it off, he read and helped edit the manuscript, which was above and beyond the call of duty. Thank you, Keith.

Keith also helped me get in touch with Freddy Rodriguez Santana, and obviously, without Freddy and his generosity, there would be no book. He and his wife, Ileana, and their son, Fredito, were my hosts while I was in Cuba, and their enthusiasm for Santiago and La Gran Piedra was contagious.

What Freddy was to Cuba, Adrián Naveda-Rodríguez was to Venezuela. He took us under his wing and showed us everything we hoped to see while giving us a grand tour of his beautiful country. At a time when tensions ran high between our countries, I found that the Venezuelan people, like Adrián, were nothing but outgoing and friendly.

Back in the United States, I first need to thank Jon Kenton, erstwhile roommate, loyal friend, and benefactor. Also many thanks to Alan Poole, not just for offering his own home again and again but for continuing to be my number-one source on all things osprey. Another member of the osprey all-star team, Rob Bierregaard, was kind enough to share information with me, as well as sharing the migratory story of the telemetry birds with anyone who was curious and had a computer. You can still visit his fabulous website, www.bioweb.uncc.edu/bierregaard/ Index.htm, and read about the continuing adventures of the telemetry ospreys.

Information from Rob's site was often relayed to me by my wife, the novelist Nina de Gramont, who, in addition to being head of my personal mission control, was, as always, completely supportive of my project, even when it meant sacrifice (and temporary single parenthood). Mark Honerkamp, always ready for an adventure, dove into the Venezuela trip even though he knew I would once again cast him as my warts-and-all sidekick, a role that he has now played in five books. And despite his pretensions to curmudgeonry and Luddism, he is also handy with a computer and a great fact checker.

As far as those who helped me along the way, the list is long. In Massachusetts, I'd like to thank my mother, Barbara Gessner, and Jim Rea for their senses of humor and for continuing to let me nest in my old family home long after I should have fledged. Also David Sears, for roof cover on the first night of my trip, and Tim Rogers and Kate Wallace Rogers, who have given my family a place to stay and work each summer on Cape Cod. In Westport and South Dartmouth, I would like to thank Gina Purtell, Brian MacNamara, Rob Powel and his family, and of course Gil Fernandez. On my spring return to Massachusetts, I was lucky enough to follow Fidel to the Outermost Inn on Martha's Vineyard, where I encountered the hospitality and openness of Hugh and Jeanne Taylor as well as the always-candid and outgoing Laurence Cabana.

Long Island was, of course, one of the trip's highlights. There I was treated like a king by that great group of online osprey followers. Special thanks to Cecilia Wheeler and Celeste Molinari, whose enthusiasm for the birds is unmatched. And to the incomparable Betty Puleston who, I hope, is still swimming her laps. Also to George C. Stoney, Jen Clement, Thomas Throwe, Dave Shore, Tim, Mickey, and the rest of the virtual gang. Also on Long Island a special thanks to Jim "Griff" Griffin and his wife, Patti. Griff: so sorry that your parts of the narrative once again fell under an editor's red pen.

In Cape May I wish to thank Mark Garland, the interns Jason Starfire, Cameron, and Jess, and Paul Kerlinger, whose books helped me begin to understand migration. In Florida I was aided by Mike McMillian, Mark "Bird" Westall, and the wonderfully generous Tim Gardner, who gave us a place to stay, guided tours, and hours of his time.

Back at my new home base of Wrightsville Beach, I need to thank Hadley for inspiration and Ace for coffee. Jack Steiner and Walker Golder are part of a generous local bird culture, and home support was provided by Kim Shable, who helped kick this project off, and the indomitable Mel Boyajian. Then there's the whole gang at the University of North Carolina at Wilmington, both my students and my fellow professors, who gave me an instant community and made me feel at home in this new place. Special thanks among this group goes to Clyde Edgerton, who gave counsel during rocky times and was an early reader of the book, to Phil Furia, for his support as department chair, and to Stan Colbert, who kicked the whole thing off.

For generous legal help with the Cuban leg of the trip, thanks to Alex deGramont and Jim Reed.

At Beacon Press, a thousand thanks to Brian Halley, for all his sweat and the many phone calls, and to Tom Hallock, whose faith and early enthusiasm were contagious.

And finally, thanks to my fabulous agent, Joanne Wyckoff, who believed in and stuck with this project through highs and lows.